GUARDIAN GUIDES

BARCELONA

GUARDIAN GUIDES
BARCELONA

FATIMA PARSONS

FOURTH ESTATE
London

First published in Great Britain in 1992 by
Fourth Estate Limited
289 Westbourne Grove
London W11 2QA
First published in 1991 by Regenbogen-Verlag Stromer & Zimmermann

Contributors: John Hooper, Manfred Sack, Imme Schröder (Ribera), Ulrike
Frenkel (Barceloneta), John London, Christian Politsch, Anuschka Seifert-Gabel,
Eulàlia Furriol, Bettina Semmer, Oliver Gardner (Sitges)

Photo credits: pages 43, 107, 110, 147, 242, 251 and 262
© Klaus Hennig-Damasko; page 261 © Elizabeth Lennard;
pages 264 and 268 © Ros Ribas

Photo credits: page 233 © Heinz Hebeissen; pages 40, 135, 137, 140, 231, 241
and 251 © Klaus Hennig - Damasko; Pages 104, 108, 114, 117, 120, 126, 130,
148, 154, 157, 158, 194, 262 and 286 © Elizabeth Lennard; pages 254 and 257
© Ros Ribas.

A catalogue record for this book is available from the British Library.

ISBN 1-85702-065-0

Designed by the Senate
Printed in Great Britain by The Bath Press, Avon

CONTENTS

CONTENTS

CONTENTS

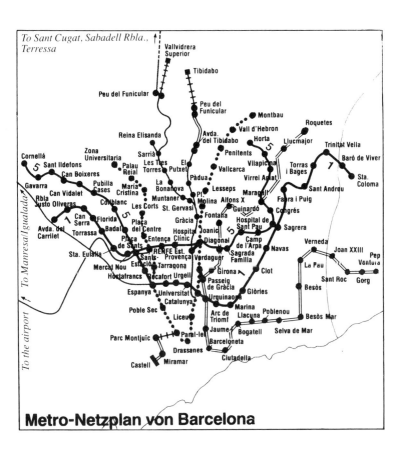

Metro-Netzplan von Barcelona

ORIENTATION

HOW TO USE THIS GUIDE

This guide is intended to get you under the surface of Barcelona. It's more than a checklist of must see's and cultural highlights; it will also lead you to the best bars and restaurants, the hottest nightclubs and the smartest shops.

Several chapters are devoted to the most important and interesting quarters of the city. Rather than drag you by the hand along a fixed route, I encourage you to dip into each area at your own pace. My idea of experiencing a city is not only traipsing through museums and churches, but also resting on the beach or sitting in a tapas bar and letting Barcelona run by like an exciting film. So while these chapters point out the notable sights in each area, they'll also help you find the right spots for people watching.

If you've come to Barcelona to indulge a passion for art and design or to explore this city's magnificent modernist architecture, there are cross references that direct you to essays on these subjects by specialist writers in their fields, designed to give you a deeper understanding of the sights you'll see. These essays are followed by extensive listings of respective museums, galleries, theatres and buildings to help you make the most of your visit.

Restaurants, shops, and bar and nightclub listings are also cross-referenced by area to help you get around quickly and easily. Our aim is to give you the widest range of exciting places in Barcelona, along with features and interviews by noted journalists that will give you an insider's view of attitudes and lifestyles in the Olympic city.

Fatima Parsons

Quartiere/Hotels

Budget hostales and pensiones

1. Hostal Goya
2. Hostal Oliva
3. Vicenta
4. Pension Fani
5. Leo
6. Hostal Colon
7. Hostal Bonavista
8. Puebla de Arenoso
9. Hostal Sena
10. Colmenero
11. Hostal Layetana
12. Hostal Levante
13. Hostal Tirol
14. Hostal Roma
15. Princesa
16. Hostal Union
17. Hostal La Paz

Comfortable and original hotels

18. Hotel Espanya
19. Hostal el Casal
20. Hostal Rey Don Jaime I
21. Hotel Nouvel
22. Hotel Meson Castilla
23. Hotel Metropol
24. Hotel Villa de Madrid
25. Hotel Suizo
26. Hotel Regina
27. Hotel Gravina
28. Hotel Wilson
29. Hotel Gran Via
30. Hostal Neutral

Exclusive hotels

31. Hotel Coron
32. Hotel Oriente
33. Hotel Rivoli
34. Hotel Alexandra
35. Condes de Barcelona
36. Hotel Gran Derby
37. Hotel Majestic
38. Hotel Ritz
39. Hotel Regente
40. Duques de Bergara

Youth hostels

41. Hostal de Joves
42. BCN Youth Hostel

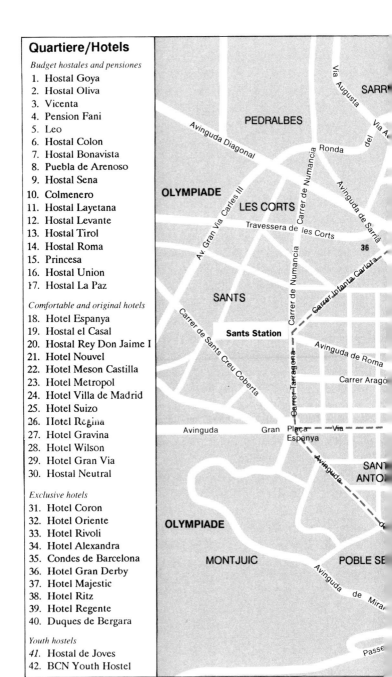

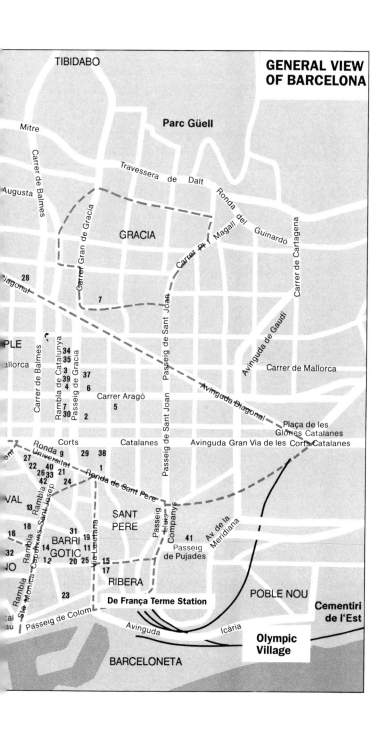

GENERAL VIEW OF BARCELONA

TIBIDABO

Parc Güell

Mitre

Carrer de Balmes

Augusta

Travessera de Dalt

Ronda del Guinardó

GRACIA

Carrer Pl Magall

Carrer de Cartagena

Diagonal

28

Carrer Gran de Gracia

7

Passeig de Sant Joan

Avinguda de Gaudi

PLE

Mallorca

Carrer de Balmes

Rambla de Catalunya

Passeig de Gracia

34
35
39
4
7
30

37

6

2

Carrer Aragó

5

Avinguda Diagonal

Carrer de Mallorca

Plaça de les
Glòries Catalanes

Corts

Catalanes

Passeig de Sant Joan

Avinguda Gran Via de les Corts Catalanes

Ronda Universitat

27
22   40
26 33
42

9   29   38

1

21

24

Ronda de Sant Pere

VAL

13

16

32

JO

18

Rambla Caputxins Sant Josep

Rambla

Rambla Sta. Mònica

31

14

12

BARRI
GOTIC

19
11
20   25

Via Laietana

SANT
PERE

Passeig Lluis Companys

RIBERA

41

Av de la Meridiana

15

17

23

Passeig
de Pujades

De França Terme Station

POBLE NOU

Cementiri
de l'Est

al
au

Passeig de Colom

Avinguda

Icària

Olympic
Village

BARCELONETA

¡BARCELONA GUAPA!

BAR-CEL-ONA: Super bars, clear blue skies, turquoise sea. This is how Javier Mariscal, designer of Cobi, the 1992 Olympic mascot, sees his dream city.

Typically Mediterranean, surrounded by the green hills and mountains of Catalonia, Barcelona is a port city. The novelist Cervantes enthused in *Don Quixote:* 'Barcelona is a treasure chest of politeness, a quiet haven for foreigners from the world over, unique in location and beauty.' And still it strives for New York's glamour and chaos, and for the grand architecture of Paris.

The Barcelonese work and play incessantly – a day is at least 36 hours long in this crazy city. The energy of the Catalans is boundless. Barcelona mes que mai! Barcelona more than ever! This is the slogan Catalonia's bold metropolis chose to promote itself and the Olympic games.

Barcelona is a modern, fully-automated city: the Metro and trains work well, the telephones hardly ever break down, the silk factories run smoothly. And yet Barcelona seems more ancient than any other contemporary metropolis. Since the Middle Ages hardly a stone has been touched in the tiny dark alleys and golden squares of the Barri Gòtic. The bullfighters on faded photographs in the bars near the Ramblas have long been buried or are great-grandfathers ten times over – or could they still be propping up the bar, black Ducados dangling from their mouths?

No other Spanish city takes as much pride in its culture, artists, writers, architects and designers. Barcelona is the genius of Dalí, Picasso and Joan Miró. Many visitors are drawn here merely by the surrealist buildings of Antoni Gaudí and the architectural masterpieces of Lluís Domènech i Montaner or Puig i Cadafalch. Their exotic Art Nouveau creations, known here as modernism, extend to the wrought-iron balconies, the rococo street lamps. Barcelona has an insatiable appetite for ornament.

A city of miracles – this is what the author Eduardo Mendoza calls his picaresque novel about his hometown. But it's also a city of small pleasures. Tapas bars in dark alleys, barely three metres wide.

¡ B A R C E L O N A   G U A P A !

Nightclubs with names like KGB that open their iron doors at six in the morning. The most delicious almond biscuits and milkshakes in the world. The view from Tibidabo, the mountain which takes its name from the Devil's tempting in St. Matthew's Gospel: All these things will I give thee, if thou wilt fall down and worship me!

Yes, all that...Barcelona is a city of contrasts. Expensive yachts lie moored right next to the poor fishermen's quarter of Barceloneta. The mountains of Tibidabo to the north and Montjuïc to the west attract visitors with Disney-style amusement parks on the one hand, and museums, the Olympic stadium and swimming pool on the other. The Eixample district with its geometric streets, imposing bars and luxury shops borders the working-class area of Gràcia, and further north lie the posh villa districts of Sarria, Sant Gervasi and Pedralbes. Barcelona is huge and bustling with a touch of anarchy and fantasy. It's Gaudí's organic dreams, the amazing flowing facade of La Pedrera - the 'stone quarry' building - or the Sagrada Familia, that fantasy of a church.

Barcelona reached its peak at the turn of the century, full of hope for a glorious future, with songs in stone, poems from wrought iron. Today it combines the best of the old world with the best of the Americas and Japan Urbane sophistication blended with sleepy Mediterranean charm. Grandeur and energy, classic beauty with postmodern style. Barcelona, the ultimate chameleon, reflects the sense of humour, passion and enterprise of the Catalans.

PLANNING YOUR TRIP

INFORMATION

Spanish National Tourist Office. 57 St James St., London SW1, tel. 071/499-0901.

AIRLINES

British Airways. 156 Regent St., London W1, tel. 071/897-4000 or toll free 0-800-247-9297.

Iberia and Viva Air. 169 Regent St., London W1, tel. 071/437-5622 or toll free 0-800-772-4642.

TRAVEL AGENTS

Air Travel Advisory Bureau. Tel. 071/636-5000.
Safe and sound charter flights and travel agents.

STA. Old Brompton Road and Euston Rd, London, tel. 071/937-9921.

Trailfinders. 42-50 Earls Court Rd and 196 Kensington High St., London, tel. 071/937-5400 or 071/938-3232.

Travel Arcade. 189 Regent St., Room 305, London W1, tel. 071/734-5873.

CLIMATE

While the Mediterranean climate is mild all year long, the best times to visit Barcelona are late spring and autumn. The temperature is pleasantly warm well into November. Many restaurants and other establishments close during the month of August when the locals rush to the beaches to escape the intense heat and humidity of high summer.

Winter and early spring vary from brisk, sunny days to rainy ones, but the temperature rarely drops below 10°C (50°F).

DRESS

Barcelona is a world capital of fashion and design and accordingly people dress in style: from chic to trendy to outrageous and avante-garde. In other words, anything goes, and given the liberal, relaxed attitude of the Barcelonese, you can wear casual clothes almost anywhere you go. With one exception – Spanish men don't wear short trousers after the age of 10, so save those shorts for the beach or you'll stick out like a sore thumb!

PUBLIC HOLIDAYS

If you're going to arrive in Barcelona on a national or local holiday, you'll have to plan ahead or you'll find that many restaurants and hostales are either fully booked or have closed their doors to join the celebration. In Catalonia, as throughout Spain, saint's days and local festivals are innumerable and dates vary each year. Check with the tourist office at Palau de la Virreina, Ramblas 99, for more information.

NATIONAL HOLIDAYS

1 January
6 January (Epiphany)
Maundy Thursday
Good Friday
Easter Sunday
Easter Monday
1 May (May Day/Labour Day)
Corpus Christi (early/mid-June)
24 June (Dia de Sant Joan)
15 August (Assumption)
12 October (National Day)
1 November (All Saints Say)
6 December (Constitution Day)
8 December (Immaculate Conception)
25 December (Christmas)
26 December

CALENDAR OF EVENTS

JANUARY

Cabalgata de Reyes. Procession of the Three Kings, great children's party (5th).

Els Tres Tombs. In the Sant Antoni quarter, procession and blessing of the animals (17th) and local festivities until the end of the month.

Piel Espana. Leather goods trade fair.

FEBRUARY

Fiesta de Santa Eulàlia. Festival of one of Barcelona's patron saints that takes place around the cathedral (12th).

Gaudi Hombre. Trade fair for men's fashion.

Gaudi Mujer. Trade fair for women's fashion.

Rally Internacional de Coches de Epoca. International vintage car rally from Barcelona to Sitges (28th).

MARCH

Alimentaria. International dietetics exhibition.

Carnival. Carnival procession on Avinguda del Paral-lel.

Romeria de Sant Medir. Local festival in Gràcia (3rd).

Salon de Anticuarios. Antiques exhibition.

APRIL

Dia del Libro. Day of the book.

Dia del Sant Jordi. Festival of honour of Saint George, the patron saint of Catalonia (23rd).

Expomovil. International motor fair.

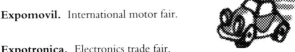

Expotronica. Electronics trade fair.

Feria de Abril. Mainly Andalusians and gypsies celebrate a big festival in the suburb Barberà del Vallès on the last weekend of the month.

Rodatur. Tourism trade fair.

Rose Market. Held in the Generalitat.

Semana Santa. Holy Week from Palm Sunday to Easter Monday with processions in several districts.

MAY

Feria del Libro. Book fair on Passeig de Gràcia (end of May and beginning of June).

Saint Ponc. Festival with lots of delicacies and stands in honour of the patron saint of flowers and fruit in Carrer Hospital (11th).

JUNE

Fiesta de Sant Joan. On the evening of the 23rd there is a great fireworks display on Montjuïc (23rd and 24th).

Gaudi Hombre. Trade fair for men's fashion.

International Film Festival. One week at the end of June and beginning of July.

Teatre Grec. Theatre festival, June – early August.

JULY

Summer Festival Productions. In the Teatre Grec and other venues.

AUGUST

Fiesta Mayor de Gràcia. In mid-August local festivals in Gràcia with live bands into the early hours.

PLANNING YOUR TRIP

SEPTEMBER

La Diadi. Catalan national holiday (11th).

Festival de Tardor. Theatre festival, September – October.

Fiesta Mayor de la Merce. Festival of Barcelona's patron saints (24th).

Gaudi Mujer. Trade fair for women's fashion.

Mostra de Cocina. Culinary week with wine tasting on Rambla de Catalunya, celebrated during the last week of September.

Sonimag. International exhibition for screen, sound and electronics.

OCTOBER

Barnajoya. International jewellery fair.

Dia de Hispanidad. It's said Columbus discovered America on this day in 1492 (12th).

Gran Teatre del Liceu. Opening of the opera and ballet season.

Liber. International book fair.

NOVEMBER

Tots Sants. All Saints is celebrated with special sweets and dessert wine, roasted almonds and chestnuts (1st).

DECEMBER

Dia dels Sants Inocents. The day of the Innocent Saints is equivalent in Barcelona to April Fool's (28th).

Feria de Santa Llucia. Christmas market in front of the cathedral (8th).

Festival de la Infancia y la Juventud. Festival for children and adolescents.

Nochevieja. New Year's Eve (31st).

THE CATALANS

You begin to notice the difference the moment you arrive at Barcelona's airport. Its huge expanses of marble and glass are kept spotless. Well-groomed executives march to and fro across the concourse with a serious, purposeful air. On your way into the city you will see that every other hoarding sports an advertisement for this or that caixa, or savings bank. And if you have already spent some time in Spain, it will strike you that the Catalans spend less time over their meals than other Spaniards, and that there are more self-service restaurants in Barcelona than in the other major cities. The Catalans' legendary industriousness has always meant that Barcelona has been among the most prosperous cities in Spain.

Its prosperity, taken in conjunction with its location - close by France on the shores of the Mediterranean - has meant that it has consistently been the most cosmopolitan of Spanish cities. Most of the ideas that have shaped Spain's modern history - republicanism, federalism, anarchism, syndicalism and communism - have found their way into Spain by way of Catalonia. Fashions - whether in clothing, philosophy or art - have tended to take hold in Barcelona several years before they gained acceptance in Madrid.

In an ideal world, one feels, the Catalans would not mind swopping places with the Belgians or the Dutch. There is a poem by Catalonia's greatest modern poet, Salvador Esprui, which captures perfectly the ambivalence of his fellow-countrymen's attitude to Spain:

Oh, how tired I am of my cowardly
old, so savage land!
How I should like to get away
to the North,
where they say that the people are clean,
and decent, refined, rich, free
aware and happy (...)
Yet I am destined never to realize my dream
and here I shall remain until death,

THE CATALANS

It is significant, however, that Espriu ends up resigning himself to his lot. Catalan dissatisfaction has always tended to be expressed as resentment, indignation and a demand for a substantial say in the running of their own affairs, rather than in terms of outright separatism.

One reason why the separatist instinct has so far been weak in Catalonia is that the Catalans, though they tend to have somewhat fairer skin and lighter hair, would not and could not claim to be racially different from other Spaniards. But it is also a reflection of the Catalans' most highly prized virtue - *seny*. There is no exact translation of *seny*. Perhaps the nearest equivalent is the northern English term 'nous' - good old common-sense. Respect for *seny* makes the Catalans realistic, earnest, tolerant and at times a bit censorious. Yet it sits uneasily with their frequently tumultuous history.

Barcelona has come under full-scale military attack by the forces of the central government on numerous occasions, usually as a consequence of uprisings and revolutions. The popularity of anarchism among the workers of Catalonia turned Barcelona into the most violent city in Europe during the early part of this century, and at the height of the civil war the Catalan capital was the scene of a bloody street war between conflicting Republican factions.

This is how the Catalan writer and academic, Victor Alba, squares the circle - 'The opposite of *seny* is *arrauxment*: an ecstasy of violence. But *arrauxment* is seen as an ultimate consequence of *seny*. Because they [the Catalans] are convinced that when they act impetuously they are being sensible... When a thing is not the way it ought to be, when a situation is not "sensible", the common-sense thing to do is to oppose it abruptly, violently.' Another explanation I have seen put forward is that the Catalans fall into two very distinct groups - those who are *sorrut* (antisocial) and those who are *trempat* (spontaneous, likeable, *simpàtico*) - and that the violent changes of direction in Catalan political history are the product of their uneasy co-existence.

THE CATALANS

A similarly paradoxical pattern can be identified in Catalan culture. For the most part, it is rather prim and humdrum. But from time to time it throws up an outstandingly original figure. In the Middle Ages, there was Ramón Llull, the multilingual Majorcan missionary who opposed the Crusades and put forward the theory that the earth was round, and Anselm Turmeda, a renegade Franciscan who converted to Islam and is regarded as a saint in North Africa. More recently, Catalonia has produced Salvador Dali and two architects whose works stand out like a string of beacons amid the stolidly bourgeois edifices of Barcelona – Antoni Gaudí, whose giant, eccentric cathedral, the Sagrada Familia, was started in 1882 and is likely to take until about 2020 to complete, and Ricardo Bofill, who has been responsible for, among other things, converting a cement works into an office block that looks like a medieval castle and for the new airport extension.

What unites this curiously heterogeneous and contradictory people is their language. Their pride in it is well-nigh limitless and they speak it at every opportunity. When two Catalan speakers and a Castilian speaker are talking together, the Catalans will address the Castilian speaker in Castilian, but as often as not they will address each other in Catalan – something that profoundly irritates other Spaniards.

Written down, Catalan looks like a cross between Spanish and French, but spoken it has a ruggedness which is lacking in either. It is unusually rich in monosyllabic words – to the point that Catalan poets have constructed entire poems out of them – and the syllables of multi-syllabic words are particularly strongly stressed. The diphthongs 'au', 'eu' and 'iu' crop up with great frequency so that to a foreigner it sounds a bit like Portuguese.

Just about the worst gaffe you can make when speaking to a Catalan is to refer to his or her language as a dialect. Catalan is no more a dialect of Castilian than Castilian is a dialect ot Catalan. Or, to put it another way, both – like French or Italian – are dialects of Latin. The first recognizably Catalan words were found in documents written in the ninth century, although the language is thought to have begun evolving in the seventh or eighth century. It spread in the wake of Catalonia's imperial expansion to an area much bigger than the four provinces of Gerona, Lérida, Tarragona and Barcelona which comprise the Principality of Catalonia itself. It is also spoken along a 15-30-

kilometre-deep strip of Aragonese territory bordering the Principality, in about two thirds of the region of Valencia, throughout the Balaeric Islands, in the Republic of Andorra and in that part of the French department of Pyrénées Orientales historically known as Roussillon. It is also spoken in Alguer, a walled town on the west coast of Sardinia, which was captured and populated entirely by Catalans in the fourteenth century and, until the early 1950s, it could still be heard in San Agustin, Florida, a town conquered by Menorcans in the eighteenth century. Catalan is the native language of something like 6,500,000 people, which makes it more widely spoken than several better-known languages such as Danish, Finnish and Norwegian.

Catalonia was the most thoroughly Romanized region of Iberia and had only the briefest of contact with the Moslems. It was, moreover, the only area to be repopulated on a large scale by *reconquistadores* from outside the peninsula. The Franks' contribution to the settlement of Catalona was only the first of the many links which were to be established between the Catalans (who were themselves originally called *francos* by other Spaniards) and the people living in what is now France. The Catalans have always been far more receptive to French ideas and attitudes than other Spaniards who tend in fact heartily to dislike the French.

The period of Catalonia's greatest glory lasted from the twelfth to the fourteenth centuries, during which time the Catalans were allied with the Aragonese. Their confederacy was a precociously sophisticated union in which the two very different partners were each allowed to retain their own laws, customs and language under the same crown. As early as the beginning of the thirteenth century, Catalonia had a *Corts* or parliament consisting of three chambers - one for the nobility, one for the bourgeoisie and another for the clergy. The sovereigns of the confederation subsequently undertook to call the *Corts* once a year and not pass any laws without its consent. The *Corts* set up on a committee of twenty-four members (eight from each chamber) whose job it was to collect taxes. In 1359 this body - the *Generalitat* - took over responsibility for the way that the money was spent as well as the way that it was collected, thus becoming what was arguably the world's first parliamentary government. As one medieval chronicler remarked, the rulers of Catalonia and Aragón were 'not the masters of their subjects, but their co-rulers'.

By the middle of the fourteenth century the Catalan-Aragonese confederation ruled not only the Balearic Islands and the city and region of Valencia but also Sardinia, Corsica and much of present-day Greece. A member of its Royal Family sat on the throne of Sicily and it controlled the gold trade with the Sudan. Today the world has all but forgotten Catalonia's golden age, but the memory of her power and influence lives on in the folk sayings of the Mediterranean. In Sicily, recalcitrant children are told to 'do what I say or I'll call the Catalans' and in Thrace you can do no worse than to wish on your enemy 'the Catalan vengeance'. A number of naval and financial terms in Castilian derive from Catalan, including probably the word *peseta.*

A banking collapse in 1381 caused by the cost of financing too many imperial wars, the rise of the Ottoman Empire and the loss of the gold trade sent Barcelona into decline even before the discovery of America shifted the geographic advantage from the Mediterranean to the Atlantic. When the city's fortunes finally took a turn for the better – in the nineteenth century – it was due not so much to commerce as to industry, and in particular the cotton business.

It was during the nineteenth century that the Catalans rediscovered themselves through their language. After the unification of Spain, the ruling class throughout the country had adopted Castilian as a mark of their status. Catalan became the language of the peasantry and the culture associated with it died out. But in the last century it became the medium for a literary revival which succeeded in enhancing the status of the language sufficiently for it to be re-adopted by the middle and upper classes, thereby regaining its repsectability and influence.

The Catalan *Renaixença,* as it is called, began in the most curious manner. In 1833 a minor poet, Bonaventura Carles Aribau, published a poem in Catalan called 'Ode to the Fatherland'. He had intended it simply as a birthday present for his patron, another Catalan called Gaspar Remisa i Niarous, who was at that time head of the Royal Treasury. But the poem was published in a Barcelona newspaper and made a great impact on the intellectual community. Aribau, a dedicated centralist, never again published anything of importance and spent the rest of his life working for the government and the monarchy in Madrid. But the renewed interest in Catalan which he had stimulated grew inexorably.

THE CATALANS

In 1859 an annual poetry competition called the Floral Games was inaugurated and in 1877 it brought to light one of Spain's greatest modern literary figures, Jacint Verdaguer. Several other outstanding writers emerged from Catalonia during the late nineteenth and early twentieth centuries - the playwright Angel Guimerá, the novelist Narcís Oller and the poet Joan Maragall.

The *Renaixença* provided the raw material and the driving force for the political movement which appeared towards the end of the last century known as Catalanism. Catalanism was a broad church, embracing all those who believed in Catalonia's separate identity and who were keen to see it recognised, whether in the form of autonomy or nationhood. The father of Catalanism, Valentí Almirall, author of *Lo Catalanisme*, was essentially a regionalist. But within a few years his ideas were given a sharper, more nationalistic edge by Enric Prat de la Riba, who provided the movement with its first political programme and whose Catalan Union supplied it with its earliest political organisation. Except during its earliest years, Catalanism was never represented by a single party. It provided the inspiration for parties of the right and the left and for parties of all classes, of which by far the most influential was the conservative upper-middle-class Lliga.

In 1934 the demagogic anti-Catalanist, Alejandro Lerroux, succeeded in forcing the *Generalitat* to accept right- as well as left-wing members. This was anathema to the left, who believed that the right could not and would not support the Republic and the President of the *Generalitat,* Lluis Companys, proclaimed 'the Catalan state of the Spanish Federal Republic'. The Civil Governor of Barcelona, himself a Catalan, declared war on the new government, and the offices of the *Generalitat* and the city hall both came under bombardment before Companys surrendered along with his entire government. The Cortes suspended the Catalan parliament and appointed a Governor-General to carry out the functions of the *Generalitat*. In 1935 the members of the *Generalitat* were each sentenced to thirty years in gaol, but benefited from the amnesty for political prisoners which was proclaimed when the left-wing Popular Front came to power as a result of the elections in February 1936.

The statute of autonomy was restored and in the period immediately after the outbreak of civil war, the *Generalitat* was able to grab many of the powers which had been denied it between 1932 and 1934. As Franco and his troops steadily gained the upper hand and the Republicans were pushed back into a progressively smaller area, the capital was moved from Madrid to Valencia and then from Valencia to Barcelona, so that it was in Barcelona that the Republic met its end. Companys fled to France only to be arrested after the German invasion by the Gestapo. They handed him over to Franco who ordered him to be executed in secret. It later emerged that the President of the *Generalitat's* last words – shouted out a matter of seconds before the execution squad opened fire – were '¡*Visca Catalunya*!' ('Long live Catalonia!')

Franco's victory unleashed a campaign against the Catalan language unparalleled in the region's history. Publishing houses, book shops, and public and private libraries were searched for Catalan books and those that were found were destroyed. Pompeu Fabra's priceless collection was burned in the street. The names of villages and towns were Castilianized, the Street of the Virgin of Monserrat (the patron of Catalonia) became the Street of the Redeemer and the Library of Catalonia was renamed the Central Library. In the mid-forties permission was granted for the publication of books in Catalan and the staging of plays in Catalan. But it remained banned from radio and television, the daily press and in schools. The *Institut d'Estudis Catalans*, which was founded in 1907, maintained a curious, half-tolerated, half-clandestine existence under Franco. It held weekly meetings, held courses on the language, literature and history of Catalonia in private houses, gave receptions and went as far as to publish books and pamphlets, some of which were even bought by the government for display at international exhibitions.

Throughout the first two decades of Franco's rule, Catalonia was the principal source of opposition to his regime. In 1944 the Communists made a disastrous attempt to invade the country through the Valle de Arán, and between 1947 and 1949 the anarchists staged a bloody but futile campaign of shootings, bombings and hold-ups in Barcelona. The failure of these attempts to overthrow Franco's regime by force ushered in a period when opposition was characterised by mass public protests. Most of the more successful ones took place in Catalonia. The pattern was set in 1948 when opponents of Franco's rule succeeded in getting 100,000 people to attend a ceremony celebrating the enthronement of the Virgin of Monserrat. In 1951 the first city-wide general strike in post-war Spain was held in Barcelona which was also the scene of mass public transport boycotts in 1951 and 1956.

But being the focus of opposition and promoting it are two very different things and the truth is that the role played by Catalan nationalists in fighting Franco was by and large a pretty tame one. There was a Catalan Liberation Front, but it never had a fraction of the support nor made a hundredth of the impact of ETA. Barcelona's students were in the forefront of the search for an independent student movement but once it had been formed the leadership was exercised from Madrid. The most dramatic acts of resistance to come out of Catalonia were symbolic ones, such as when the audience at the *Palau de la Música* sang the unofficial national anthem of Catalonia in front of Franco when he was on a visit to the area in 1960.

In short, the Catalans' response to Franco owed a good deal more to *seny* than to *arrauxment* and this, I think, has somewhat diminished their status and influence in a democratic Spain. Moreoever, the virtual absence of violent nationalism has meant that the inhabitants of Catalonia were not subjected to the same relentless oppression that helped to homogenise the population of the Basque country and so the differences between 'native' and 'immigrant' have not been erased – or disguised – in Catalonia to the same extent as in the Basque country. If Catalonia has not occupied a centre stage since Franco's death, it is partly because today's Catalan nationalists are having to struggle to create a sense of nationhood in an area which is manifestly less different from the rest of the country now than it has been at any time in its history.

Immigrants have been pouring into the Principality from other parts of Spain for almost a century. The growth of industry, first in and around Barcelona and then in the other provincial capitals of Catalonia, created a demand for labour that the Catalans were quite unable to satisfy by themselves. About half the population of Catalonia today is of immigrant stock and it has been estimated that there will be no 'pure' Catalans left by the year 2040.

In the 1920s the newcomers were predominantly from Murcia,

which - although Castilian speaking - was partly conquered by Catalans. But the influx after the civil war and during the *años de desarrollo* consisted of an increasing proportion of Andalusians. Since this was by far the largest and longest 'wave', the Andalusians now form the biggest single group of immigrants in Catalonia. With their gracious but passionate temperaments and their love of flamenco, the Andalusians are not merely not Catalan but the heirs to a very potent alternative culture. This is only one of several reasons why it is proving more difficult to assimilate the most recent wave of immigrants than it was to integrate those who arrived before the civil war.

The most important reason is their sheer numbers - a quarter of a million in the forties, nearly half a million during the fifties and almost a million during the sixties. The tidal wave swept over Barcelona and into the rest of Catalonia. When Spain's 'economic miracle' came to an end almost one in five of the population of the other three provinces was of immigrant stock. Because of their numbers, the immigrants of the forties, fifties and sixties often live in areas where only the priest, the doctor and perhaps the schoolteachers and the shopkeepers are Catalans by origin. The new immigrants represent a far higher proportion of Catalonia's total population, which is now nearing six milliion, than their predecessors ever did and since the return of democracy numerical strength has acquired a political as well as a social significance. The new immigrants sense their importance and it enables them to resist Catalanization longer.

The repressive measures taken by Franco's government and the influx of this new wave of immigrants presented a dual threat to the Catalan language which, by the time the dictatorship ended, was facing a crisis. According to a report published by the Spanish government in 1975, the proportion of the population who could speak Catalan was 71 per cent in the Principality, 91 per cent in the Balaeric Islands and 69 per cent in the three provinces of Valencia. The percentage who actually did speak it at home was somewhat lower in all cases. In Catalonia proper the figure was reckoned to be about half.

Contrary to everything that had been assumed, Catalan remained the social language of Catalonia but was gradually ceasing to be the family language of its inhabitants.

HISTORY

400 BC Iberians, then known as the Layetanos, settle in the Mediterranean coast and establish Barcinona.

From 600 BC Greek settlers arrive at Empurias.

Around 200 BC Roman conquest begins. The Carthaginians arrive from Africa and the Roman Empire lands with the first legions at Empurias.

Around 100 BC The Romans establish Augusta Barcina, today Barcelona.

100 BC – 200 BC The economy blooms in the Roman colony as oppressed Iberians adopt laws, architecture, culture and even the language and currency of the Roman Empire. Hispania, or Iberia now comprises three major Roman provinces. Two great Caesars come from Italica, today's Sevilla: Trojan, who ruled the empire from AD 98-117, and Hadrian AD 117-138. Catalonia is part of the Roman province Hispania Citerior with its capital city Tarragona. Because of its port, Barcelona becomes a major commercial centre.

Around AD 300 Crisis in the Roman Empire. Barcelona and Tarragona are destroyed.

414 Visigoth invasion. Barcelona becomes capital of the Visigoth Empire under King Teudis.

713 Moorish conquest of Barcelona.

801 Reconquest by Ludwig the Pious; Barcelona becomes capital of the Spanish mark of the Carolingian Empire.

HISTORY

1137 Unification of the earldom Barcelona with the kindgom of Aragón.

1258 The treaty of Corbeil frees Catalonia from being a theoretical part of France, through the marriage of Ramón Berenguer III to Douce de Provence. Economic boom for Barcelona. Jaume I establishes the first democratic urban government: the Consejo de Ciento, the Council of the Hundred.

1300-1360 Peak of Catalonia's prestige and power. Parts of Greece are conquered. Catalonia has 500,000 inhabitants.

1356-1375 War between Peter of Aragón and Peter the Terrible of Castile. Banks declare bankruptcy, Jews are massacred, French invasion and wars with Sardinia and Sicily under Martin the Humane.

Around 1400 Fall of Catalonia. Castile becomes the dominant state in the Iberian peninsula through its wool and corn trade with Holland and Germany.

1469 Unification of Aragón and Castile through the marriage of the Catholic Kings Ferdinand and Isabella. Barcelona's importance diminishes, partly through a royal decree granting Seville and Cadiz monopoly of trade with the overseas colonies.

1492 Columbus discovers America. The advent of Christianity in Spain is completed after 200 years with the reconquest of Granada and liberation from the Moors.

1493 Columbus is greeted by Ferdinand and Isabella in Barcelona after his first voyage to the new world.

1701-1714 Spanish war of succession. Barcelona sides with the Habsburg Charles, troops of Bourbon King Phillip V conquer the city on 11 September 1714; loss of many privileges. The university founded in 1430 is relocated and the Catalan language is gradually banned from daily use.

1716   Phillip V passes a new law, the Nueva Planta.   The Catalan kingdom is dissolved and declared a province of Castile.   The bourbon dynasty strengthens the Catalan economy.

1700–1800   Economic and industrial upturn.

1763   Foundation of the Barcelona chamber of commerce.   Textile industry expands through trade with the Americas.

1783   One of the first textile dyeing factories in the world is established in Barcelona.   In the preceding 60 years Barcelona's population has doubled to 860,000.   The textile industry alone employs 75,000 workers.   The first large vineyards are planted in Penedés.

1793   After Louis XIV is guillotined, Charles IV goes to war with revolutionary France.

1804   Napoleon becomes Emperor and only a year later draws Spain into war with him against England.

1808   The people dethrone the monarch Charles IV and his heir, the future Ferdinand VII.   Napoleon installs his brother, Joseph Bonaparte, as king of Spain.   Napoleonic troops occupy Spain.   On 2 May the War of Independence begins against the French occupation.   Catalan is the official language of Catalonia.

1812   Parliament proclaims a liberal constitution in Cádiz.

1814   Spain wins the battle of Vitoria with English help.   Ferdinand VII ascends the throne, declares the liberal constitution illegal and resumes his absolutist reign.

1821–1824   Mexico, Venezuela and Peru declare independence from Spain.

1830   Coronation of Isabella II.

HISTORY

1833-1839 First Carlist War between partisans of the Bourbon Don Carlos and friends of Isabella II.

1847-1849 Second Carlist War.

1848 Construction of the first railway from Barcelona to Mataró.

1850 Catalonia now has 1.6 million inhabitants.

1858 Barcelona's city walls are pulled down in order to extend the urban area.

1868 General Prim forces the abdication of Isabella II.

1869 A progressive and liberal constitution is introduced.

1872-1876 Third Carlist War.

1873 The First Republic is proclaimed and Catalonia declared an independent state within the Republic.

1874 The Cortes, Spain's parliament, is dissolved. Peasants and workers revolt. The bourgeoisie hopes for the reinstatement of the monarchy. A military coup brings Isabella's son. Alfonso XII, to the throne. Thanks to their textile industry, the Catalans are the richest people in Spain.

1893 Barcelona's opera house, the Liceo, is bombed by anarchists. Catalan nationalism under Prat de la Riba is revived.

1888 and 1929 World exhibition in Barcelona.

1898 Spain loses its colonies in Cuba, Puerto Rico and the Philippines in the Spanish-American War.

1901 The Catalan party, in the form of the Lliga Regionalista, is voted into City Hall. Prat de la Riba modernises schools, the arts, transport and the police.

1907 Prat de la Riba founds the Instituto d'Estudis Catalans in Barcelona.

1909 Semana Trágica (Tragic Week), anarchists demonstrate in Barcelona.

1923-1930 The Catalan General Primo de Rivera installs a military dictatorship.

1931 King Alfonso XII abdicates. Proclamation of the Catalan Republic on 14 April.

1936-1939 Spanish Civil War. Barcelona/Catalonia is a Republican stronghold.

1939-1945 General Franco's dictatorship forces into exile intellectuals, artists, politicians, anarchists, in short all prominent Republicans. The Catalan language and culture are brutally suppressed. The Sardana, the national dance, is outlawed and even those speaking Catalan within the family are imprisoned.

1953-1955 Spain becomes a member of the United Nations. American aid facilitates economic recovery after years of stagnation. Many countries refuse to support Franco's regime with financial aid. Thousands die in Barcelona and Catalonia from malnutrition.

1959 New economic policy opens up Spain's isolated economy. Investment from all over the world floods into the Iberian peninsula. Mass tourism discovers the costas and Barcelona.

1975 Death of Franco. Juan Carlos I takes the throne.

1977 The transition, the road to democracy, begins with Adolfo Suarez as prime minister. Under his government Catalonia is given autonomy. Political parties are legalised.

HISTORY

1978 The Catalan language is taught at school.

1981 A military coup in Madrid's parliament building on 23 February is averted by the skilful intervention of the King.

1982 The socialist Felipe González is voted prime minister.

1986 On 1 January Spain gains admittance to the EEC.

1992 Barcelona hosts the Olympic games, Sevilla hosts the Expo and Madrid becomes the Cultural Capital of Europe. Celebrations mark the quincentenary of the discovery of America by Columbus.

GETTING THERE

BY AIR

Unfortunately getting to Barcelona stress-free by air has its price. Even the cheapest scheduled flights with British Airways and Iberia will cost between £150 and £250 depending on the season. Only a few charter flights from Britain and the USA fly to El Prat, Barcelona's airport.

Many charter flights, student and budget travel agencies fly to the provincial capital Girona, which is only an hour's train ride inland from Barcelona. Spanish trains are very economical; however, you must add the cost of a taxi from the airport to the station. Nevertheless, this somewhat laborious arrival is worthwhile for large families or tourists travelling on a budget. Girona itself, with its Roman baths, early Gothic churches, many street cafes and romantic old quarter make the detour well worth it.

Girona Airport. Tel. (972) 20-75-00.

Renfe. Railway information, tel. 20-70-93.

El Prat Airport. Tel. (93) 370-0101.

Tourist Information. International Arrival Hall, tel. 325-5829. Mon.- Sat. 9:30 a.m.-8 p.m., Sun. and holidays 9:30 a.m.-3 p.m.

All the important information is available here, as well as city maps, Metro plans, information on he useful tourist bus 100, monthly calendars, hotel reservations, and tips for excursions. Many of the top hotels in Barcelona will meet you at the airport with their courtesy buses. Find out here or when you book!

BY TRAIN INTO TOWN

There is a city-airport train which covers the 12 kilometres from El Prat

GETTING THERE

to the Sants station in the west of the city and Plaça de Catalunya station in the centre. Timetable: daily, Sants-airport, 5:42 a.m.- 10:12 p.m.; airport-Sants, 6:12 a.m.-10:42 p.m. Plaça de Catalunya-airport, 6:35 a.m.-10:05 p.m.; airport-Plaça de Catalunya, 6:12 a.m.-10:12 p.m.

BY CAR INTO TOWN

All major car rental firms are available at the airport. Compare prices.

BY TAXI INTO TOWN

A standard surcharge of 225 pesetas is made for the 12km ride from the airport into town. On top of that a further 175 pesetas are added as airport and station surcharges to the meter charge. During rush hours it's an expensive and nerve-racking experience!

BY TRAIN

If you travel to Barcelona by train you'll arrive absolutely whacked, unless you take the super-fast and expensive TALGO. Due to typically anarchic/Spanish reasons the track gauge differs from that of other European countries, which means that in most cases you'll have to change to a RENFE train in the border towns of Port Bou, La Tour de Carol or Irun. A tiresome affair! By 1993 all RENFE tracks are supposed to have adapted to the European standard and by 1995 they should be connected to the french TGV network. However, whether this tight deadline can be met is still in the lap of the gods.

RENFE (Red Nacional de los Ferrocariles Espanoles). Round-the-clock train information, tel. 490-0202 and 490-0480.

TRAIN STATIONS

Sants. Plaça dels Països Catalans, tel. 490-0202. M: Estació Sants.

This cold and modern station with international connections, is currently Barcelona's main railway station as Terme Francia is being renovated. The Barcelona Talgo from Paris Austerlitz station, the Pablo

Casals Talgo from Zurich and Milan, and the Catalan Talgo from Geneva arrive here.

The airport train leaves every half hour from platforms 3 and 4. Trains to the Spanish provinces dash from Sants in all directions.

The ticket counters are somewhat confusing and always have queues. For the airport and local trains buy your ticket at the window on the far right marked 'Cercanïas'. That applies to all stations.

Estacio de Francia, Terme. Avinguda Marqués de l'Argentera, tel. 490-0202. M: Barceloneta.

This beautiful turn-of-the-century station, with ornate wrought iron construction spanning the giant hall, is the most central and convenient station, right by the Barri Gòtic. Following renovation, normal trains and Talgos for France will depart from here from summer of 1992.

Passeig de Gracia. Tel. 490-0202. M: Passeig de Gràcia.

This mini station is hidden in the Metro station of the same name. Many of the national and international trains that stop here at its only two platforms also pass through Sants, but since the stop at Passeig de Gràcia is more central and much less hectic it is worthwhile to get on and off trains here; above all, for trains to Sitges, which are always overcrowded from Sants. This way at least you get a seat. It's also good as a meeting place, as you an hardly miss each other.

Plaça d'Espanya. Tel. 205-1515. M: Espanya.

The airport train also stops here. This station is run by the F.G.C. (Ferrocarils de la Generalitat de Catalunya). Trains leave for the shrine of Montserrat and Gaudí's most genial construction, the chapel commissioned by his patron Güell in Santa Coloma de Cervelló.

Plaça de Catalunya. Tel. 205-1515. M: Catalunya.

Another F.G.C. station for trains to the surrounding mountains, the university and to Sant Cugat and Sabadell.

GETTING THERE

BY CAR

The fastest connection between the French border and Barcelona is the motorway. The A-7 begins at the Pyrenean pass of La Jonquera and ends on the wide Gran Via de les Corts Catalanes, or Gran Via for short, right in the centre of the Catalan capital. However, the motorway costs pesetas. The toll from the border at La Jonquera to Barcelona is about £6. Cheaper and more picturesque is the national highway N-2 from Port Bou through Figueres, where Dalí's theatre-cum-museum beckons, and then Gothic Gerona.

In the centre of Barcelona, parking is hard to come by and in the Barri Gòtic, virtually impossible. Leave your car in the smart residential area north of the Avinguda Diagonal and take one of the famously cheap taxis or public transport, otherwise you will be inundated with parking tickets or even towed away. In the evening it is marginally easier to find a space, if not in the old part of town, then in the Ribera quarter or in the vicinity of the university. Spaniards are savage parkers and take pleasure in ramming and scratching other cars. So, careful with that new car!

In any case, caution is called for with the deft thieves. Never leave anything behind in your car, not even in the boot. Thieves are only too pleased to break in, especially when it comes to expensive cars with foreign number plates. All Spaniards carry their car radios on them, even if they only pop out for a loaf of bread. Jackets and raincoats, even umbrellas and bulging plastic bags attract the opportunist thief. And car thieves here work pretty fast.

INFORMATION AND HELP

Acesa–Autopistas Concesionaria Española. Plaça Gal.la Placída, tel. 217-2800.
Information on toll-motorways.

RAC. Muntaner 239-253, tel. 200-8800.
Information and help in the case of breakdown.

Reial Automovil Club de Catalunya. Santaló 8, tel. 200-0754.
The Catalan automobile club offers round-the-clock information,
possibly in English and French, depending on the time you call.

REPAIRS

All the major makes have branches and garages. Here are but a few:

BMW. Buïgas, 21-23, tel. 204-5552.

Fiat. Balmes 212, tel. 237-9704.

Mercedes. Urgell 233, tel. 230-8600.

Peugeot. Capità Arenas 68, tel. 203-3240.

Volvo. Urgell 259, tel. 239-0483.

VW, Audi, Seat. Gran Via de les Corts Catalanes 90, tel. 332-1100.

Detroit. Biscaia 326, tel. 351-1203.
24-hour recovery and repairs.

Graus Gàrcia. Nou Pins 24, tel. 350-7535.
Round-the-clock recovery.

GETTING AROUND

Barcelona is a real paradise for public transport enthusiasts. It is such a pleasure to ride, glide and wander on land, over the water and in the air, that a car can only be a liability. Tourists shuttle back and forth all day between cultural and sporting sights on the number 100 bus. Children love the many cable cars and funiculars, but I love best to ride along the long streets of the Eixample on the ordinary bus routes. Luckily, prices are very reasonable in comparison with the rest of Europe.

Info-Telefon. Tel. 412-0000. Offers information on all means of transport, unfortunately mostly in Spanish and Catalan. However, Barcelona's transport system is not complicated.

Kiosk Plaça de Catalunya. At the two or three white kiosks belonging to the city transport company you can get Metro maps and bus information, as well as the 10-journey tickets valid on routes T-1 and T-2, and friendly advice.

BUSES

Times. Daily 6:30 a.m.–10 p.m. Night buses 11:00 p.m.–4 a.m. from Plaça de Catalunya.

Tickets. 10-journey tickets for route T-1, Tarjeta Multiviaje, cost 450 pesetas. Singles cost approximately twice as much. The T-1 ticket is also valid on the FFCC, the Metro, the Tibidabo funicular and the Tramvia Blau. The tourist day-pass at 275 pesetas is hardly worth it, unless you make eight journeys a day of the bus, Metro or FFCC. You can only obtain these tickets in the Botiga del Metro and at the Sants and universitat stations.

GETTING AROUND

ROUTES

Buses can be recognised easily by their three colours:

Red. Buses travelling through the centre, or departing from the Plaça de Catalunya and through the city.

Yellow. Buses crossing the city but not the Barri Gòtic or city centre.

Blue. Night buses all travelling through the centre, many departing from the Plaça de Catalunya.

SUPER-BUS ROUTES

Bus 100. Only between June 24 and September 29, daily 10 a.m.-7.15 p.m. Tourist day passes for 600 pesetas (400 pesetas after 2 p.m.) are available on the bus. These sightseeing buses, called Descobreixi Barcelona (Discover Barcelona), go around the metropolis covering 15 interesting locations. The point of departure is the Pla de Palau by the main post office, although I prefer to get on at the Columbus monument or by the city hall at Plaça Sant Jaume. The round trip takes approximately two hours, but is not worthwhile if you don't get off the bus occasionally. The bus 100 takes you to parks and sights that would otherwise be hard to reach, such as the Monestir de Pedralbes with its Thyssen collection, the new swimming pool with its sculpture by Chillida, the Parc la Creueta del Coll, the Parc Güell, and the Anella Olímpic on Montjuïc. The bus also climbs halfway up the neighbouring mountain, the Tibidabo, and even tickets for the Tramvia Blau, the Teleferic and the Funicular de Montjuïc are included.

Bus 14. From the zoo to the Ramblas up to Gràcia and Sarrià as far as Passeig Bonanova in the new area above Diagonal.

Bus 17. From Passeig Nacional, Barceloneta's boulevard, to Plaça de Catalunya, Via Augusta and San Gervasi, Plaça Molina as far as the Vall d'Hebron Olympic Centre.

Bus 24. From the Paral-lel Metro station to the Plaça de l'Universitat and via Passeig de Gràcia as far as Parc Güell.

Bus 38. Leaves from Plaça de Catalunya and travels via the Ramblas up to Montjuïc and via Plaça de Espanya to near the Sant Antoni market.

Bus 64. From Monestir de Pedralbes through the smart Sarrià, Tres Torres and Eixample districts as far as the scruffy Boulevard Paral-lel, the Columbus monument and the beach at Barceloneta.

METRO

Times. Mon.-Fri. 5 a.m-11 p.m., Sat. 5 a.m.-1 a.m., Sun. 6 a.m.-1 a.m.

Tickets. The T-2 10-journey ticket, Tarjeta Multiviaje costs 400 pesetas. Singles cost about twice as much at 75-80 pesetas; weekends are more expensive. So it's worth it to buy a T-2 ticket. They are available in Metro stations and are not valid on buses where the more expensive T-1 is required. However, the T-2 is valid on the FFCC and the Tramvia Blau.

FFCC–Ferrocarrils. Plaça Catalunya, tel. 205-1515. Times are the same as the Metro, T-2 tickets are also valid here.

These modern, air-conditioned trains are considerably more pleasant and faster than the antiquated Metro. Unfortunately, they only run to the north through the better districts of Sarrià, Tibidabo and Vallvidrera to Sabadell. You must buy a new ticket if you change from the Metro at Plaça de Catalunya onto the FFCC.

FUNICULARS AND CABLE CARS

The standard 10-journey tickets for bus and Metro are valid on many funiculars and cable cars, as is the day-pass for bus 100.

Funicular de Tibidabo. Tel. 211-7942. Daily 7:15 a.m.-9:45 p.m.

This funicular with standing room only buzzes up to the Cumbre

GETTING AROUND

del Tibidabo from the Plaça Doctor Andreu, which you can reach via FFCC Tibidabo and the Tramvia Blau. It stops right next to La Muntanya Màgica amusement park.

Funicular de Montjuïc. Daily in summer every 15 minutes; 11 a.m.–9:30 p.m. winter, weekends and holidays only.

This funicular runs from Palal-lel Metro station to the Estació Miramar halfway up Montjuïc. Nearby is the Fundació Miro with its restaurant offering a good view, and the newly laid-out Botanical Gardens.

Teleferico de Montjuïc. Tel. 256-6400. June–Sept.: daily 12-8:30 p.m.; Sept.–June, Saturdays and holidays 11-a.m.-2:45 p.m. and 4-7:30 p.m.

Runs directly from the Miramar terminus of the Montjuïc funicular up to the Parc d'Atraccions and the castle and military museum.

Funicular Vallvidrera. The steepest of all the funiculars lurches up from the Peu Funicular FFCC station to Barcelona's highest point at the Plaça Pep Ventura in the suburb of Vallvidrera.

Transbordador Aeri del Port. Harbour cable car, Torre de Sant Sebastiá, tel. 317-5527, M: Barceloneta, or Torre Sant Jaume, harbour quay, M: Drassanes, up to Miramar or Montjuïc. June-Sept.: Mon.-Fri. 11 a.m.-9 p.m.; Oct.-June: Mon.-Fri. 12 noon-5:45 p.m.; weekends and holidays 11:30 a.m.-7 p.m.

Wonderful! And the first thing that any visitor to Barcelona should do.

Tramvia Blau. Plaça Kennedy to the Funicular del Tibidabo, tel. 412-000. Daily 7:15 a.m.-9:45 p.m.

Romantic and over 100 years old, the last blue tram in operation. Currently being restored, but has been replaced by a bus.

Golondrinas del Puerte. Plaça Portal de la Pau, tel. 412-5944. M: Drassanes. July-Sept., daily 10:30 a.m.-9 p.m.; Oct.-June, daily 11 a.m. 6 p.m. Children under 5 free.

It's a horror trip for vertigo sufferers, but for others the greatest pleasure in Barcelona is a cable car ride on the **Transbordador Aeri.** Moll de Barcelona, Torre Sant Jaume - or from Barceloneta, Torre Barceloneta-Montjuïc, Torre Miramar, tel. 317-5527. Oct.-June: Mon.-Fri. 12 noon-5:45 p.m.; July-Sept.: Mon.-Fri. 11 a.m.- 9 p.m.; weekends and holidays 11:30 a.m.-7 p.m.

The fastest route to get from the beach in Barceloneta to the Ramblas and Montjuïc is unfortunately rather expensive, but the view of the harbour, the old town and the mountains is well worth it.

After the Columbus Statue, turn left towards the harbour, with its newly-built walkway, **Moll de Fusta** and the snazzy bars and restaurants right on the quayside.

TAXIS

Barcelona's 7,000 taxis are black and yellow, like bees. The Catalan metropolis is even listed in the Guinness Book of Records as the European city with the most taxis. Free taxis can be recognised by a green light on the roof and a sign in the window saying 'Lliure'

Charge.   225 ptas basic charge, 200 ptas surcharge for journeys to railway stations and the airport. Taxis are good value compared to most other western countries.

Calling a Taxi.   Information number: 336-000. Reliable companies can be called on the following numbers: 212-2222, 322-2222, 330,0300, 330-0804, 358-1111, 300-3811 and 387-1000. But it's no problem to hail a taxi in the street. There are **taxi ranks** in all main railway stations and larger streets.

CAR RENTAL

On the whole, international companies such as Hertz, Avis and Budget are slightly more expensive than their smaller Spanish counterparts. It's worth it to make enquiries and compare prices. Here are a few to try:

Atesa.   Balmes 141, tel. 235-8140, and at the airport, tel. 302-2832.

Docar.   Montnegre 18, tel. 322-9008.

Europcar.   Viladomat 214, tel. 439-8403, and at the airport, tel. 317-6980.

Rental Auto.   Avinguda Sarrià 32, tel. 230-9071.

Tot Car.   Avinguda Josep Tarradellas 93. tel. 321-3754.

Vanguard.   Londres 31, tel. 439-3880 and 322-7951. M: Diagonal.
   You can also hire **motorcycles** from here, from Vespinos for 2,500 ptas a day to a Yamaha 400 for approximately 6,700 ptas per day. But beware: Spaniards are real Kamikaze riders and love to whiz round corners without crash helmets.

CAMPERS

Caravanes Catalanes. Premià 23, tel. 253-3387.

Rent-Esplai. Roger de Flor 191, tel. 257-7275.

Old Cars. Masria Victòria 13-14, tel. 421-1549.

CYCLES

Bicitram. Marquès de l'Argentera 15, tel. 204-3678. M: Barceloneta. Saturday, Sunday and holidays, 10 a.m. - 8 p.m.

This tiny shop with a very helpful owner can be found near the renovated Estació Franci (or Terme). Possible flat rates for weekly rental.

Filicletas. Passeig de Picasso 38, tel. 319-7811. M: Barceloneta. Open weekends. Daily rental about £7.

Biciclot. Sant Joan de Malta 1, tel. 307-7475. M: Clot. Open daily.

INFORMATION

TOURIST INFORMATION

Barcelona Informacio. City Information, tel. 010, or 318-2525.
This number is usually engaged but if you get through information is available in English and French about everything from street festivals and museums to opening times of beach huts and swimming pools.

Oficinas de Informacio Turistica

In **Sants main railway station:** tel. 490-9171. Open daily 8 a.m.-8 p.m.

At **El Prat airport:** tel. 325-5820. Open Mon.-Sat. 9:30 a.m.-8 p.m., Sun. 9:30 a.m.-3 p.m.

In the **city centre.** Gran Via de Corts Catalanes 658, tel. 301-7443. Open Mon.-Fri. 9 a.m.-7 p.m., Sat. 9 a.m.-2 p.m.

Summer only:

In the **Ajuntament de Barcelona:** Plaça de Sant Jaume, tel. 302-4200. Open 24 June-30 Sept., Mon.-Fri. 9 a.m.-8 p.m., Sat. 8.30 a.m.-2:30 p.m.

In the **Palau de la Virreina:** Ramblas 99, tel. 301-7775. Open 24 June-30 Sept., Mon.-Sat. 9:30 a.m.-9 p.m., Sun. 10 a.m.-2 p.m.

These tourist offices provide a wide range of information and services, including free city maps and Metro plans, hotel reservations, theatre tickets and addresses of local festivals, nightclubs, bars and restaurants. You can get free detailed maps in English and with photos of art/history walks through the area, as well as pamphlets on Modernism, Gothic and Romanesque sights and the different Catalan regions around Barcelona.

Cultural Information. Palau de la Virreina, Ramblas 99, and opposite at No. 118, in the Generalitat bookshop, where you can get information from two computers.

INFORMATION

Magazines. The weekly city magazine *Guia del Ocio* is helpful for newcomers but also valued by Barcelona experts. This very comprehensive little booklet lists almost all cinema, music and theatre programmes as well as most bars, clubs and restaurants. The glossy **Barcelona Concept**, magazine with lots of shopping addresses, appears twice yearly.

BANKS AND MONEY

Between June and September, banks and bureaux de change are generally only open from 8:30 a.m.–2 p.m. Monday to Friday. During the rest of the year they are also usually open on Saturdays from 8:30 a.m.–1 p.m. In the city centre, some banks stay open until 4:45 p.m.

The Banco at the **airport** is open daily from 7 a.m.–11 p.m. and at **Sants** station, tel. 410-3915, during the summer, Monday to Saturday from 8 a.m.–10 p.m., Sundays from 8 a.m.–2 p.m. and from 4–10 p.m.

The **Banco Bilbao Vizcaya**, Plaça de Catalunya on the corner with Bergara (M: Catalunya), and at Ramblas 52 (M: Drassanes) is open Monday to Saturday from 8:15 a.m.–2 p.m. and from 4-10 p.m. Further brances of this bank will soon introduce longer opening hours. Enquire at each particular branch. Those mentioned above are the most central.

Beware of the many Cambio offices at popular tourist points that are open at weekends and late at night. You pay for this extra service with poor rates of exchange and high commissions. When you buy pesetas, banks and *caixas* (savings banks) are more numerous and offer better exchange rates.

Because of the many pickpockets, travellers cheques in pounds or dollars are a good idea as they are easily replaceable in the event of loss. You can cash them everywhere. Again, the exchange rate is poorer in hotels and pensiones than in banks, for both travellers cheques and cash.

Those carrying Eurocheques and the Eurocheque card can withdraw spending money up to 25,000 pesetas per cheque. Ask for a pin number, this way you can use the card in cashpoint machines in hundreds of caixas and banks.

Important: Without a passport or ID card you cannot exchange money or cash cheques. Many Spaniards carry only photocopies of their passports or ID because of the threat of theft. Unfortunately, photocopies are seldom accepted in banks and bureaux de change.

You can, of course, withdraw pesetas at cashpoint machines with a credit card and pin number. But beware: many of these machines are in small enclosed lobbies that only open by sliding your card into a slot by the door. Once inside, be sure to close the door or a thief may slip in behind you and relieve you of your cash. Be especially careful after dark.

If you take your Girobank savings book to Barcelona you can top up at the main post office. You can also cash pesetas up to £300 per withdrawal from other post office branches. There is a monthly maximum, currently £600, but you can enquire at your post office and possibly increase this limit. International Girocheques, debited to your account, are also very convenient and can be easily cashed at all branches. It works really well, but watch out for opening times!

American Express. Passeig de Gràcia 101, on the corner with Rosselló, tel. 217-0070.

Visa and Mastercard. Tel. 315-2512

Diners Club. Tel. 302-1428.

POSTAL SERVICES

The Spanish post office! When you buy stamps or mail a parcel, be sure to count your change and stamps. "Miscalculations" can occur, often to your disadvantage. Parcels and books should be sent by recorded delivery. This is what the locals do, and they should know. Post is often tampered with in ports, according to a friendly man behind the counter.

Correo Central. Plaça Antoni López. M: Barceloneta.

You can buy stamps *(sellos)* at the main post office Monday to Friday from 8:30 a.m.-10 p.m., Saturday from 9 a.m.-2 p.m., and Sunday 10 a.m.-12 noon, at the sellos counter in the basement. Mail can be

INFORMATION

collected Monday to Saturday from 9 a.m.-2 p.m. at the Post Restante counter on the left of the hall. Telegrams can be sent daily from 8:30 a.m.-10 p.m. Additional counters for air mail (Via Aerea), recorded delivery (Certificades) and express post (Postal Express) are open Monday to Friday from 8:30 a.m.-8 p.m. and Saturdays from 9 a.m.-2 p.m.

Post Office Savings Bank. Caixa Postal. The counter is on the left in the hall and is open Monday to Friday from 8:30 a.m.-2 p.m. It is also open on Saturdays from October to the end of May, though unfortunately not in the summer.

TELEPHONE

In Spain the **Telefónica** is entirely separate from the post office. Telephone calls can be made from wherever you see the illuminated blue or sometimes green circle with the white T. Public telephones can be found on any street corner, but frequently they are vandalised. Instructions are also given in English in all booths. Telephones for international calls are marked **Teléfono Internacional**. More convenient is to call from public telephones in bars, cafés or restaurants. Collect calls are not possible from public telephones, only from a Telefónica bureau.

National calls are cheaper after 8 p.m. and at the weekend, and international calls cost less during the week after 10 p.m. and all day at weekends.

The area code for Barcelona is 93.

Directory Enquiries. Barcelona city and province, 003. Other provinces, 009. Europe, 008. Rest of the world, 005.

Operator. 008 for international calls and 009 for national calls.

Prefixes. England: 44. USA: 1. Ireland: 353. To call London, for example, dial the following number: 07, wait for the tone, then 44-71, then the private number. Omit the first 0 of the prefix as with international calls.

48

Useful Numbers.   Talking clock, 093.   Weather, 094.   Sport, 097.
Wake-up calls, 096.

Telefonica.   Plaça de Catalunya, Fontanella 4, nearby Portal de
l'Angel. M: Catalunya.   Mon. - Sat., 8:30 a.m.-9 p.m.
     The call must be booked beforehand and paid for afterwards. Major
credit cards such as Visa, Eurocard, or American Express are accepted
for charges over 500 pesetas. Information in other languages is available
at the information desk.   Collect calls can be made and must be
requested as '*Llamada de cobro revertido*'.

USEFUL ADDRESSES AND NUMBERS

Airport Information.   Tel. 370-1011.

AIRLINES

British Airways.   Passeig de Gràcia 85, tel. 215-2112.

Iberia.   Plaça Espanya, Passeig de Gracia, tel. 325-7358 (reservations
and sales), 301-3993 (flight information).

TWA.   Passeig de Gràcia 55, Tel. 215-8188.

AU PAIR AGENCIES

Asociacion Internacional, Intercambio Cultural Au-Pair.   Passeig
de Gràcia 67, tel. 215-4895.
     Apply to this agency in writing, enclosing a photograph and giving
personal details. A basic knowledge of Spanish is useful, although many
families also speak French and English.

See also British Council Institute.

Barcelona Information.   Tel. 010, or 318-2525.
British Council Institute.   Amigó 83, tel. 209-6388.

INFORMATION

Chemists. Farmacias de Guardia, night duty chemists, are listed at all chemists, or you can find them in the local paper under this heading.

CONSULATES

British Consulate. Diagonal 477, tel. 419-9044.

Canadian Consulate. Via Augusta 125, tel. 209-0634.

Irish Consulate. Gran Via Carles III 94, tel. 330-9652.

U.S. Consulate. Via Laietana 33, tel. 319-9550.

Fax. You can send a fax in the photo shop **Forsire**, Gran de Gràcia 120. M: Diagonal. Open Mon.-Fri., 10 a.m.-2 p.m. and 4-8 p.m. Or at **Eco Press**, Plaça  Castellà 2, tel. 318-0603. M: Universitat. Both shops are cheaper than the main post office.

Firemen. Bomberos, tel. 080.

GUIDES AND INTERPRETERS

Barcelona Guide Bureau (BGB). Via Laietana 54, 6-5 (08003), tel. 268-2422.

The Professional Association of Tourist Information Guides. Pl. Berenguer el Gran 1 (08002), tel 345-4221 or 319-8416. Open 4-8 p.m.

LOST PROPERTY

Oficina de Objetos Perdidos. Ayuntamiento, Plaça Sant Jaume, tel. 301-3923. M: Jaume I.
With a bit of luck, you may recover your stolen handbag or briefcase here, if it was dropped by the bag snatchers.

INFORMATION

LANGUAGE COURSES

Asociacion Catalana de Escuelas de Idiomas. Balmes 217 (08006), tel. 237-8596.

The umbrella organisation for language schools. Write to this address for a full list of schools, some of which can arrange lodgings for foreign students.

Escuela Oficial de Idiomas. Avinguda de les Drassanes (08001), tel. 329-3412. M: Drassanes.

In contrast to private Spanish language courses, this state language school is extremely economical.

Universitat de Barcelona. Estudis Hispànics, Plaça Universitat, Gran Via C.C. 585 (08007), tel. 318-4266 and 318-9926. M: Universitat.

Intensive summer courses in Spanish and Catalan. There is also a full year course, 'Spanish Language and Culture', aimed at foreigners with a basic knowledge of Spanish.

LEFT LUGGAGE OFFICES

Sants Central Railway Station.
Tel. 490-0202.

You can leave your luggage here in lockers for 200-400 pesetas per day. Open daily, 6:30 a.m.–11 p.m.

International Maritime Station. Tel. 302-4192.
Storage space is available here for 200 pesetas per day. Open daily 8 a.m.–3 p.m.

Belears Maritime Station. Tel. 317-0217.
Storage space available. Open daily 9 a.m.–1 p.m. and 4–10 p.m.

Sarfa. Plaça Duc de Medinaceli 4, tel. 318-9434.
Storage space available for 150 pesetas per day. Open daily 8 a.m.–8.15 p.m.

51

INFORMATION

Alsina Graells. Ronda Universitat 4, tel. 302-6545.

Storage space for 50 pesetas per day. Open daily 9 a.m.-1.30 p.m. and 4-8 p.m.

Motorway Information. Tel. 204-2247.

Rail Information. Tel. 490-0202.

TRAVEL AGENCIES

Barnastop. Pintor Fortuny 21 (08001), tel. 318-2731. M: Liceu. Open Mon.-Fri. 10 a.m.-2 p.m. and Sat. 11 a.m.-2 p.m.

This agency puts travellers in touch with drivers who have passenger space available (prices are governed by international agreements), and also books cheap bus journeys in Europe and charter flights to the Balearic and Canary Islands. An accommodation service is available, mainly in summer, for holiday flats in Barcelona.

Viatges l'Arc. Ronda Sant Pau 46, 4th floor, tel 301-2836. M: Parallel; and Passeig del Born 10 (Ribera), tel. 315-0098 and 319-4028. M: Jaume I.

Cheap but reliable flights to Europe, U.S., Latin America and other cities in Spain. Friendly, English-speaking staff who will also give advice on rail or ferry travel to the Canaries and to Ibiza and Formentera.

WOMEN'S CULTURAL CENTRES

Ca la Donna. Gran Via de les Corts Catalanes 549, 4°-1a, tel. 323-3307. M: Urgell.

Approximately 15 different women's groups meet here.

Centre de Documentacio de la Donna. La Sedeta, Sicilia 321, tel. 257-4578. M: Joanic.

WOMEN'S INFORMATION CENTRE

Donna-Prisma Cultural. Rambla de Catalunya 101, tel. 215-1533.
M: Diagonal.

LESBIANS AND GAY MEN

Sextienda. Raurich 11, Barri Gòtic. Open Mon.-Sat. 10 a.m.-9 p.m.
This shop distibutes free maps of gay Barcelona and Sitges.

Zeus Gay Shop. Riera Alta 20, tel. 242-97950. M: Sant Antoni.
Open Mon.-Sat. 10 a.m.-9 p.m.
This shop also gives away gay maps of the city.

Grup de Lesbianes Feministes de Barcelona. Ca de la Donna,
Gran Via de les Corts Catalanes 549, tel. 323-3307.

Barcelona Lesbian Group. *L'Eix Violeta*, a young lesbian group, also
meets here.

YOUTH SERVICES

Oficina de Turisme Juvenil de Catalunya. (Catalonia Young
Tourists Office). Gravina 1 (08001), tel. 302-0682.
Student ID cards and youth hostel cards are available here.

Direcció General de la Joventut. (Youth Department). Generalitat
de Catalunya, Viladomat 319 (08029), tel. 322-9061.

HELP IN BARCELONA

If you want to call the police because your handbag or camera has been stolen, your car broken into ro vandalised, dial the free **emergency** numbers 092 and 091.

Although city policemen wearing blue uniforms, the so-called Guardia Urbana or Policía Municipal, carry guns on their belt, they are exceptionally friendly and helpful, even if you're only looking for an obscure alley.

Ideal for minor problems are the *casacas rojas*, recognisable in their bright red jackets. They assist tourists and stroll along the Ramblas and Passeig de Gràcia between the months of June and September.

POLICE

Theft and robbery are best reported immediately in person at the central police station, where some officers speak English.

Tourist Attention. Ramblas 43, tel. 301-9060.

Open 24 hours a day during summer, Christmas and Easter, and regular office hours the rest of the year. Here you can be sure that the staff speak your language; they'll assist with legal information, put you in touch with lawyers and doctors, make telephone calls to friends or relatives back home, and will even arrange to have money sent to the police station or the hotel. If you lose your credit card, you will find people here who can inform the credit card company and order a replacement in Spanish - very helpful in this country, as few Spaniards speak English fluently.

Policia. Ample 23, tel. 318-3689. M: Drassanes. And **Central Police Station**, Laietana 49, tel. 302-6325 and 301-6666. M: Jaume I.

MEDICAL HELP

In case of emergency dial 092. The police will then contact the ambulance. Otherwise contact the following directly:

Ambulancias de la Ciudad. Tel. 329-7766 and 300-2020.

Medico de Urgencia. Tel. 212-8585 and 317-1717. Emergency doctor.

Hospital Sant Pau. Avinguda Sant María Claret 167, tel. 347-3133. M: Hospital Sant Pau.

Hospital Clinic. Casanova 143, tel. 323-1414. M: Hospital Clínic.

Hospital Creu Roja. Dos de Maig 301, tel. 235-9300. M: Hospital Sant Pau.

All three hospitals have round-the-clock emergency service.

ENGLISH-SPEAKING DOCTORS

Your embassy will have a list of all English-speaking doctors and paramedics. Before leaving Britain, get hold of an E-111 form from any post office. Some doctors will accept this certificate and attend to you. Unfortunately, many surgeries and medical centres are closed in August. Therefore, medical insurance is recommended, particularly if you are travelling by car.

ACCIDENT ASSISTANCE

You should contact your consulate in the event of an accident and they will arrange everything for you from repatriation, legal aid, interpreters, vehicle repair and telephone calls home.

AA. Tel. 339-7824.

RAC. Tel. 200-8800.

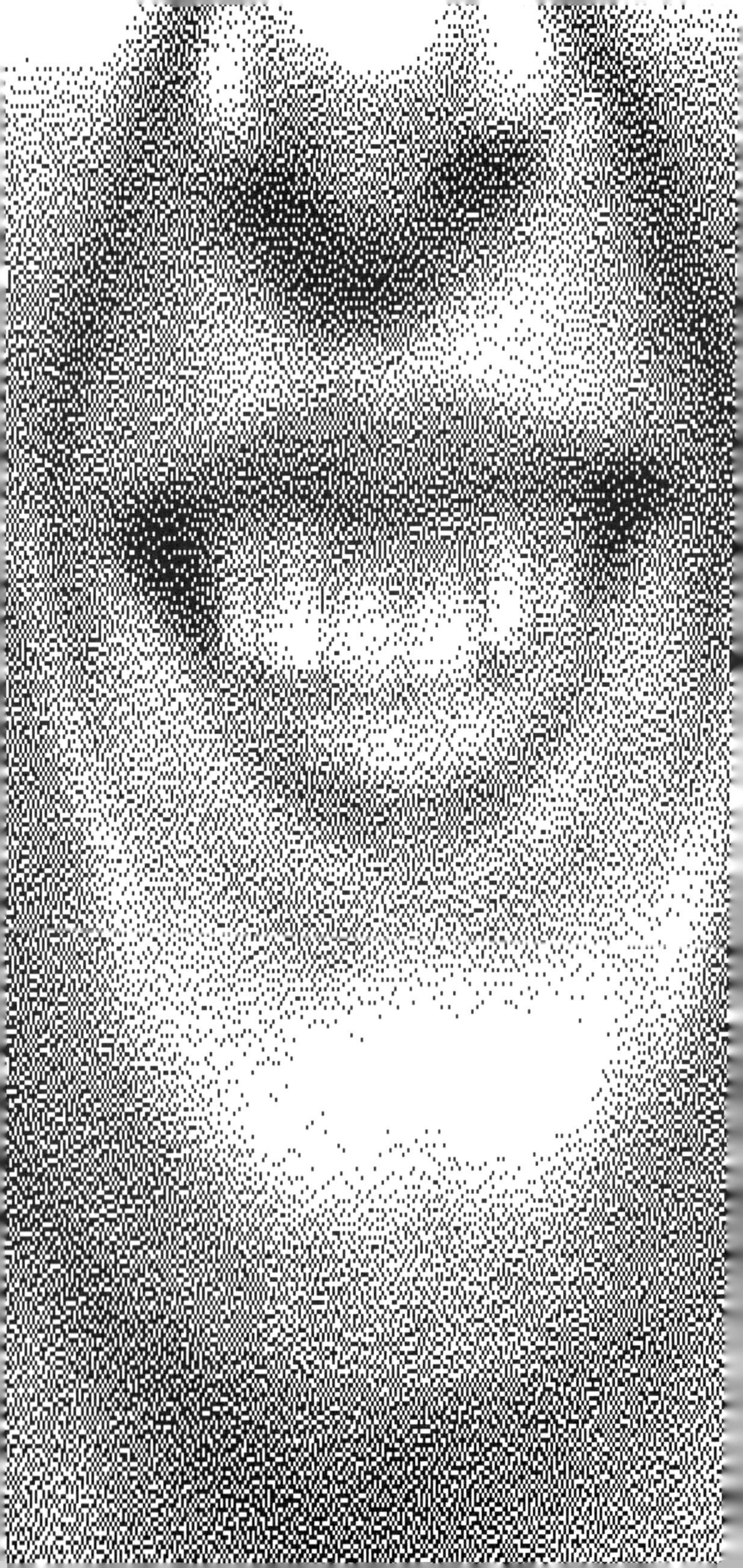

LANGUAGE

Barcelona is the capital of Catalonia and people here are very proud of their national language, Català (Catalan, that is). Even the European Parliament, when pressed by the Generalitat of Barcelona, was obliged to admit Català as an official language. True Catalans stand out from the 'guest workers' from Andalucia, Galicia and the Basque country. All over Spain, Catalans are considered arrogant, devious and obsessed with money and work. They, however, see themselves as the only true Europeans among Spaniards. Someone who wasn't so keen on the Spanish once said, 'Africa begins at the Pyrenees'. But the people of Barcelona believe that Moorish influence is still predominant in Spain, apparent above all in the architecture of Granada and Seville, and they want to remain aloof.

The people in Barcelona despise the main language spoken in the rest of the country - Castilian - after the region of Castile, which has Madrid as its capital and seat of government. Because Català was banned under Franco and many even ended up in jail for using this language, Catalans still breathe an air of revolution. Resistance fighters once whispered their secrets in Català and the priests of Montserrat continued to preach in their language regardless.

If you want to get in with Catalans, you should say *Si us plau* and *Bona nit*, rather than *Por favor* and *Buenas noches*!

The following list includes a few important words in English, Catalan and Castilian (in that order). There is a special Gourmet glossary in the Food and Drink section.

one *un*; *uno*
two *dos*; *dues* (m./f.); *dos*
three *tres*; *tres*
four *quatre*; *cuatro*
five *cinc*; *cinco*
six *sis*; *seis*
seven *set*; *siete*
eight *vuit*; *ocho*

nine *nou*; *nueve*
ten *deu*; *diez*

Monday *dilluns*; *lunes*
Tuesday *dimarts*; *martes*
Wednesday *dimecres*; *miércoles*
Thursday *dijous*; *jueves*
Friday *divendres*; *viernes*

LANGUAGE

Saturday *dissabte; sàbado*
Sunday *diumenge; domingo*

January *gener ; enero*
February *febrer; febrero*
March *març; marzo*
April *abril; abril*
May *maig; mayo*
June *juny; junio*
July *juliol; julio*
August *agost; agosto*
September *setembre; septiembre*
October *octubre; octubre*
November *november ; noviembre*
December *desembre; diciembre*

spring *primavera; primavera*
summer *estiu; verano*
autumn *tardor ; otoño*
winter *hivern; invierno*

Christmas *nadal; navidad*
Easter *setmana santa; Semana Santa*
New Year *cap d'any; año nuevo*
yesterday *ahir; ayer*
today *avui; hoy*
tomorrow *demà; mañana*
day *dia; dia*
week *setmana; semana*
weekend *cap de setmana; fin de semana*

year *any; año*
yes/no *sí/no; sí/no*
thank you *(moltes) gràcies; (muchas) gracias*

it's nothing *de res; de nada*
please *si us plau; por favor*
excuse me *perdoneu/dispenseu; perdone/disculpe*

Sir *Senyor ; Señor*
Madam *Senyora; Señora*
Miss *Senyoreta; Señorita*

hello! *hola!*
good morning *bon día; buenos dias*
good afternoon *bona tarda; buenas tardes*
good evening *bona nit; buenas noches*
good night *bona nit; buenas noches*
good-bye *adéu-sia; adios*
How are you? *Com està?; Como està?*
see you tomorrow *fins demà; hasta mañana*
What time is it? *Quina hora és?; Quéw hora es?*
Where can one ...? *On es pot ....?; Dónde se puede ...?*
Where is ...? *On és pot ...?; Dónde està ...?*
I am looking for ... *Cerco ...; Busco ...*
I would like ... *Voldria ...; Quisiera ...*
I need ... *Necessito ...; Necisito ...*
Do you speak English/German/French? *Parleu anglès/alemany/francès?; Habla Usted inglès/alemán/francès?*

60

What is this in Castilian/Catalán? *Com es diu això en castellà/català?*; *Cómo se llama esto en castellano/catalàn?*

Please speak more slowly *Parleu una mica més lent, si us plau*; *Hable un poco más lento, por favor*

What is your name? *Com us dieu?*; *Cómo se llama Usted?* (formal)

What is your name? *Com te dius?*; *Cómo te llamas?* (familiar)

My name is ... *Em dic ...*; *Me llamo ...*

What time is breakfast? *A quina hora es pot esmorzar?*; *A qué hora se puede desayunar?*

to have lunch *dinar*; *almorzar*

to have dinner *sopar*; *cenar*

Do you have a menu? *té menú?*; *tiene menú?*

the menu *la carta*

the bill *el compte*; *la cuenta*

a glass *un vas*; *un vaso*

a plate *un plat*; *un plato*

a bottle *una ampolla*; *una botella*

cutlery *coberts*; *cubiertos*

knife *ganivet*; *cuchillo*

fork *forquilla*; *tenedor*

spoon *cullera*; *cuchara*

How do I get to ...? *Per anar a ...?*; *Para ir a ...?*

Where is the nearest petrol station/garage? *On és la pròxima gasolinera/el pròxim taller de reparació?*; *Dónde està la próxima gasolinera/el próximo taller de raparación?*

Please fill up the tank *Ompliu el dipòsit, si us plau*; *Llene el depósito, por favor*

exit *sortida*; *salida*

water *aigua*; *agua*

air *aire*; *aire*

Do you have any rooms? *Us queda alguna habitacio?*; *Le quede alguna habitacion?*

For one night/two people *Per una nit/dues persones*; *Para una noche/dos personas*

How much is that? *Quant val?*; *Cuánto vale?*

beds *llits*; *camas*

price *preu*; *precio*

open *obert*; *abierto*

closed *tancat*; *cerrado*

Have you ...? *Vosté té ...?*; *Tiene Usted ...?*

more *més*; *más*

less/fewer *menys*; *menos*

no more *res mes*; *nada más*

How much is that? *Quant val això?*; *Cuànto vale esto?*

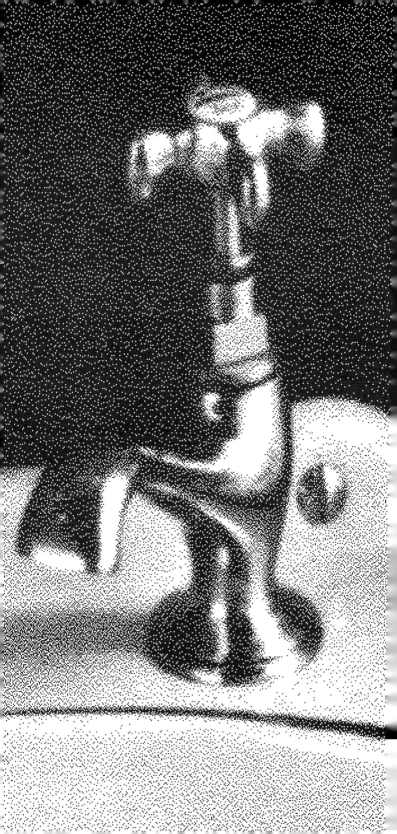

ACCOMMODATION

The extremely helpful tourist offices (see Information), mostly with young staff, will book you into any kind of hotel and *hostal*. Unfortunately, two-star establishments are not a guarantee of a clean and quiet room. And some three-star hotels offer less comfort and service than good two-star hostales. Often, my choice was influenced more by location than by the accommodation itself.

Warning: Even the most beautiful view of the ornate cathedral towers and the coral-red roofs of the Gothic quarter do not make up for sleepless nights. Spaniards have an unbelievable resistance to noise. Such disturbance, either from ghetto-blasters or rowdy neighbours, stray dogs or amorous cats, is a major problem all over Spain but especially in the narrow streets of the old town. For months I couldn't sleep without earplugs. Light sleepers should take some along as a precaution.

Because many of the budget hotels and hostales occupy one or two floors of an apartment building, often with inner wells not unlike a Swiss cheese, all sorts of noise reverberates freely throughout. Acoustic scientists find this wide range of echoes emanating from all corners a dreaded study project. And it is astonishing how many cocks in Barcelona can't resist crowing into the morning every quarter hour. So, don't just inspect the beds!

My favourite area for hotels is behind the Plaça de Catalunya in the Eixample, the pleasant shopping and residential district with its straight, chequer-board streets. Here hardly any bag snatchers or junkies armed with knives lie in wait at night to jump exhausted tourists. Unfortunately, such a horrific experience is not uncommon in the port area of the old town. Single women travellers above all should avoid accommodation to the left and right of the Ramblas below Carrer Escudellers. Although you will find the most economical *pensiones* here, they are little more than seedy dosshouses and should only be a last resort. Barcelona is small enough for you to stroll from your hostal in the quiet Eixample to the Barri Gòtic. The buses and Metro are also safe, reliable and cheap.

Other recommendable areas are those between the Ramblas and

ACCOMMODATION

Plaça Sant Jaume, the area around the university near Plaça Universitat and Plaça de Catalunya.

BUDGET HOSTALES AND PENSIONES

EIXAMPLE

Hostal Goya. Pau Claris 75, tel. 302-2565. Singles from 1,850 ptas, doubles from 2,800 ptas.

A tiny, quiet 11-room hostal in a super location, and the rooms are not too small.

Hostal Oliva. Passeig de Gràcia 32, tel. 317-5087. Singles from 1,850 ptas, doubles from 3,400 ptas.

This hostal occupies 16 rooms in an old apartment building, almost right next door to Gaudí's beautiful Art Nouveau houses. Rooms facing the street are rather noisy.

Ch Vicenta. Ramblas de Catalunya 84, tel. 215-1923. Singles from 1,200 ptas, doubles from 2,400 ptas.

Wonderful location, you can look straight onto the street cafés on the Ramblas. This modest Casa d'Hostes (pensión) has 28 rooms with wash basins only; however, the bath on the corridor is clean. Those who like the nearby designer bars and nightclubs can walk back at night and save on taxi fares.

Pensione Ciutat Comtal. Mallorca 255, tel. 215-1040. Singles from 3,500 ptas, doubles from 5.500 ptas.

Tiny Pensione on one floor of an apartment building. Each of the 11 rooms has bath and telephone. Very good and safe area, near many shops and bars.

Pension Fani. València 278, tel. 215-3645. Singles from 1,000 ptas, doubles from 1,650 ptas.

Located in an ideal, safe area, this pensión has 27 small rooms with bath and shower on the corridor.

Ch Leo. Roger de Llúria 54, tel. 301-4191. Singles 2,400 ptas, doubles 3,600 pts.

Eleven rooms on one floor in a large, old apartment building.

Hostal Colon. Arago 281, tel. 215-4700. Singles from 2,000 ptas, doubles from 2,400 ptas. Rooms with telephone.

One-star hostel with 15 rooms in a beautiful apartment building. A lot of traffic, so better to get a room at the back.

Hostal Bonavista. Carrer Bonavista 21, tel. 237-3757. Singles from 1,500 ptas, doubles from 2,000 ptas.

Very comfortable for the price. The old furniture also gives this house its charm. Tasteful and clean. Many tapas bars and restaurants on the squares in the nearby Gràcia area.

UNIVERSITY AREA

Ch Puebla de Arenoso. Aribau 29, tel. 253-3138. Singles from 1,500 ptas, doubles from 2,000 ptas.

This pensión has only eight rooms but is quietly located.

Hostal Sena. Ronda Universitat 29, tel. 318-9097. Singles from 1,400 ptas, doubles from 2,000 ptas.

Friendly proprietor, clean rooms and baths. Near Plaça de Catalunya and the Ramblas.

ACCOMMODATION

BARRI GOTIC

Ch Colmenero. Petritxol 21, tel. 302-6634. Singles from 2,000 ptas, doubles from 2,400 pts.

Tiny pensión with 10 rooms, in the old town. An excellent *granja* (milk bar) right next door will entice you for breakfast.

Hostal Layetana. Plaça Ramon Berenguer el Gran 2, tel. 319-2012. Singles from 1,300 ptas, doubles from 2,100 ptas.

High above the roofs of the town, with fantastic views of the cathedral. Quiet and clean, with a friendly proprietor. I enjoyed my stay here very much!

Hostal Levante. Baixada de Sant Miquel 2, tel. 317-9565. Singles from 1,600 ptas, doubles from 2,100 ptas.

Right in the old town bustle. The showers on the corridors are clean. Not too noisy at night.

Hotel Oasis. Plaça del Palau 17, tel. 319-4369. Singles from 4,500 ptas, doubles from 5,500 ptas.

Lovely views over the harbour and the post-modern bars of the Moll de la Fusta or, from the back, the Ribera quarter with the Picasso Museum. The 65 rooms are small, without much luxury, but at least they have telephones.

Hotel Peninsular. Sant Pau 34, tel. 302-3138. Singles 2,700 ptas, with bath 3,400 ptas. Doubles 4,300 ptas, with bath 5,600 ptas.

This green and white Art Nouveau hotel has a brilliant light-filled glass roof in the courtyard. Wonderfully old-fashioned, even though the friendly owners renovated it in 1988. Smallish rooms, no TV or mini-bar, but what do you expect for one-star prices?

Hostal Tirol. Rambla de las Flores 85, tel. 318-1538. Singles from 1,800 ptas, doubles 2,400-3,000 ptas.

From the windows there are wonderful views of the flower sellers on the Ramblas. However, if you are looking for peace and quiet, take an interior room as the 'most romantic street in the world' never sleeps.

Hostal Roma. Plaça Reial 11, tel. 302-0366. Singles from 1,700 ptas, doubles 2,200-3,500 ptas. Rooms with telephone.

At the moment the Plaça Reial is not a good address, as many drug dealers hang out and peddle their merchandise on the benches and under Gaudí's lovely street lamps. However, the hostal has two stars, and the city promises to clean up the square for the Olympics, as it is one of Barcelona's finest.

Ch Princesa. Princesa 7, tel. 319-5031. Singles from 1,500 ptas, doubles from 2,100 ptas.

This pensión, with 41 rooms is located in a reasonable area and near the Picasso museum.

Hostal Union. Unió 14, tel. 318-1581. Singles 900-1,800 ptas, doubles 2,100-3,000 ptas.

Located behind the Opera Liceu in a small side street off the Ramblas, this one-star 21-room hostal offers parking places and telephone in the rooms. However, the area is considered rather down-market and not too safe, being so near the Barrio Chino.

Hostal la Paz. Argenteria 37, tel. 319-4408. Singles from 1,000 ptas, doubles from 1,500 ptas, with bath from 1,800 ptas.

A surprisingly good value hostal, with 38 rooms. Near the Picasso museum, the wonderful Santa María del Mar church and the Born, with its many bars.

ACCOMMODATION

COMFORTABLE AND ORIGINAL HOTELS

BARRI GOTIC AND RAMBLAS

Hotel Atlantis.   Pelai 20, tel. 318-9012.   Singles from 10,000 ptas, doubles from 13,000 ptas.

This new designer-hotel, with 41 rooms, is right in the centre, near Plaça de Catalunya. at the start of the Ramblas.   Extremely comfortable beds and fully air-conditioned, naturally.

Hotel Espanya.   Sant Pau 9, tel. 318-1758.   Singles from 1,900 ptas, doubles 3,800-4,600 ptas.

One of the few modernist hotels in the city constructed by the Art Nouveau master, Domenech i Montaner.   As the hotel is in the Barrio Chino, wealthier clients are deterred, and consequently the management lacks the funds for a much needed renovation.   The rooms are only gradually being refurbished.   Beds, curtains and carpets are ancient.   However, you should see the lobby with its elaborate fireplace and the wonderful dining room with its nymph and water-lily tiles.

Hostal el Casal.   Carrer Tapineria 10, tel. 319-7800.   Singles with bath 3,100 ptas, doubles with bath 5,400 ptas.

This three-star hotel is the best located in Barcelona: right next to the cathedral, whose towers seem within reach from the breakfast room.   Three floors in a well-kept old building, with a great roof terrace for taking photos.   Very helpful proprietor.   You'll sleep like a baby.

Hostal Rey Don Jaime I.   Jaume I II, tel. 315-4161.   Singles with bath 2,700 ptas, doubles with bath 4,400 ptas.

This two-star hostal, with 30 rooms, is near the city hall and 30 seconds away from Jaume I Metro station.   Though very small, the rooms are very comfortable.   Good quality/value ratio.

Hotel Nouvel.   Santa Anna 20, tel. 301-8274.   Singles 2,900 ptas, doubles 4,400-5,800 ptas.

This well-kept, old-fashioned hotel has traditional Spanish floor tiling, a different pattern in each room.   The 76 rooms are tastefully decorated and furnished. It's in a quiet side street off the Ramblas and near Plaça de Catalunya.

Hotel Meson Castilla. Valldonzella 5, tel. 318-2182. Singles with bath 5,400 ptas, doubles with bath 8,000 ptas.

This two-star hotel is near the future museum and art gallery complex in the old Casa Caritat. The house looks antique, but the rooms have recently been refurbished. My insider tip: extremely comfortable!

Hotel Metropol. Ample 31, tel. 315-4011, fax 319-12760. Singles with bath 11,000 ptas, doubles with bath 14,500 ptas.

The hotel's super-modern decor, right in the port district, attracts young Japanese and Americans with a taste for design. Surprisingly good value considering rooms have TV and telephone, new beds and good service.

Hotel Villa de Madrid. Plaça Vila de Madrid 3, tel. 317-4916. Singles with bath 6,500 ptas, doubles with bath 10,000 ptas.

A three-star hotel with 28 rooms on a quiet square in the middle of the old town. There is room to breathe, and the traffic noise is bearable because of the many surrounding pedestrian zones. Near Plaça de Catalunya.

Hotel Suizo. Placa de l'Angel 12, tel. 315-4111, fax 315-3819. Singles with bath 9,200 ptas, doubles with bath 12,500 ptas.

This turn-of-the-century three-star hotel is near the cathedral. Picasso loved the Suizo, and sometimes celebrities still stay here, attracted by the slightly shabby charm of the bourgeoisie, the excellent service, TV and air-conditioning in rooms, and room service into the small hours.

UNIVERSITAT

Reding. Gravina 5-7, tel. 412-1097. Singles from 10,000 ptas, doubles from 12,000 ptas.

Another brand-new hotel that opened its doors in January 1991.

ACCOMMODATION

Modern, but boring decor, though the 44 rooms have colour TV. There's even a garage underneath - useful, as there is a great shortage of parking spaces in the centre of Barcelona.

Hotel Regina. Bergara 2, tel. 301-3232, fax 318-2326. Singles with bath 10,000 ptas, doubles with bath 15,000 ptas.

This three-star hotel is more in the style of a grand hotel. Rooms have antiques, room service and TV.

Hotel Gravina. Gravina 12, tel. 301-6868. Singles with bath 9,000 ptas, doubles with bath 13,000 ptas.

A three-star Art Nouveau hotel with 60 rooms, all with TV and grand comfort.

EIXAMPLE

Hotel Wilson. Diagonal 568, tel. 209-2511. Singles 9,600 ptas, doubles 12,000 ptas.

Though it's right in the middle of Barcelona's number one shopping avenue, the double-glazing doesn't let the traffic noise in. Ideal for night owls, because many of the bars and discos are just around the corner.

Hotel Gran Via. Gran Via 642, tel. 318-1900. Singles with bath 7,200 ptas, doubles with bath 10,500 ptas.

This grandiose hotel is decorated with fantastic antiques and the lobby is straight out of Versailles. At the beginning of the shopping area in Passeig de Gràcia, the location is ideal for uptown or downtown.

Hostal Neutral. Rambla de Catalunya 42, tel. 318-7370. Singles from 1,600 ptas, doubles 2,600-3,200 ptas.

This two-star hostal has a peaceful location, with a view of the Eixample's finest promenade. All 28 rooms have a telephone.

ACCOMMODATION

EXCLUSIVE HOTELS

BARRI GOTIC AND THE RAMBLAS

Hotel Colón. Catedral 7, tel. 301-1404, fax 317-2917. Singles 12,000 ptas, doubles 19,000 ptas.

A grand hotel like the Suizo, the Colón has the super location opposite the cathedral.

Hotel Oriente. Ramblas 45-47, tel. 302-2558. Singles 8,600 ptas, doubles 13,000 ptas.

This three-star hotel with 142 rooms is in one of the oldest buildings on the Ramblas. Little can be recognised from the erstwhile monastery of San Bonaventura built in 1670. Today you can dance in the ballroom where monks once strolled in the cloister.

Ramada Renaissance. Rambla 111, tel. 318-6200 or reservations tel. 318-4432. Singles 25,000 ptas, doubles 36,000 ptas.

Very American in style and comfort. The entrance is in a side street off the Ramblas. This gigantic hotel, with fax and translation service for business travellers, is popular with opera stars who like to stay almost next door to the Liceu Opera.

Hotel Rivoli. Rambla Estudis 128, tel. 302-6071. Singles 17,500 ptas, doubles 21,000 ptas.

Barcelona's most post-modern hotel, designed by Germany's Camilla Hamm in the Mediterranean colours of azure blue, yellow and turquoise. The restaurant and Philippe Starck's bar with its crooked aluminium lighting are also impressive. Each room has a video and, on request, a wordprocessor. Ideal for business travellers.

EIXAMPLE

Hotel Alexandra. Mallorca 251, tel. 215-3052, fax 216-0835. Singles 17,500 ptas, doubles 22,000 ptas.

The cool high-tech design is already apparent from the lobby of the

ACCOMMODATION

Alexandra. This stylish, 75-room, four-star hotel, located in one of uptown Barcelona's most beautiful streets, is a hub for fashion designers, film producers and politicians.

Condes de Barcelona. Passeig de Gràcia 75, tel. 215-0616, fax 216-0835. Singles 18,000 ptas, doubles 25,000 ptas.

This 1896 building is a fine example of modernism; note the detailed tile work on the facade and the excellent wrought-iron decoration. A known address for the landed gentry and aristocracy, with a pleasant bar and stately restaurant. Diagonally opposite Gaudí's famous apartment house, La Pedrera.

Condes de Vedruna. Carrer Pau Claris 150, tel. 322-3215, fax 410-0862. 124 suites from 39,000 ptas.

This new five-star hotel is in a modernist corner building, built up with three more storeys in a glass tower which hovers over the original house and spans the corner. Swimming pool, satellite TV, garden, and shops.

Gran Hotel Catalonia. Balmes 142, tel. 217-6517, fax 415-9667. Singles 18,500 ptas, doubles 25,000 ptas.

A new five-star hotel which opened in the sum of 1991 in the upper parts of Eixample, near Diagonal. Nice views over the city, and satellite TV in rooms.

Hotel Gran Derby. Loreto 28, tel. 322-3215, fax 410-0862. Doubles 22,000 ptas. Apartments.

The Diagonal area, one of the four important venues for the Olympic games, is located in the far north of the city near F.C. Barcelona's football stadium, the Royal Polo Club and the Estadio Central Sants. It is surrounded by high-rise buildings belonging to hotel chains such as the Meliá Barcelona-Sarrià and the Princesa Sofía. The Gran Derby, however, is wonderfully old-fashioned. This turn-of-the-century hotel has only 39 rooms but offers great comfort.

Havana Palace. Gran Via de les Corts Catalanes 647, tel. 412-1115 or reservations tel. 215-7981. Singles 23,000 ptas, doubles 30,000 ptas.

Six floors with 145 rooms and extras like private fax machines in the suites and roof terraces on the top floor. For book lovers, the small Barcelona Library is nestled next to the bar.

Hotel Majestic. Passeig de Gràcia 70, tel, 215-4512, fax 215-7773. Singles 18,000 ptas, doubles 22,500 ptas.

Not a mammoth hotel, despite its four stars and 336 rooms. Relatively old-fashioned, with unrenovated rooms, but a great location!

Hotel Ritz. Gran Via les Corts Catalanes 668, tel. 318-5200, fax 318-0148. Singles 32,000 ptas, doubles 41,000 ptas.

Barcelona's only hotel in the five-star/Grand-Luxe category. And still, the Ritz in Madrid is a thousand times more imposing. All the same, the name once lured people like Helmut Schmidt and the late Andy Warhol, more recently Julio Iglesias and his starlets.

Hotel Regente. Rambla de Catalunya 76, tel. 215-2570. Singles 13,000 ptas, doubles 19,000 ptas.

A four-star Art Nouveau building with 78 rooms and a swimming pool. Wonderful location, surrounded by the best cafés, restaurants and bars in the city.

UNIVERSITAT

Diques de Bergara. Berbara 11, tel. 301-5151, fax 317-3442. Singles 20,500 ptas, doubles 24,000 ptas.

Like the Grand Hotel des Bains in Venice, this majestic turn-of-the-century hotel boasts miles of marble Greek statues, a wrought-iron elevator and fresh flowers in each of the 68 rooms. Near the Plaça de Catalunya and the Café Zürich. One of my favourite hotels.

YOUTH HOSTELS

If you're travelling as a pair, it is hardly worthwhile staying in a youth hostel considering the low price of a pensión. Prices run between 450 and 650 pesetas per person per night. Some youth hostels also have a canteen where you can eat a small meal for a few pesetas.

ACCOMMODATION

Hostal de Joves. Passeig Pujades 29, tel. 300-3104. M: Ciutadella, Arc de Triomf or Bogatell. Bus: 40, 41, 51,141, NL. Open 3 p.m.-12 noon.

Central and near the Ciutadella park and the Norte bus station. 68 beds.

Albergue Verge de Montserrat. Passeig de Nostra Senyora del Coll 41-51, tel. 213-8633. M: Vallcarca. Bus: 25-28. Open 24 hours.

Miles out of town, but bigger than the Hostal de Joves (180 beds). A last resort only. Youth hostel card required.

BCN Youth Hostel. Pelai 62, tel. 317-3095. M: Catalunya.

Not an official state youth hostel, but it's centrally located, right by Plaça de Catalunya. Friendly, young staff, but accommodations are somewhat scruffy.

Pere Tarrés. Numància 149-151, tel. 410-2309. M: Les Corts and Maria Cristina. Bus: 7, 15, 34, 43, 59, 66. Open 8:30 a.m.-10 a.m. and 4 p.m.-12 mid. 100 neds. Youth hostel card required.

Albergue Kabul. Plaça Reial 17, tel. 318-5190. M: Drassanes. Bus: 18, 14, 59, NL, NS, ND. Open 24 hours. 160 beds.

Albergue Studio. Ptge. Duquessa d'Orleans 58, tel. 205-0961. M: Reina Elisenda (Generalitat R.R.) Bus: 22, 34, 64, 66. Open July-Sept. 24 hours. 40 beds.

APARTMENTS

Hotel Apartamento Rekor'd. Muntaner 352, tel. 200-1953. FFCC: Muntaner. Doubles 16,000 ptas. Apartments from 160,000 ptas per month.

In this apartment hotel you can stay economically by the month - interesting for those on business or involved in the Olympic games. This is the place for those who want self-catering. You can really feel at home, as the Carrer Muntaner is in the city's most desirable residential area.

ACCOMMODATION

Hotel Apartamento Victoria. Avinguda Pedralbes 16, tel. 215-2540, fax 489-3227. M: Maria Christina. Doubles 19,000 ptas. Monthly rate better value (negotiable).

Large, comfortable apartments in the Zona Alta, Barcelona's most desirable residential area. Each room has a sun terrace. The best apartment hotel in town, with a swimming pool and good restaurant.

Hotel Apartamento Silver. Bretón de los Herreros 26-30, tel. 218-9100. M: Fontana. Doubles 6,500 ptas. Monthly rate better value (negotiable).

Clean apartments, not luxurious. Lots of families and business travellers. Pleasant and safe surroundings.

Hotel Apartamento Portamar. Paral-lel 46, tel. 329-9111, M: Paral-lel. Approximately 110,000 ptas per month.

This apartment hotel only lets its 80 self-contained studios on a monthly basis. The district is central, though much less chic than the Eixample.

Interhome. Diputació 300, tel. 302-2587.

This international agency arranges holiday apartments on the coast, in Sitges and a few in Barcelona. Phone them from home and request a brochure.

Tandem Language School. Ronda Sant Antoni 100, tel. 318-5434 and 317-1132. M: Universitat.

The helpful German partners of this language school also arrange flats for a small fee for longer stays in Barcelona. But because many students look for accommodation during the summer you had better contact Tandem a few weeks in advance to assess your chances.

CAMPING

Unfortunately, camping sites are in the sticks at least four kilometres from Barcelona. However, if you'd rather not leave your car on the Ramblas and want to spend the night for as little as possible, there is a wide choice of first-class sites with all mod cons. The **Barcelona**

ACCOMMODATION

Asociacion de Campings, Via Laietana 59, tel. 317-4416, provides information on camping sites.

Cala Gogo. Carretera de la Platja, 08820 El Prat, tel. 379-4600.
   The best site, 8km south of the city. 1,500 places.

Camping Barcino. Laurea Miró 50, 08950 Esplugues de Llobregat, tel. 372-8501. M: Can Vidalet on line L5.
   This small site, with 150 places, is only about 4km south of the city. Category 1.

SIGHTS

Barcelona is an ideal city for sightseeing. It is difficult to point out the most important places for your agenda in a few sentences, because in the Barri Gòtic, Ribera and Barrio Chino each house tells a story and each brick is fascinating.

Think of Barcelona as one gigantic masterpiece. Don't just rush from one sight to the other. Forget about tourist stress, and don't settle for any official sightseeing programme of whatever description. It's much better to take your time and stroll through the ancient quarters. Wherever you go, it's fun to watch the Catalans at their favourite pastimes - eating, gossiping and drinking.

Here's a list of the top sights for first-time visitors.

HIGHLIGHTS

Antic Hospital de la Santa Creu. See Barrio Chino.

Casa de la Caritat. See Museums.

Casa Mila, La Pedrera. See Gaudi.

Catedral. See Barri Gòtic.

Estadi Anillo Olimpico (Olympic stadium). See Montjuïc.

Hospital de Sant Pau. See Modernism.

Monestir de Pedralbes. See Museums.

Monestir de Sant Pau del Camp. See Barrio Chino.

Monument a Colom. See Ramblas.

Museu Picasso. See Ribera.

SIGHTS

Museu de Zoologic. See Museums.

Palau de la Musica Catalana. See Modernism.

Sagrada Familia. See Gaudí.

Santa Maria de Mar. See Ribera.

Vil.la Joana. See Modernism.

THE TEN MOST BEAUTIFUL VIEWS

Barcelona is ideal for those people who like to appreciate a city from a birds-eye view. Five different funiculars, a rack railway and cable cars shuttle over the harbour, the city and up Montjuïc and Tibidabo. Here is a list of the most beautiful views. Have fun up there!

From the **Transbordador Aeri** cable car leaving Barceloneta via Moll de Barcelona by the Columbus monument, past Miramar station to Montjuïc. (See Ramblas)

From **Torre de Barceloneta** and **Torre Jaume** on the **Transbordador Aeri**, looking onto Barceloneta's beach and the harbour.

From the **Monument a Colom** at Plaça Portal del Pau. M: Drassanes. (See Ramblas)

From the carousel in **La Muntanya Magica** amusement park on Tibidabo. FFCC: Avinguda de Tibidabo, then onwards with the Tramvia Blau and finally by funicular to the park.

From the terraces of the restaurants **La Balsa**, **La Venta**, and the bars **Merbeye**, **Mirablau** and **Tres Torres** at the foot of Tibidabo. FFCC: Avinguda de Tibidabo, then onwards to the Tramvia Blau terminus.

From a cabin on the **Teleferic**, on your way up to the Castell de Montjuic. M: Paral-lel, then onwards on the funicular to Montjuïc and the Teleferic.

From the terrace on the upper floor of the **Corte Ingles** department store, looking onto Plaça Catalunya.

From the roof of **Casa Mila**, La Pedrera. Gaudí's grandiose residential building on Passeig de Gràcia.

From the towers of **Sagrada Familia**, Gaudí's unfinished cathedral.

From the terminus of the **Funicular de Vallvidrera**. (See Sant Gervasi, Sarrià, Pedralbes and Tibidabo)

PARKS

Parc de la Ciutadella. Passeig de Picasso and Passeig de Pujades. M: Ciutadela and Arc de Triomf. Dail 8:30 a.m.-9 p.m.

    In 1715 Felipe V built a fortress near the harbour, marking the conquest of Barcelona. The citadel was demolished in 1850, but the remaining park, despite its 31 hectares, is more conveniently laid out than the parks on Montjuïc or the Parc Güell. The 1888 world exhibition took place in this park. Domènech i Montaner's curious castle, today the Zoological Museum, right at the entrance, served as a café-restaurant during the exhibition. The castle also featured prominently in Eduardo Mendoza's novel *The City of Miracles*. The park offers something for everyone: boating on the lake, the zoo, and the Museums of Zoology, Geology and Modern Art next to the Parliament of Catalonia.

Parc Güell. Olot. M: Lesseps. Bus: 24, 25, 31, 74 or T 100. Daily. Autumn and winter: 9 a.m.-5 p.m.; spring: 9 a.m.-7 p.m.; summer 9 a.m.-9 p.m.

    The park of all parks! One of the wonders of the world. Walking through Gaudí's early piéce de résistance, you'll feel immersed in the world of Salvador Dalí. I love the long snake-like benches with their

glittering tile surfaces as fine as mosaic. It is said that Gaudí achieved
their gentle shapes with the help of a worker, who had to sit naked on a
lump of soft plaster. Without doubt, Gaudí was a genius. For years he
worked up here with hundreds of labourers on this utopian project,
patiently financed by his benefactor, Count Güell. The work was never
fully completed, as Barcelona's bourgeoisie had not yet discovered the
hills around the city. The two entrance gates are like fairytale fantasies.
You can also admire the fascinating earth-coloured columns, tilted and
twisted to resemble stalagmites and tree roots. Don't forget the small
Gaudí museum in one of the two villas.

Parc de la Creueta del Coll. Castellterçol, tel. 213-2514. Bus: 28
and T 100. Pool open 20 June-15 Sept., Mon.-Fri. 10 a.m.-4 p.m.,
weekends and holidays 10 a.m.-7 p.m.

This modern park, located in a former quarry, is very popular
during the summer for its swimming pool and man-made waterfall. An
Eduardo Chillida sculpture, weighing several tons, hangs precariously
over the blue pool. In winter, people boat on the lake, surrounded by
palms. The American artists Ellsworth Kelly and Roy Lichtenstein
produced sculptures for this park, which was designed by the architects
Josep Martorell and David Mackay.

Parc de l'Espanya Industrial. Muntadas. M: Estació Sants. Bus: T
100.

This five-hectare high-tech park was created in 1985 and its
hallmarks are the futuristic towers and the red Chinese steel dragon.
Children can slide out of the dragon's mouth, and lovers go boating on
the elongated lake. The park is especially idyllic in the evening, when it
is bathed in red and green light.

Parc del Velodrom d'Horta and Parc del Labirint. Passeig de
Vall d'Hebron and Germans Desvalls. M: Montbau (and a long walk).
Bus: 26 and 27.

It's a pity that these overlapping parks are so far from the Metro and
the city. The green spaces (around the velodrome) designed by
architect Bonell i Rius and sculptor Joan Brossa are particularly
beautiful. There you'll find question marks made of concrete next to

brackets and quotation marks, and the fractured columns announce the adjoining 18th-century labyrinth. This romantic park, with statues, fountains and a Moorish palace, built for a count and in private hands until 1971, is well worth the long journey. During the Olympiad, competitions will take place in the velodrome, so let's hope that by then there will be better public transport.

Els Jardins de la Vil.la Amelia. Santa Amélia. M: Maria Cristina.

Lovers of architecture and art shouldn't miss this ultra-modern park designed by architects Martínez Lapena and Torres, in spite of the long journey north of Diagonal through the villa districts of Pedralbes and Sarrià. Francisco López's realistic sculpture of a drowned woman is particularly fascinating.

Parc Joan Miró. Aragó, at the corner with Tarragona. M: Tarragona.

Joan Miro's statue *Dona i Ocell* (Woman and Bird), rises out of a pond - a yellow, red and blue tower whose mosaic surface is reminiscent of Gaudí. The palms and shrubs do not quite succeed in sheltering the visitor from traffic noise on the wide Avinguda. In the evening elderly Spaniards play their version of *pétanque*.

CEMETERIES

Cementiri del Sud-Oest. Mare de Déu del Port, Plaça Davant del Cementiri and Carretera del Foment i les Banderes, tel 332-8847. M: Paral-lel, onwards with the Montjuïc funicular. Open daily, 10 a.m.-1 p.m. and 4-8 p.m.

SIGHTS

Most visitors arrive by car. Long siesta, but during summer, open until at least 8 p.m. This huge cemetery on Montjuïc was opened in 1883 and is the resting place for many famous names which you can discover along the labyrinthine alleys. You can wander up and down steps and along avenues lined with plane trees, and gaze at elegant chapels and miniature houses where Barcelona's high society were buried at the beginning of the century. Exponents of Modernism such as Puig i Cadafalch and Domènech i Montaner not only built palaces for the aristocracy and textile barons, but also their memorials.

The fact that mourners can take their cars or motorbikes right up to the grave is somewhat disconcerting. However, after an hour in this hilly, open space, you might need a comfortable vehicle in order to further explore this seemingly endless cemetery. The modern park, with its asymmetric benches was built in memory of the victims of the civil war and the dictatorship. Famous personalities buried here include: the anarchists Buenaventura Durutti and Francisco Ascaso, politicians such as Francesc Mácia, and the crazy mayor Francesc de Paula Rius i Taulet, the sculptor Josep Clara, architect Ildefons Cerdà, whose 'Plan Cerda' was responsible for the Eixample, as well as poet and priest Jacint Verdaguer. Nearby, the gypsies also built spectacular caravan parks, which you can find in streets around the ring road to the left of the cemetery and the Zona Franca industrial zone, complete with life-size plaster statues of swinging flamenco guitarists.

MUSEUMS

Casa de la Caritat. Montalegre 5 (Barrio Chino), tel. 301-0174.
M: Plaça de Catalunya.

The Museum of Contemporary Art is scheduled to open in 1992 in
this monastery. The Goethe Institute is also planning an annexe in this
building. Exhibitions still take place in the old *palau,* and the café in the
atrium is an ideal place to relax after a stroll on the nearby Ramblas.

Casa-Museu Gaudí. Parc Güell, tel. 284-6446. M: Lesseps. Mar.-
Nov.: Sun.-Fri. 10 a.m.-2 p.m. and 4 -7 p.m. Admission.

Gaudí lived in this house while he was building the park for his
patron, Güell. Have a look upstairs in the small spartan room with its
iron bed, crucifix on the wall and the cupboard which only contained
the same old black suit. This small museum could be better organised.
Chairs and sofas of Gaudí's design are haphazardly arranged among
modernist furniture, and there is no information available. Still, it's very
atmospheric and somehow touching.

Fundació Joan Miro. See Montjuïc.

Fundació Tapies. Aragó 255, tel. 487-0315. M: Passeig de Gràcia.
Tues.-Sat. 11 a.m.-8 p.m., Sun. 11 a.m.-3 p.m. Admission.

This former publishing house now contains Antoni Tàpies's
collection. Symposia on international art and visiting exhibitions of
contemporary art along the lines of the Fundació Miró are planned.
The original facade by Domènech i Montaner is an architectural
masterpiece (see Modernism).

Gabinet de Fisica Experimental Mentora Alsina. Carretera de
Vallvidrera-Tibidabo 56, tel. 417-5734. Funicular del Tibidano.
Guided Tours only.

Exhibition of classic physics apparatus and instruments.

Gabinet Postal. Palau Reial, Diagonal 686, tel. 280-1874. M: Palau
Reial.

Museum of the post office.

Galeria de Catalans Illustres. Bisbe Cassador 3, tel. 315-0010.
M: Jaume I.
   Portraits of famous Catalans.

Monestir de Pedralbes. Baixada del Monastir 9, tel. 203-9282. Bus:
22, 64, 75 and T 100. Tues.-Sun. 9:30 a.m.-2 p.m.
   City hall will install Baron Thyssen-Bornemisza's collection of old
masters in this 1326 monastery, which opens in the summer of 1992.
The trip to Pedralbes is lovely, as the monastery, with its romantic
three-storey cloister, is located in a green and open space among luxury
villas.

Museu Arquelogic. See Montjuïc.

Museu d'Art de Catalunya. See Montjuïc.

Museu de les Arts Decoratives. Palau Reial de Pedralbes, Diagonal
686, tel. 280-5024. M: Palau Reial. Tues.-Fri. 10 a.m.-1 p.m and 4
p.m.-6-p.m., Sat.-Sun. 10 a.m.-1:30 p.m.
   This pavilion, on the estate belonging to Count Güell became a
palace for the Royal Family in 1919. As Alfonso XIII hated Barcelona,
he spent little time here, but the 1929 world exhibition was one of
those occasions. During the Spanish Civil War the palacio served as
residence for the president of the republic. Today the Museu de les
Arts Decoratives is particularly interesting for its 16th-20th century
clocks, furniture, jewellery and porcelain. If you're interested in
carriages, you can admire the gold-plated Baroque exhibits in the
Museu de les Carrosses. The gardens surrounding the palace are full of
statues, shrubs in bloom, fountains and hungry cats. Take some cat
biscuits and cats will appear out of nowhere. The many benches are
excellent for relaxing after an exhausting shopping spree in nearby
Bulevard Rosa.

Museu de les Arts del Espectaculo. See Barrio Chino.

Museu de les Arts Grafiques. Poble Espanyol, Montjuïc, tel. 426-1999. M: Espanya. Admission included in entrance fee for the Spanish Village.
Typography, lithography, engravings and prints.

Museu d'Arts, Industries i Tradicions Populars. Poble Espanyol, Montjuïc, tel. 423-6954. M: Espanya. Tues.-Sun. 9 a.m.-2 p.m. Admission included in entrance fee for the Spanish Village.

Museu d'Art Modern. Parc de la Ciutadella, Plaça d'Armes, tel. 319-5728. M: Arc de Triomf. Tues.-Sat. 9 a.m.-7:30 p.m., Sun. and holidays 10 a.m.-3 p.m., Mon. 3-7 p.m. Admission.
This small museum is unbearably hot during the summer. Unfortunately, a visit is hardly worth it as no exceptional modern masterpiece, no Picasso or Dalí adorn the greying walls. You get the impression the museum is rather neglected, and it is expected that the collection of Catalan impressionists, including Fortuny, Rusinol and Casas, will soon be moved to the newly designed art centre in order to make room for the Catalan parliament.

Museu del Calcat. See Barri Gòtic.

Museu de Carrosses Funebres. Sancho de Avila 2, tel. 300-5061. M: Marina.
Hearses and carriages of Barcelona's city undertaker.

Museu de la Catedral. See Barri Gòtic.

Museu i Centre d'Estudis de l'Esport Dr. Melchior Colet. See Sports.

Museu de Ceramica. Palau de Pedralbes, Diagonal 686, tel. 280-1621. M: Palau Reial.
Museum of ceramics that exhibits plates and tiles from the 12th to the 20th century.

MUSEUMS

Museu de la Ciencia. Fundació Caixa de Pensions, Teodor Roviralta 55 (entrance on Avinguda Tibidabo), tel. 212-6050. FFCC: Avinguda Tibidabo. Bus: 17, 22, 58, 73, T 100. Tues.-Sun. 10 a.m.-8 p.m. Admission.

This science and engineering museum combined with a planetarium, is very popular with physics, computing and engineering enthusiasts as well as kids. Discover the secrets of the solar eclipse, analyse the chemical composition of your body and study Catalonia as seen from a satellite in space.

Museu Clara. Calatrave 27, tel. 203-4058. FFCC: Tres Torres. Sculptures and other works by Josep Clara exhibited in his studio.

Museu Etnologic. Plaça Santa Madrona, tel. 424-6402. M: Espanya. Mon. 2-8:30 p.m., Tues.-Sat. 9 a.m.-8:30 p.m., Sun. 9 a.m.-2 p.m. Admission.

The ethnological museum specialises in Latin American cultures (Guatemala) as well as the peoples of Papua New Guinea and the Philippines, but many other races are represented through interesting exhibits.

Museu del Futbol Club Barcelona. Arístides Maillol, in Barcelona's football stadium, tel. 330-9411. M: Collblanc, Maria Christina. Bus: 7, 15, 54, 56, 57. Tues.-Fri. 10 a.m.-1 p.m. and 4-6 p.m., weekends and holidays 10 a.m.-1 p.m. Admission.

This gigantic stadium and the museum displaying trophies, photographs and documents of the history of Spain's oldest football club (founded in 1899) is one of the most visited sights in Barcelona. Under Franco the F.C. was a symbol of Catalan national pride, and before his death the club had a 120,000-strong membership, a symbol of protest against the dictator and Castilian dominance. Pope John Paul II is an honorary member.

Museu d'Historia de la Ciutat. See Barri Gòtic.

Museu d'Historia de la Medicina de Catalunya. Ptge. Mercador 11, tel. 216-0500. M: Diagonal. Thurs. 10 a.m.-1 p.m.

This curious museum of medicine, with impossible opening times, has 2,500 exhibits ranging from syringes to preserved brains. Torture instruments from the Middle Ages are especially gruesome.

Museu i Laboratori de Geologia del Seminari. Diputació 231, tel. 245-1600. M: Universitat.

Centre of geological research. More than half a million fossils.

Museu Frederic Mares. See Barri Gòtic.

Museu Militar. See Montjuïc.

Museu de la Musica. Diagonal 373, tel. 416-1157. M: Diagonal. Tues.-Sun. 9 a.m.-2 p.m. Admission. Children free.

This museum is a must even if you're not interested in music and musical instruments, as it is housed in one of Barcelona's most beautiful Modernist buildings (see Modernism).

Museu del Perfum. Passeig de Gràcia 39, tel. 215-7238. M: Passeig de Gràcia. Mon.-Fri. 10 a.m.-1:30 p.m. and 4-7:30 p.m.

This scent museum located behind a perfumery, is worth a quick visit. It's a bit dusty, but the antique flasks might well inspire packaging designers. Among the 5,000 exhibits you'll find Marie Antoinette's and Grace Kelly's perfume as well as Dalí's lip-shaped bottle.

Museu Picasso. See Ribera.

Museu del Templo Sagrada Familia. Plaça Sagrada Familia and Mallorca 401, tel. 255-0247. M: Sagrada Familia. Open daily Jan.-Mar. 9 a.m.-7 p.m., Apr.-June 9 a.m.-8 p.m., July-Aug. 9 a.m.-9 p.m. Admission.

Only for absolute Gaudí enthusiasts and those interested in architecture. The genesis of the cathedral is illustrated in documents, plans, letters and drawings by Gaudí.

MUSEUMS

Museu Taurí. Gran Via de les Corts Catalanes 749, tel. 245-5803. M: Glories. Apr.-Sept., daily 10 a.m.-1 p.m. and 3.:30-7 p.m. Admission.

If you don't abhor bullfights, come here to admire the gold embroidered matador jackets and enormous stuffed bulls.

Museu Textil y de la Indumentaria. See Ribera.

Museu Verdaguer. Vil.la Joana, Vallvidrera, tel. 204-7805. FFCC: Baixador de Vallvidrera. Tues.-Sun. and holidays 9 a.m.-2 p.m.

Artworks and personal scripts in possession of the Catalan poet Jacint Verdaguer.

Museu de Zoologia. Parc de la Ciutadella, Passeig de Picasso, tel. 319-6950. M: Arc de Triomf. Tues.-Sun. 9 a.m.-2 p.m. Admission. Housed in a colourful Art Nouveau building by Domènech i Montaner (see Modernism), today you can study dinosaur skeletons and stuffed animals here. The library contains recordings of animal sounds from all over the world.

BARCELONA'S ARCHITECTURE

Sometimes Barcelona seems like a figment of Antoni Gaudí's imagination. Certainly what makes the city's architecture so matchless is Gaudí's personal and potent response to Art Nouveau. The Güell Park, his Garden of Mysteries. The huge wrought-iron gates of Güell Palace. The view from the roof of Casa Mila. They remain with you long after you have left Barcelona, like fragments of the best dream you ever had.

But there is life in Barcelona beyond Gaudí. Barcelona has more magic in its gutterings, balconies and spires than most cities can boast in their finest monuments.

In order to appreciate Barcelona as a prolific centre of Spanish architecture you must examine the history of Catalan tradition and cultural identity. It is history full of contradiction and oppression, uprising and open rivalry with Madrid. Whereas the Catalan capital was the base of the international brigades during the civil war, Madrid became the seat of Franco's regime. Fascist victory in 1939 delayed the arrival of the modern age for many years. Only when Franco ceded power to King Juan Carlos in 1975 was the way paved for free elections and cultural liberalisation. At the same time the central government in Madrid granted Catalonia its long-awaited autonomy. The Català language could once more develop, and the cultural traditions of the people were accepted. These factors, combined with the pent-up energy resulting from 30 years of oppression, shaped the development of modern architecture and design in Barcelona.

Franco's regime had not only hampered foreign relations, but also made the work of progressive architects very difficult. During the 1970s, young architects looked abroad, and their enthusiasm for international trends, which is still particularly intense today, was understandable in the wake of this 'opening up'. Barcelona dons a truly modern European face.

Barcelona also drew inspiration from its own tradition, such as Modernism, the Catalan Art Nouveau (Antoni Gaudí, Joseph Puig i

ARCHITECTURE

Cadafalch, Lluis Domènech i Montaner), and from the rationalist tendency of Le Corbusier's student, Josep L. Sert, whose later work, the **Fundacio Joan Miro** (1972-5), on Montjuïc is the most beautiful museum building in the city. Nowhere else can you find a clearer expression of Sert's concept of 'white Mediterranean architecture'. His residential buildings, such as **Casa Bloc** (1932-6) or the **Maisonette Building** (1931), are no longer recognisable in their original form. His **Joyeria Roca** (1934), a jewellery shop, deservedly became an interior design model for a number of homes and shops.

Caught between internationalism and tradition, Baarcelona's young designers and architects have prospered over the last decades. Efforts to gain recognition and the greatest possible cultural and economic autonomy peaked in buildings for the 1992 Olympiad. The 'new' Montjuïc **Olympic Stadium** was reconstructed and extended by the Italian architect Vittorio Gregotti. He superimposed his own construction on the 1929 body, so that the building now combines its former awesomeness with the cool professionalism of today's sporting venues. Despite this, visitors are not sheltered from the rain. International collaboration is still no guarantee of quality. Further projects included Arata Isozaki's **Sant Jordi Sports Hall** and the **Olympic Village** with its marina. **Moll de la Fusta** was also rebuilt, a collaboration involving Luxembourg's Rob Krier.

The main objective of city planning policy remains to bring Barcelona closer to the sea. Strange as it may seem, many Catalans believe that Barcelona has its back to the sea. In the south, the city is cut off by the harbour; further north the coastal railway prevents the Poble Nou district from reaching the coastline. In order to achieve this closeness to the sea, the Avinguda Diagonal has to be extended, the harbour relocated and the old industrial zone pulled down. This is of little concern to most people here, as they welcome progress. The 'Plan Cerdà' is, in a sense, being extended and partially corrected. This plan formed the foundation for the city's expansion around 1855, and its focal point, the Eixample (in Castilian *el ensanche*, meaning 'the expansion'), though well meant, failed to a degree.

In 1840, the civil engineer Ildefons Cerdà arrived in the bulging metropolis, which was suffering from property speculation, inadequate sanitation and overpopulation. Cerdà had a dream of a city of the future, but Barcelona was locked within its ancient city walls. Fifteen years later these fortifications were coming down, and Cerda - by then head civil engineer at city hall - could start implementing his plans with the ruling of a royal decree. His new city was based on two principals: an ample street grid for transport and infrastructure, and space between the streets for residential and social purposes, peace and leisure. Cerdà's perfect model included apartment buildings of not more than four storeys and ample green spaces, all built on 133.33 metre blocks of land. He wanted a green, humane and airy district that would 'create a sense of fraternity between people'.

The reason that the central government in Madrid approved this plan so quickly was not due to idealistic conviction but rather to the fact that law and order could be better enforced through this system. Cerdà's wide boulevards (not unlike Haussmann's in Paris) facilitated quicker military intervention. To this day you can feel the disadvantage of this layout. Nowhere is traffic noise and pollution so in evidence as in Eixample, intended as a green utopia. Conceived to curb property speculation at the time, the Plan Cerdà soon provoked it. In time, each block was fully exploited for construction, causing the disappearance of all green spaces. Instead of the 250 inhabitants per hectare, as anticipated by Cerdà, by 1925 there were already eight times that number, reaching 3800 per hectare in 1960.

Even though Cerdà's original dream was not achieved, Barcelona is indebted to this visionary for one of the most beautiful urban planning projects of the 19th century. It became a model for many cities. The Eixample is an exhibition of the most elegant buildings in the style of Catalan Art Nouveau Modernism. Walk through this district, look at the ornate gables and marvel at the many solutions that architects came up with in such a limited system with narrow guidelines.

But the Eixample is also impressive after dark. You'll find many of the architecturally innovative bars and nightclubs that have made Barcelona famous. Young designers and architects often move on to greater things, depending on the success of these design débuts. Two such bars are **Nick Havanna** (1986) by Eduard Samsó, one of the first focal points for new Spanish design, and **Café Network** (1987), a bar-restaurant conceived by Samsó and Alfredo Arribas. The latter has also collaborated with Javier Mariscal on the quayside bar **Gambrinus**, with

ARCHITECTURE

plenty of sand-blasted glass and a huge *lobster* on the roof. Inside, the story of a shipwreck is told through architectural images. Arriba's design school, **Escola Elisave**, where he himself is a lecturer, is another must-see.

Samsó is also noted for his shop extensions. His designs are simple and clear, yet not lacking hidden Spanish temperament. The **Boutique Lurdes Bergada** (1989), the **Boutique de Vetements Hommes Jean-Pierre Bua** (1984), the shoe shop **Zapateria Bis de Bis** (Samsó's first project from 1982), and particularly the jewellers **Joyeria Oller** (1986) are examples of how architectural design in Barcelona is carried out with great taste and a fine sense for trends.

There are a few more bars that you ought to visit when you're out in Eixample at night. **Zsa Zsa**, with its lovely back-lit marble bar, and **Trenta-Tres** are two brilliant night environments designed by Dani Freixes.

Otto Zutz (1985) is not only famous as a nightclub and disco. The conversion of the old watch factory into a bar shows Studio Per's understanding of old building materials. Oscar Tusquets, head of Studio Per, has shown the same sensitivity in the restoration of the old music hall **Palau de la Musica Catalana** (1905 Lluis Domènech i Montaner, restoration 1986-8 Studio Per).

Studio Per was among the first design schools to explore Catalan tradition and architecture. Their chair design and street furniture testify to this interest in historical design. The metal benches that can be seen all over town (particularly on the Ramblas) are the work of Tusquets. The cast iron shapes are based on Gaudí's wall benches in Parc Güell.

This studio has left its mark everywhere in this Mediterranean metropolis. The **Casa Gil Sala** (1971, Clotet and Tusquets) was one of the first examples of 'experimental architecture' towards the end of Franco's regime.

Jordi Garcès and Enric Soria were equally successful at employing traditional building materials in the conversion of an old palace in to the **Picasso Museum** in the Barri Gòtic (1986).

The other giants of Catalan architecture are MBM: Martorell, Bohigas, and Mackay. As Barcelona's official city planner, Oriel Bohigas has been one of those responsible for urban development over recent years, as well as planning for the 1992 Olympiad. MBM specialises in bigger projects, for example, the two schools **Escola Thau** (1974) and **Escola Catalunya** (1981-3).

The large housing complexes by these architects, such as the **Conjunto Residencial** (1971-4) or the **Codas Meridiana Building** (1959-65), are also worth seeing. On the latter you can admire the traditional Catalan skill of employing decorative brickwork. The windows exploit light and shadow - a main feature of architecture in this country of endless sunshine. To avoid excessive heat in the summer, windows often angle away from the direction of the sun. A classic example is the apartment building **Edificio Vivendes** by Josep Coderch de Sentemenat in Barceloneta. The play of its window units in the light is impressive, and when the shutters are closed in the midday sun, the facade seems to shimmer.

A very controversial 'disciplie' of Catalan architecture is Ricardo Bofill. He is famous for his spectacular projects in the outskirts of Paris, where he hid municipal housing behind palatial architecture. In Barcelona he was only permitted to experiment outrageously in his early days. His most spectacular building is perhaps his own workshop and residence, the **Taller d'Arquitectura de Ricardo Bofill** (1977) in the industrial suburb Sant Just Desvern. A huge, converted cement factory houses studios and apartments. Adjoining this structure is an immense residential complex with four inner squares housing 1,000 people.

The most tangible improvements in Barcelona are the remodelling and revitalising of squares, parks and open spaces, intended to enhance the quality of life in those areas of the metropolis totally void of trees and greenery. Another element of this scheme is the conversion and modernisation of the old town. These plans, implemented over the last few years, are the result of a long process of restructuring in nearly all areas of public life. These new public facilities are functional works of art. This is especially in evidence in two areas: in Sants, the district surrounding the railway station, and in Gràcia, the former village gobbled up by Barcelona.

Right next to Estació Sants is the **Park de l'Espanya Industrial**. Its green spaces, lakes, arena and expressive sculptures and towers serve as a kind of barrier between the station and adjoining residential areas.

The remodelled squares in Gràcia have been integrated into their surroundings exceptionally well. The **Placa del Sol**, rebuilt by Jaume

ARCHITECTURE

Bach and Gabriel Mora in 1985, is the centre of the annual fiestas. The integration of the subterranean car park into the surroundings met with international acclaim. What creates the atmosphere in the square are the small things, the attention to detail, such as the streetlamps and benches. It is enjoyable just to sit down and admire the Catalan talent of uniting new and old, emphasising both in the process.

Today, Barcelona is a major example of the important transition that took place in the larger Spanish cities after Franco's death in 1975. This democratic renaissance posed fundamental questions to the way people saw themselves and to their perception of their towns and civic life. Post Franco architects define the town as a place of democratic existence and multiplicity. Barcelona is a vivid example of this endeavour, with all the advantages and disadvantages that accompany experimentation during a period of restructuring.

ADDRESSES

Boutique des Vetements Hommes Jean-Pierre Bua. Diagonal 496. M: Hospital Clinic.
Eduard Samsó, 1989.

Bridge. Bac de Roda/Felip II. M: Navas.
Santiago Calatrava, 1987.

Café Network. Diagonal 616. M: Maria Cristina.
Alfred Arribas and Eduard Samso, 1987.

Casa Bloc. Passeig Torras i Bages 91-105. M: Sant Andreu.
Joseph L. Sert, 1932-6.

Casa Gil Sala. Sant Marius 36. FFCC: Puxtet.
Studio Per (O. Tusquets and L Clotet), 1971.

Codas Meridiana Building. Meridiana 312-318. M: Trinitat Vella.
MBM, 1959-65.

Conjunto Residencial. Passeig de la Bonanova 92-94. FFCC: Sarrià.
MBM, 1971-4.

ARCHITECTURE

German Pavilion. Avenida
Marquès de Comillas, former
exhibition ground on Montjuïc.
M: Espanya.
Ludwig Mies van der Rohe,
1929. Reconstruction: Studio
Per (Christian Circi), 1986.

Edificio Vivendes. Passeig
Nacional 43. M: Barceloneta.
Josep Coderch de Sentemenat,
1951.

Escola Catalunya. Mare de
Dèu del Carme, in Sant Adrià de
Besós. M: Joan XXIIII.
MBM, 1981-3.

Escola Elisave. Augusta 205,
corner with Vallmajor 11.
FFCC: Bonanova.
Alfredo Arribas, 1986.

Escola Thau. Esplugues 49–
53. M: Zona Universitaria.
MBM, 1974.

Fundació Joan Miró. Plaça
Neptu, Miramar, Montjuïc. M:
Paral-lel, then Montjuïc
funicular.
Josep L. Sert, 1972-5.

Gambrinus. Moll de la Fusta.
M: Drassanes.
Alfredo Arribas and Javier
Mariscal, 1989.

Hilton. Diagonal 589. M:
Hospital Clínic.
Pinón and Viaplana, 1990.

Joyeria Oller. Santaló 41.
FFCC: Muntaner.
Eduard Samso, 1986.

Joyeria Roca. Passeig de
Gràcia 18, corner with Gran
Via. M: Passeig de Gràcia.
Josep L. Sert, 1934.

Maisonette Building.
Muntaner 342-48. FFCC:
Muntaner.
Josep L. Sert, 1931.

Exhibition Centre. Plaça
Espanya. M: Espanya.
Renovation: Studio Per, 1984.

Moll de la Fusta. M:
Drassanes.
Conversion and square design by
Rob Drier, among others.

Nick Havanna. Rosselló 208.
M: Provenca.
Eduard Samsó, 1986.

Olympic Stadium. Avenida
Estadi, Montjuïc. M: Paral-lel,
then Montjuïc funicular.
Built in 1929, renovation by
Vittorio Gregotti, 1989.

ARCHITECTURE

Olympic Village. Poble Nou.
M: Ciutadella.

Otto Zutz. Lincoln 15. M:
Fontana, or FFCC: Gràcia.
Studio Per (Pep Bonnet), 1985.

Palau de la Musica Catalana.
Hospital 56. M: Urquinaona.
Reconstruction and extension:
Studio Per (O. Tusquets), 1986-8.

Parc de l'Espanya Industrial.
Next to Estació Sants. M: Sants.

Picasso Museum. Montcada
15-17. M: Jaume I.
Conversion: Jordi Garcès and
Enric Soria.

Plaça del Sol. M: Fontana.
Jaume Bach and Gabriel Mora.

Plaça dels Paisos Catalans.
M: Sants.
Pinón, Miralles and Viaplana,
1987.

Sports Palace Sant Jordi.
Olympic grounds, Montjuïc.
Arata Isozaki, 1990.

**Taller D'Arquitectura de
Ricardo Bofill.** Avenida de la
Indústria 14, in Sant Just
Desvern, tel. 371-5950.
Ricardo Bofill, 1977.

Trenta-Tres. Diagonal 510.
M: Diagonal.
Dani Freixes, 1982.

Zapateria Bis de Bis. Galerias
Bulevard Rosa, Passeig de
Gràcia 55. M: Passeig de Gràcia.
Eduard Samsó, 1982.

Zsa Zsa. Rosselló 84. M:
Hospital Clínic.
Dani Freixes, 1988.

GAUDI -
ARCHITECT OF GENIUS

Gaudí is timeless. Whether you've just come across one of his monuments or are viewing it for the umpteenth time, what you walk through, observe, touch and breathe is at the same time strange and familiar, enlightening and confusing, lucid and crazy, overwhelming and miraculous. Each of these buildings is the result of a soul close to the people, a man obsessed with searching, tirelessly exploring, courageous, pragmatic, overflowing and faithful. Antoni Gaudí was much more gifted and versatile than his contemporaries in this field, a universal artist, a master builder with the medieval manual skill and a modern scientific curiosity.

Measured by his fame you'd think he'd covered half of Barcelona with his magnificent buildings. However, they number only a dozen, including a park, a crypt and his great unfinished votive cathedral, **Sagrada Familia**, in a new district of Barcelona at that time. This is his best known building, as famous as the Pyramids, Cologne Cathedral, the Eiffel Tower and Sydney Opera House, a landmark whose completion, whenever it may be, incessantly preoccupies Gaudí lovers. So wonderful, they rave, that, still far out at sea, sailors would see it and rejoice: Barcelona!

The news from the Sagrada Familia is that someone new has succeeded Gaudí as sculptor: the sixty-year-old Catalan, Josep Maria Subirachs. Only 24 years ago, hundreds of famous artists from all over the world demanded rather brusquely in a petition that the building cease immediately. The imposing skeleton should remain as it was, an unfinished masterpiece of Antoni Gaudí, an original, a great utopian idea. In sympathy with the medieval church masons' build, it is likely that the master would have contradicted them in favour of a 'work in progress', a project for generations. Gaudí once said, 'God isn't in a hurry'. He himself had spent 43 years on this cathedral, and exclusively for the last 12 years of his life. He even hid away in a builders' hut, a construction monk.

Antoni Gaudí i Cornet was born in 1852 in Reus, one hundred

kilometres south of Barcelona, the son of a coppersmith. When, in 1926, he was run over by a tram and killed on the way to church, the first of four towers on the east facade, the Christmas portal and the crypt in which he was subsequently buried had been completed. At present work is being carried out on the columns that will carry one of the five naves by the end of the millennium. Donations of around £1,000,000 are received annually, plus the revenue from half a million visitors to the eternal building site during the same period. The book dealer Bocabella i Verdaguet, who had the idea for this atonement church and who laid the foundation stone in 1882, wanted this colossal project to be pursued with donations alone.

When the Union for the Worship of Saint Joseph fell out with the first architect it engaged - an academic of the neo-Gothic - it contracted the 31-year-old Gaudí. It remains a mystery why the Union of Joseph, which through this church wanted to protest against the industrialisation and secularisation of Catalonia and proclaim old values, chose Gaudí in particular. He was a young man, well-built, blond and blue-eyed, at the time sceptical of the church, a nationalist who would only speak Catalan, unknown in his field. Gaudí subscribed to new social ideas, was interested in old construction techniques, preoccupied himself with workers' issues, loved Catalonia and showed political awareness.

Catalonia, which had lost its independence to Spain one hundred years earlier and was now in the process of rediscovering its identity, was contemplating its past universally through language, literature and art. Gaudí's great colleague, Lluis Domènech i Montaner (1850-1923), was also president of the separatist Unio Catalana; the equally great architect, Josep Puig i Cadafalch (1867-1956), was president of the first united regional government of Catalonia. The entire province was experiencing a nationalist, economic and cultural renaissance. At the same time, an aristocracy of merchants open to the arts was born. They read Ruskin, Goethe, Viollet-le-Duc and Richard Wagner in Catalan, they studied their own history and sought, in the guise of Catalan Modernism, to extract something new and something that was theirs from this - their independent Art Nouveau.

Puig accurately described the state of architecture in a book which introduced his work. "Some dared to undertake the impossible task of reviving romantic architecture, others imported the New Gothic of

Viollet-de-Duc, others still sought a modern style in Germany, Austria and France or strove for architectural rationalism by emphasising the specific characteristics of materials and constructive logic. Perhaps the most positive result of all these attempts is that we have created a modern art based on our own traditional forms which we have enhanced through the splendid characteristics of new materials. This way our national spirit found solutions for today's problems. We have added some of the richness of our medieval tradition to this art, reminiscent of Moorish style and which displays faint oriental attributes. It was a common effort by independent visionaries as well as their conservative predecessors - the work of masters and their apprentices. All this was sustained by a literary, social and historic renaissance..." (*L'Oeuvre de Puig i Cadafalch Architecte*, Barcelona 1904; the Catalan Renaixença).

Gaudí was right in there with them. But he was always himself, defying all influences, without comparison right from the start, unmistakable. A lecturer once said he was either a genius or mad. Probably he was both, an assumption difficult to deny considering his creations in Barcelona. Let's see.

First study: **Casa Vicens** (1888) in Carrer les Carolines 24. The construction materials manufacturer Manuel i Montaner commissioned Gaudí to build this house and almost went bankrupt in the process. It's a fairy-tale castle in Catalan-Moorish style with lots of turrets, chimneys, oriel windows, galleries and balconies built with blunt, brown, undressed stone and brick, decorated with sparkling blue, white and yellow tile patterns. It soon becomes apparent that the black wrought-iron doors and window grilles were not designed to ward off intruders so much as to please the eye. You'll find yourself standing in front of a colourful and overwhelming vision shimmering in the sunlight and discovering traces of many different styles; but the eclectic caprice is evidently pure Gaudí. Unfortunately, you cannot enter the fantastic and seemingly oriental splendour of the interior.

Second study: **Palacio Güell** (1889). By now Gaudí had met and won over the wordly Eusebio Güell i Bacigalupi, textile manufacturer and patron of the arts. Both entered into a relationship that must have

GAUDI

been similar to that of Palladio and Trissino, the merchant from Vicenza educated in the humanities.

As a test, the young Gaudí was allowed to build the entrance to Güell's estate (on Avenida de Pedralbes) in 1887: on the left a gatehouse, on the right a stable with a bridle path. Between them he built a gate which has attracted much fame: a wrought-iron abstract dragon, a prime example of Catalan skill in wrought-iron work, the first of Gaudí's many similar designs. This small complex has unmistakably Moorish qualities, the stable has a roof of tubular terracotta tiles cut in half and arranged perpendicularly. If you ask for the key you can go upstairs and study the secret of its construction from above.

Shortly afterwards, Güell commissioned the talented architect to build his residential palace in the narrow Carrer Nou de la Rambla. After adding a few pictures of inconsequential actors and scenes from plays, the building was declared a theatre museum: an eclectic nightmare bulging with many beautiful objects, sombre and ostentatious. The closely packed decorations are indescribably loud, and so are the heavy, ornate coffered board and stalactite ceilings, wall decorations, banisters, alcoves, arches, paintings, columns and plinths, everything finished with the greatest craftsmanship in wood, stone, iron, varnish and stained glass, mainly in black, brown, grey and gold. Individually, these decorations will make you sigh in admiration, collectively, they cancel each other out.

And still, the genius stands out: not in the thousands of details, but in the many practical inventions, especially in the overall room layout. They are arranged in such a way that the first and second floor make up one surprisingly multi-faceted room, used for concerts and social events - Güell kept an open house. On leaving, you will feel a little exhausted from this intake of heavy, sweet and exotic cocktails. The eyes become intoxicated and begin to long for daylight and the banalities of the street.

Third study: **Colegion Teresiano** (1889). The school and mother-house of the order of Saint Teresa of Avila. What a surprise, what a relief! While Gaudi was allowed to literally squander money on the Palacio Güell, here he was urged to be as frugal as possible, and the architecture benefited as a result. This convent school is a rectangular structure in a fantastic Gothic style which had been initiated by another architect as far as the first floor, but which nevertheless bears all the hallmarks of Gaudí. The most beautiful sections are the two narrow corridors that run parallel along the entire length of the building on the first floor. Both are characterised by close-knit rows of white, plastered, parabolic arches which support the floor above - fascinatingly beautiful, fascinatingly effective. The space between the corridors is dominated by white air wells typical of the Mediterranean. You can sense a pleasant and meditative mood.

Fourth study: **Casa Batlló** (1906). You can't possibly miss this building on the wide and elegant Passeig de Gràcia. The rich textile baron Josep Batlló i Casanovas commissioned Gaudí to convert this house. Casa Batlló is flanked by an historic and equally impressive house by the architect Puig i Cadafalch, dating from 1902.

You'll want an hour to behold this wondrous and strangely beautiful, perhaps the most beautiful of Gaudí's houses. The whole building was sold by Sotheby's in 1991. First of all, you'll find yourself standing in front of the building, gazing in astonishment. At ground level, the natural stone columns are shaped like elephant feet; above, the first floor sports wide oriel windows and small columns with curious knots and blossoms. The balustrades resemble masks, and on the undulating, grey, natural stone facade, with a hint of brown, there are innumerable glistening blue, green and ochre tessera tiles of increasing intensity. Crowning it all, the turret and wavy roof, with its shimmering green-brown ceramic tiles and a backbone made of spheres creating the overall image of a giant reptile.

Similar allusions to nature continue inside. The staircase leading up to the flat is a winding ceramic backbone; undulating walls and ceilings, painted like veined skin; on the ceilings, mysteriously illuminated, round, high windows. Finally, the flat itself, where everything seems to flow. The doors appear as though they have been kneaded from wood. There is not one corner of this refined house that has not been well thought out. Even the narrow air-well tries to deceive and at the same time reconcile the eye: the blue and green of the tiles become increasingly intense as it descends. You can only imagine what must be happening up top; the terrace, reptilian roof, the bizzare chimneys, the striking mosaic. But a few blocks further down Passeig de Gràcia you can actually experience similar creations close-up.

Fifth study: **Casa Mila** (1906). This is Gaudí's most famous house, his last secular building before he became engrossed in work on the Sagrada Familia. The Milá House is an enormous corner edifice with bulging balconies made of solid natural stone, and balustrades of monstrously knotted, engraved wrought-iron, as if it were recycled scrap - curiously attractive structural sculptures. The facade was superimposed on the building and the house itself is supported by an iron skeleton. The building was recently bought by a savings bank and is since being restored a tiresome business to remove corrosion and halt ruin. Eventually it will be used for cultural events.

There are guided tours every hour, not through the house with its totally organic ground plan, but in the adventurous, undulating landscape of the roof and its ghostly vents and chimneys, where inevitably you'll make out masked figures. The large number of chimneys on the roof is due to the fact that traditionally rooms were heated individually and not centrally.

The sculptor Gaudí reached his peak with the roof of Casa Mila. Here he created abstract, multicoloured sculptures anticipating Miró and Picasso, and delightful decorations of sometimes aggressive sculptural power, as opposed to the natural figures from the New Testament that, together with snails, lizards and snakes, cover the east portal of the Sagrada Familia. However, there is a square in Barcelona, on Carrer Olot, where Gaudí further improved his art of mosaic sculptures.

Sixth study: **Parc Güell** (1914). Nowhere else did Gaudí (assisted by two colleagues, Josep Maria Jujol and Francesc Berenguer) prove himself such a universal artist: sculptor, 'painter' of glass and tile mosaics, landscape designer, architect and, last but not least, planner of urban and social environment. On this terrain, at the time unpopular, he wanted to build a settlement in a park-like landscape whose 60 villas would group within reasonable distance around a market square mounted on Doric columns. Patron (and probably designer) of the project was Eusebio Güell. However, the venture lacked investors, and therefore the people of Barcelona only inherited the park, the most curious park in the world, a grotto-like, brightly coloured, natural landscape of architecture. There is also evidence of true Gaudí through his conspicuously sloping columns and walls supporting streets, paths and viaducts.

What Gaudí displayed here, and on Sagrada Familia, he only ever surpassed in vision, rigour and courage in the crypt of the church of Santa Coloma de Cervello, which was intended to tower above the workers colony of Güell's textile mill 23 kilometres south of Barcelona. He only really built its crypt, but it is the boldest, most modern, if not the most interesting creation that Gaudí ever embarked upon.

His partly arithmetical, partly empirical method was based on the idea of simulating the church's dynamic lines with suspended chains weighed down at their neuralgic points by small lead-filled sacks. Turned on its head, according to Gaudí's thinking, it would create the arch structure of the church. Gaudi never intended to copy Gothic arches, but to develop and correct the Gothic lines. He wanted to rediscover the pure Gothic ideal.

Asked what his inspiration was, Gaudí, the ultimate innovator and genial maverick, answered: 'A tall tree. It supports its branches, and they their twigs, and they their leaves. And each part grows harmoniously and magnificently since God the artist created it'. Gaudí had read Ruskin, who emphasised 'that all the loveliest shapes and ideas emanate directly from nature'. Shape follows construction, and the most beautiful shapes consist of curves.

Gaudí's doctrine is still relevant today, if one removes all the bizarre excesses unique to an unrepeatable period of Catalan history and the struggle for an artistic and natinalist renaissance: the artist, builder and visionary of shapes. Gaudí is modern – as always during an age not sure of itself.

GAUDI SIGHTS

Bellesguard (1900-1902). Bellesguard 16-20. FFCC: Tibidabo, Tramvia Blau and by foot into the hills.

Although you cannot enter the house, today owned by a family of doctors, the trip is well worth it as this villa is wonderfully located and

GAUDI

resembles a fairy-tale castle.

Casa Batlló (1904–1906). Passeig de Gràcia 43. M: Passeig de Gràcia.
  You can enter the lobby and admire the sublime staircase. At press time, it was up for sale through Sotheby's.

Casa Calvet (1898–1900). Casp 48. M: Passeig de Gràcia.
  The visitor can only contemplate the simple facade of this five-storey apartment building, Gaudí's dullest in Barcelona.

Casa Mila (1905–1910). La Pedrera, Passeig de Gràcia 92. M: Diagonal.
  Guided tours of the roof and its wonderful chimneys nearly every hour.

Casa Vicens (1878–1885). Carolines 18-24. M: Fontana.
  You can only see the outside of this multicoloured, geometrically tiled villa which Gaudí designed for a rich tile manufacturer.

Col.legi de les Teresianes (1889–1894). Ganduxer 95-105. FFCC: Bonanova.

My favourite of Gaudí's designs, the Palau Güell off the Ramblas. Now a museum of theatre and show business.

You can only visit this convent upon prior arrangement. For me, it is one of Gaudi's least important buildings, as he was forced to drop many brilliant ideas through lack of funds and time.

Colonia Güell. Santa Coloma de Cervelló, tel. 634-0532. FFCC: from Plaça Espanya to Santa Coloma. Open Mon.-Fri. 10:15 a.m.-1:15 p.m. and 4-6 p.m. (Closed Thurs. afternoon.) Sun. and holidays 10 a.m.-1:30 p.m.

Entrada Finca Güell (1884-1887). Avinguda de Pedralbes 7, corner at Passeig Manuel Girona. M: Palau Reial.

Only the ornate wrought-iron dragon gate and a pavilion remain of Count Güell's mansion. Still, a visit is worthwhile. Near the university.

The Lamps on Plaça Reial (1859). Plaça Reial. M: Liceu.

The two candelabra-like gas lamps at each end of the Royal Square are early works by the master. They illuminate this slightly scruffy square, though today electrically powered.

Palau Güell (1886-1890). Nou de la Rambla 3-5. M: Liceu.

My favourite Gaudí creation. Today the museum of theatre and show business (see Museums).

Parc Güell (1900-1914). Olot. M: Lesseps. Bus: 24, 31, 32, 74, 100.

Sitting on a wavy, mosaic bench or under a stony arcade, you can dream of Gaudí until dusk.

Sagrada Familia (1884-1926). Corner of Marina, Provenca and Mallorca. M: Sagrada Familia.

The building works have continued ever since Gaudí's death. A trip up the tower is well worth it. Give the museum a miss.

MODERNISM

Modernism - the Catalan version of German Jugendstil, French Belle Epoque, the Anglo-Saxon Arts and Crafts movement, the Italian Style Liberty, and the Viennese Sezession - developed here between 1880 and 1914. Following the Great War, hard Art Deco lines and cold technique replaced the ornaments and flowers of Modernism.

Walking through Barcelona you will come across wonderful tiles, wrought-iron balconies and street lamps, playful portal designs and letter boxes, fantastic water tanks and rooftop ornaments. So keep you eyes peeled!

Since 1990, when Eixample hosted a special exhibition called *Quadrat d'Or* (the Golden Square), many of the most famous Catalan Art Nouveau buildings have been designated plaques displaying the year of completion and names of the architects. The most successful and spectacular architects - apart from the great master of Modernism, Antoni Gaudí - were Lluis Domènech i Montaner (1850-1923) and Josep Puig i Cadafalch (1867-1957). Puig is pronounced 'putsch'.

The following list of the most interesting Modernist buildings is subjective. The tourist office distributes a 24-page pamphlet with excellent photographs on the theme 'Modernism in Catalona'. In it you'll find many more addresses.

EIXAMPLE

Casa Amatller. Passeig de Gràcia 41. M: Passeig de Gràcia.

(Puig) In 1898 Puig superimposed this classical facade on a residential building which remotely resembles the Römer in Frankfurt, and has Dutch-style gables. He also altered the patio, staircase and first floor, which today houses the Institut Amatller d'Art Hispanic. The windows, tile floors, lamps and furniture are all original Puig. The statue of Sant Jordi, the dragon killer and symbol of Catalan nationalism, is also worth noting.

Casa Fuster. Passeig de Gràcia 132. M: Diagonal.

The genius of architect Domènech i Montaner is evident in the surreal Palau de la Musica Catalana.

(Domènech, 1910) The floral ornaments and bow windows on this apartment building, reminiscent of Gothic churches, are typical of Domènech. An ideal blend of harmonious proportions and sensitive use of materials.

Casa Lleo Morera. Passeig de Gràcia 35, tel. 215-4477. M: Passeig de Gràcia.

(Domènech, 1905) This residential building today houses the Patronat Municipal de Turisme de Barcelona. Visits can be arranged. Unfortunately the lanterns and the sculptures on the facade were removed years ago; however, every lover of architecture must see the first floor apartment with its precious glass cupola above the patio, the tiles on the walls and the splendid masonry above the doors. Also have a look at the second floor facade. The sculptures with technical achievements of the day, such as telephone, camera, lightbulb and gramophone, seem rather curious today.

Casa Quadras. Diagonal 373. M: Diagonal.

(Puig) The Museu de la Música is yet another masterpiece by Puig. Modelled on Barcelona's Gothic palaces such as Picasso Museum in

MODERNISM

Carrer Montcada, the ex-residence of the Baró de Quadras has a central patio and a grandiose staircase. I like this building better than Gaudí's cathedral, and it is almost always empty. Worth a visit! (See Museums for opening times).

Casa Terrades. Diagonal 416-420. M: Diagonal.

(Puig) A corner building known as Casa de les Punxes, this fairy-tale palace reflects Puig's interest in Central European Gothic.

Casa Thomas. Mallorca 291-293. M: Passeig de Gràcia.

(Domènech) Built in 1898 as a residential building, extended by his son-in-law Guardia i Vial, it is today the headquarters of the avant-garde B.D. design firm. The showrooms are open to the public (see Shopping). Don't miss the opportunity to visit the interior of this opulent Domènech house.

Editorial Montaner i Simon. Aragó 255. M: Passeig de Gràcia.

(Domènech) This was Domènech's first great project, built between 1878 and 1886. Recently it was substantially renovated by his great grandson, Lluis Domenech i Girbau, to house the exhibitions of the Fundació Tàpies (see Museums). Only the ornate facade remains of the original building, which was the headquarters of a leading Catalan publisher.

Eixample Plan Cerda. Roger de Lluria, corner at Counsell de Cent. M: Passeig de Gràcia.

This first block with its large courtyard, was built between 1860 and 1863 outside the city walls, according to the design of the city planner Ildefons Cerdà. The origins of Modernism can be seen in the decoration of the facade.

AROUND THE CITY

Casa Golferichs. Gran Via 491. M: Urgell.

(Joan Rubio i Bellver, 1871-1952) Joan Rubio was Gaudí's student. This 1901 house was his first major project and is located on one of the most elegant streets of its time. Neighbours recently saved the building from demolition. This experiment in Gothic shapes and materials today houses the district council.

Casa Macaya. Passeig de Sant Joan 108. M: Verdaguer.

(Puig, 1901) An elegant prototype of the villas typical of turn-of-the-century textile barons, this house is today the Centro Cultural de la Caixa de Pensions de Barcelona. It periodically houses temporary exhibitions. Everything is centred on an enormous atrium. Puig salvaged the massive staircase from a medieval palace that was being demolished. Go and feast your eyes!

Casa Marti. Montsió 3. M: Jaume I.

(Puig, 1896) Café-restaurant Els Quatre Gats (The Four Cats) was Puig's first important building. It is interesting for its Moorish and neo-Gothic influence and special brick.

Casa Muntadas. (Puig, 1901) See Tibidabo.

Casa Quadros. Rambla Sant Josep 82. M: Liceu.

(Josep Vilaseca, 1848-1910) This elegant 1896 apartment building, right on the Ramblas, displays a Japanese influence in its tile and facade art work. It has an eccentric sculpture of a dragon holding an umbrella, as this building originally housed an umbrella shop.

Casa Roviralta. (Rubio, 1913) See Tibidabo.

Castell dels Tres Dragons. Passeig Picasso. M: Arc de Triomf.

(Domènech) Built as a café for the 1988 world exhibition in the then revolutionary style of plain iron and unplastered red brick, the building is adorned with colourful heraldry, fairy-tale battlements and Moorish tiles. Today it houses the Museu de Zoologa in Parc de la Cuitadella (see Museums).

Fonda Espanya. (Domènech) See Barrio Chino.

Hospital de Sant Pau. Avinguda de Gaudí. M: Sant Paul.

(Domènech, 1902-1930) The idea was to build a different pavilion

M O D E R N I S M

for each field of medicine, joined by subterranean passages. Coloured roof tiles and the quality workmanship that went into the tiled facades and sculptures on the gables and windows make a visit to this complex a must. Be considerate and quiet, it's still a hospital. Also of interest is the new sloping pedestrian zone, Avinguda de Gaudí, with bronze Art Nouveau street lamps by local architect Pere Falques dating from 1900. Falques also designed the curious street lamps and round mosaic benches for Passeig de Gràcia.

Palau de la Musica Catalana. Sant Pere més Alt. M: Urquinaona.

(Domènech, 1908) The concert hall, decorated with Eusebi Arnau's sculptures of Wagner and other composers, is a dream for lovers of Art Nouveau, a nightmare for purists. The auditorium has impressive windows and a cupola in the most radiant colours. Also wonderful are the floral mosaic columns at the entrance and on the facade, the tile walls in the lobby, and the plaster sculptures on the ceiling, almost surreal through their opulence. Visits by prior agreement, or buy a concert ticket.

Vil.la Joana. Vil.la Joana, Vallvidrera, tel. 204-7805. FFCC: Baixador Vallvidrera. Tues.-Sun. 9 a.m.-2 p.m.

The poet Jacint Verdaguer wrote his poems and novels in this beautiful house. Here is a rare opportunity to see the interior of a typical Modernist villa high up in the elegant suburbs.

THE RAMBLAS

The Ramblas are two thousand metres of history covered with tourist tack. Like the Champs Elysées and Oxford Street, the Ramblas is a once proud thoroughfare that has fallen on hard times. There are whores down by the statue of Columbus, there are small birds crammed into cages further up, there are tacky souvenir shops everywhere in between. But though the Ramblas might be a tourist trap, it is often only a breath away from the timeless heart of Barcelona. One step off the Ramblas and the dark mysteries of Barcelona proper begin.

The Ramblas has five different names from the Plaça Catalunya down to the Columbus Statue. Along this thoroughfare a stream once flowed down to the sea by the city walls built by King Jaume I in the 13th century. It's probably for this reason that the boulevard is called Rambla de Canaletes at its northern end. It is said that those who drink from the fountain, **Font de Canaletes**, will always return to Barcelona. Nowadays it is here that F.C. Barcelona's football fans, draped in red and blue striped scarves and armed with litre bottles of beer, argue vociferously about the future of their beloved Barca.

Next is the Rambla dels Estudis, in honour of the university which, in the 16th century stood on the right near what is today the Iglesia Belén but which was converted by Felipe V into barracks at the beginning of the 18th century. Animal lovers shudder with horror in the Rambla dels Ocells, popularly known as the 'boulevard of the birds'. Budgies, canaries and nightingales are packed into tiny cages, cats sit in their own mess, rabbits are painfully crowded together, as are garishly dyed chicks and small tortoises. Protest against this abuse of animals at the nearly police station, the only post-modern building in the Ramblas. Or launch a spontaneous protest right in front of the stalls which, by the way, are simply locked for the night without any consideration for the animals!

Console yourself as the Rambla Sant Josep turns into a colourful flower market, known as the Rambla de les Flors. The name derives from **Mercat de Sant Josep**, the city's best market, known simply as

A ramble on the Rambles (the Catalan spelling of the Ramblas).

the **Boqueria**. This imposing market hall opened its wrought-iron doors in 1840. Wander inside, where you'll gape at the pyramids of fish, shrimps and lobsters. Boar's heads dangle above the stalls alongside wild pheasants, ducks and rabbits (a favourite Catalan dish). There are gigantic displays of herbs, wild mushrooms and hundreds of sausages, from the simple chorizo to varieties you've never heard of!

Opposite the Boqueria you'll unexpectedly walk onto a true Miró work, a star made of cobblestones in his favourite colours - yellow, red and blue. Here on the **Plaça de la Boqueria**, known simply as the **Pla**, between the Ramblas de Sant Josep and the Rambla de Caputxins, the rivers Pi and Hospital once flowed into the Rambla. The **Palau de la Virreina** (Ramblas 99, tel. 301-7775), stands next to the market. The palace of the vicereine of Peru, who married a citizen of Barcelona in 1778, is the location for the Ministry of Culture, an art museum which houses temporary exhibitions and the **tourist office**.

A visit to the **Gran Teatre del Liceu** opera house (Sant Pau 1, on the corner of the Ramblas, tel. 318-9122) is just as interesting as a visit to the **Cafe de l'Opera** (Ramblas 74. Open daily 8 a.m.-2 a.m.) across the road, with its fading wall decorations, ancient waiters and a regular crowd of transvestites, students, artists, tourists and professors. The sun terrace is good for people-watching on the Ramblas.

With 3,000 seats, the Liceu is Europe's second largest opera house after the Scala in Milan. You can visit this glamorous 1847 building upon prior arrangement over the phone with the public relations department (visits Mon.- Fri. 11:30 a.m. and 12:15 p.m. Closed Aug.). The lobby, with its slightly tacky ceiling frescos depicting writers ranging from Aristophanes to Lope de Vega, is worth seeing. It is not easy to obtain tickets for concerts and opera, as 90% are allocated to subscribers. So write to the threatre before your trip and request a booking form. If you queue for four hours before the evening performance, you might stand a chance of getting a ticket.

This stretch of the Ramblas is named after the long gone Capuchine monastery, one of the palaces on the **Plaça Reial**. Josep Maria Carandell, Barcelona's best chronicler, writes about it in his book. *Nueve Guía Secreta de Barcelona*: 'At the beginning of the 18th century this Capuchine monastery with its church in the middle stood on this lively square. In 1848 the monks left the square and the French architect Daniel Molina gave the royal square its present aspect. The fountain was built in honour of the Three Graces and the playful street lamps are early designs by Antoni Gaudí'.

Unfortunately thieves, beggars, prostitutes, alcoholics, and junkies injecting in full view of the patrolling police, loiter day and night on this wonderful square. A rehabilitation programme, recently launched in an effort to clean up the area for the Olympic Games, will hopefully improve the situation.

The Ramblas Santa Monica, after the church of the same name, begins on the Plaça del Teatre and extends to the Columbus statue. This stretch of the Ramblas is the shabbiest. On the right is the Barrio Chino, and on the left row upon row of doss houses, junk shops and over-priced bars.

At the port end of the Ramblas is the **Museu Cera** Passatge de la Banca, tel. 317-2649. Open summer, daily 10 a.m.-8 p.m.; winter, Mon.-Fri. 10 a.m.-2 p.m. and 4-8 p.m., Sat.-Sun. 10 a.m.-8 p.m. Admission). This rather mediocre wax museum has appalling historical wax figures such as Columbus and the Spanish kings.

The colossal 60-metre **Monument a Colom** (Plaça Portal de la Pau, tel. 302-5224. M: Drassanes) was inaugurated for the world exhibition in 1880. Many celebrations around the statue are planned for 1992 during the quincentenary of the discovery of America. Columbus hasn't forgiven the world for only naming Colombia after him: America derives its name from the Florentine explorer Amerigo Vespucci. A lift takes you to the visitors' platform from where you can enjoy a super view of the city, smog permitting (open 24 June-24 Sept., daily 9 a.m.-9 p.m; rest of the year, Tues.-Sat. 10 a.m.-2 p.m. and 3:30-6.30 p.m., Sun. 10 a.m.-7 p.m. Admission).

Opposite the statue are the medieval, royal shipyards, one of the oldest in Europe and one of the finest examples of Gothic architecture. They house the excellent **Museu Maritim** (Portal de a Pau 1, tel. 318-3245. M: Dressanes). Open Tues.-Sat. 10 a.m.-2 p.m. and 4-7 p.m., Sun. and holidays 10 a.m.-2 p.m. Admission. Anchored nearby there used to be a reproduction of Columbus's flagship, the *Santa Maria*, but sadly it was burned down by ETA terrorists in 1990.

Every 30 minutes a little pleasure boat chugs from the wharf near the Columbus statue towards Barceloneta and around the harbour.

CAFES AND BARS

Amaya. Ramblas 20, tel. 302-1037.

   At the front, a long bar where you can breakfast on croissants and tortillas; at the back, a popular restaurant which also features in thrillers by Vázquez Montalbán.

Escriba. Antigua Casa Figueres, Ramblas 83.

   Beautiful tile mosaics adorn this corner house containing the Escriba bakery. Treat yourself to an *ensaïmada*; they are exceptionally good here.

Pinocho. Mercat de la Boqueria. Mon.-Sat. 6 a.m.-4 p.m. Closed in August.

   Tasty tapas, tortillas and fast fried food. Everything is very fresh due to its location in the market, to the right of the entrance.

Cafe de l'Opera. Ramblas 74, tel. 317-7585. M: Liceu. Daily 9 a.m.- 2 a.m. Closed Feb.

   Traditional café, whose cast of characters rivals the opera house across the Ramblas.

Cafe on the Ramblas

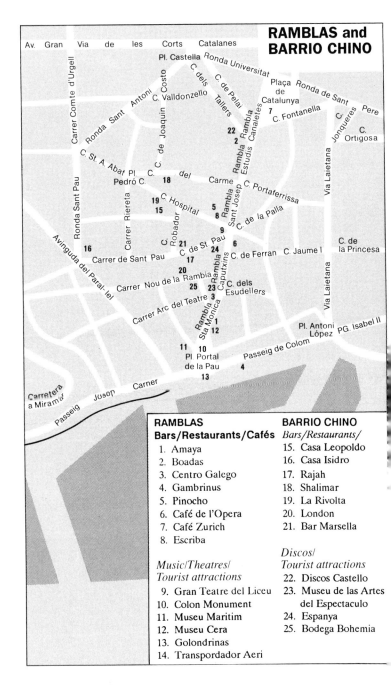

RAMBLAS and BARRIO CHINO

RAMBLAS
Bars/Restaurants/Cafés

1. Amaya
2. Boadas
3. Centro Galego
4. Gambrinus
5. Pinocho
6. Café de l'Opera
7. Café Zurich
8. Escriba

Music/Theatres/
Tourist attractions

9. Gran Teatre del Liceu
10. Colon Monument
11. Museu Maritim
12. Museu Cera
13. Golondrinas
14. Transpordador Aeri

BARRIO CHINO
Bars/Restaurants/

15. Casa Leopoldo
16. Casa Isidro
17. Rajah
18. Shalimar
19. La Rivolta
20. London
21. Bar Marsella

Discos/
Tourist attractions

22. Discos Castello
23. Museu de las Artes del Espectaculo
24. Espanya
25. Bodega Bohemia

BARRI GOTIC

The Barri Gòtic is best explored at night. This way your eyes are not distracted from the pure Gothic by garish neon and packed shop windows. A stroll through the narrow alleys zaps you back in time to the Middle Ages, watched by dragons, damsels and stony ogres which romp about under the roofs and on the towers of palaces and churches.

The Gothic quarter is certainly not a dull, open-air museum. People live behind these historic facades, unfortunately mostly in overcrowded mini-flats in need of urgent repair, with a primitive toilet on the landing and rising damp. Ragged underwear, grey long johns and flowery bed linen hang over the streets, the sound of flamenco music and *pasadobles* wafts out of rear patios and barred windows. Spaniards would rather spend their money on copious meals, Cava, fancy clothes, jewellery and luxuries than on their four walls. But that's precisely why the old town's authenticity has been preserved: no modern trash, no insensitive renovations, and and above all, no new buildings.

Even if you can only spend one day in Barcelona, you must visit the cathedral with its beautiful cloister, the History Museum and the Plaça Jaume. The heart of the Gothic quarter around the cathedral and the former palace of the Counts of Barcelona stand on the remains of a Roman forum and the city walls of **Mons Taber**.

Let's begin our tour at the **Plaça Nova**, the Roman place of execution and later marketplace. The Portal del Bisbe, next to today's **Palau del Bisbe** (Bishop's palace) is flanked by two restored towers of the old city wall. The 13th-century Bishop's palace was extended with a stern facade. Inside, in the courtyard, you can stroll through a Roman arcade beside colourful Gothic stained glass windows. Opposite is the **Casa de l'Ardiaca**, today's city archives, with a Gothic fountain in its courtyard.

On the right the **Carrer Montjuïc del Bisbe** leads us to the romantic **Plaça Sant Felip Neri**, once the heart of the Jewish ghetto. A fountain splashes quietly and you can sit under an old acacia tree, contemplate the ancient facades and dream for hours of the Middle

Street-lamps by Gaudí on the Plaça Reial in the Gothic quarter.

Ages. The church **Sant Felip de Neri**, dating from 1752, stands where the synagogue probably once stood.

The history of shoemaking is illustrated in a medieval palace on this enchanting square. The **Museu del Calcat** (tel. 302-2680. M: Jaume I, Liceu. Open Tues.-Sun. 11 a.m.-2 p.m. Admission) features footwear from the dim and distant past up to the beginning of the 20th century. Marvel at the tiny, richly embroidered silk pumps that women wore 200 years ago.

Let's leave the square and walk left along the Carrer Sant Sever which leads to the Porta de Santa Eulalia. Behind lies the most unusual part of the cathedral, the 1385 **cloister** with its overgrown garden. Palms, magnolia and mistletoe proliferate behind wrought-iron fences, and geese swim in the mossy pond. No one really knows why geese in particular have lived here for generations. Some believe the white birds represent Santa Eulalia's virginity, others say they are a reminder of the legendary geese that saved Rome with their trumpeting.

The **cathedral** (Pla de la Seu. Open daily 7:30 a.m.-1:30 p.m. and 4-7:30 p.m.) with its three naves and 29 side chapels, was the third place of worship built on this site. Hardly a stone remains of the first early Christian basilica, destroyed during a raid on the city by Al-Mansur in 985. Two portals remain of the Roman chapel of Ramon Berenguers II dating from 1058, the Porta de Sant Sever, and the entrance to the chapel of Santa Lucia.

Jaume II laid the foundations of today's cathedral in 1298; however, the western facade was completed only in 1892 by the Frenchman Carli, based on ancient designs from the year 1408. The cathedral is dedicated to Santa Eulalia and her crypt lies beneath the high altar. Also visit the altar of Saint George: the dragon slayer was immortalised on the ceiling in the 15th century. The moor's head under the organ once dispensed bonbons for children, and don't overlook the ornate chancel with its magnificent carved choirstalls. The prized treasures of **Museu de la Catedral** (Plaça de la Seu, tel. 315-3555. M: Jaume I. Open daily 11 a.m.-1 p.m. Admission) are the Gothic tabernacle and gold-plated silver throne of King Marti I.

Leave the cathedral through the main door onto the **Plaça de la Seu** where wrinkled old women peddle their tacky holy pictures and candles. Here on Sunday mornings the Catalans celebrate their austere national dance, the Sardana (though not in August). On the right you can get to the Baixada Canonja which leads to the remains of the Roman wall on Carrer Tapineria behind the **Casa de la Pia Almoina**. the alms house, where food was handed out to the poor in the Middle Agles.

Going back the same way and turning left along Carrer dels Comptes, you arrive at the **Museu Frederic Mares** (Condes de Barcelona 10, Plaça Sant Iu, tel. 310-5800. M: Jaume I. Open Tues.-Sat. 9 a.m.-2 p.m. and 4-7 p.m, Sun. and holidays 9 a.m.-2 p.m.). The Catalan sculptor, born in 1893, lived until 1990 in this palace of the counts of Barcelona and exhibited his scurrilous collection of fans, sculputres and souvenirs in the upper living quarters. His valuable collection of Roman, Romanesque and Gothic artifacts and sculptures, dating from the 12th to the 19th centuries, are exhibited on the lower floors.

To the left of the Plaça Sant Iu stands the pope's palace, and behind it the **Palau Reial Major**, residence of the counts of Barcelona, next to the Plaça del Rei. Opposite is the **Museu d'Historia de la Ciutat** (Plaça del Rei, tel. 315-1111. M: Jaume I. Open Tues.-Sat. 9 a.m.-8:30 p.m., Sun. and holidays 9 a.m.-1:30 p.m. Admission). Children love this city museum because the Roman foundations, discovered in the cellar in 1931, are now imaginatively illuminated and create a three-dimensional impression of the ancient streets, houses and sculptures. Upstairs the history of Barcelona is uninspiringly illustrated in city plans and medals, engravings and portraits of kings. You can reach another section of the museum through a passage which leads to the royal palace dating from the 14th century. In the Tinnell hall and the chapel of Santa Agata you'll come across ornate wooden ceilings and colourful stained glass. As in many other museums in Barcelona, exhibits are only labelled in Catalan and Spanish.

Back on the Baixada Santa Clara where it meets Carrer Paradis you can visit the three Corinthian columns, remains of the Roman Augustus temple, in the house of the **Centre Excursionista de Catalunya** (the Catalan walking club, open Mon.-Sat. 6 p.m.-10 p.m.) If you're in luck, the entrance will also be open during the day, and you can just make out the columns through the glass door.

It's only a few steps to Plaça de Sant Jaume, where the forum was located in Roman times. Today you can visit the Gothic palace, **Palau de la Generalitat**, which houses the regional government after prior written arrangement (or on the 23 April). For security reasons, it's necessary to write 15 days in advance stating the number of visitors and their ID/passport numbers, address: Cabinet de Protocol i Relations Externes, Plaça Sant Jaume 08002, Barcelona. The tour lasts 30 minutes. Commentary is only in Spanish and Catalan. 1532 **Pati dels Tarongers**, with its magnificent double arcaded gallery and orange trees in the marble courtyard, is worth a visit.

The palau was the seat of the royal court of justice from the end of the 18th century to 1908. In 1931 Francesc Macià proclaimed the Catalan Republic from its balcony, which ended five years later with the Spanish Civil War. The new Generalitat only moved back into the palace in 1977 after Franco's death. Also of interest are the murals dating back to the 1920s in the Saló de Sant Jordi, as well as Josep Sert's golden frescos dating from 1928 in the Saló de les Cròniques in the **Ayuntament**, or city hall, located opposite.

CAFES AND BARS

Bar del Pi. Plaça de Sant Josep Oriol. Daily 8 a.m.–12:30 a.m.

Coffee, sandwiches and Horchata in one of the prettiest squares in the old town, a long way from the noise of the Ramblas.

Gelateria Pagliotta. Jaume I 15. Daily 9 a.m.–9 p.m.

Good homemade Italian ice cream from the chubby and friendly proprietor.

Meson del Café. Llibreria 16. Mon.–Sat. 7 a.m.–12 mid.

Like a gingerbread house, in one of the narrowest streets of the quarter between the city hall square and the Plaça del Rei. Knock back a strong coffee at the bar.

Paraigua. Pas de l'Ensenyanca 2. Mon.–Sat. 10 a.m.–12 mid. Closed in August.

A popular bar, frequented by young bureaucrats from nearby city hall and the Ministry of Culture.

Portalon. Banys Nou 20. Mon.–Sat. 9 a.m.–12 mid.

Tapas bar with low prices and great atmosphere. Not for sticklers for cleanliness: it's at least 20 years since the rough plastering has been scrubbed.

BARRI GOTIC

Bars/Restaurants/Cafés

1. Portalon
2. La Vinateria
3. Paraigua
4. Los Caracoles
5. Can Culleretes
6. Meson del Cafe
7. Bar del Pi
8. Gelateria Pagliotta

Museums/Tourist attractions

9. Palau de la Generalitat
10. Museu Frederic Mares
11. Museu d'Historia
12. Museu del Calcat
13. Catedral
14. Temple Roma d'Augusti
15. Santa Maria del Mar

Fashion/Design/Music

16. Mercat Portaferrissa
17. Manual Alpargateria
18. Coses de Casa
19. Beardsley
20. La Cubana
21. Papirum
22. La Caixa de Fang
23. Los Tarantos

RIBERA

Ribera is not a big barrio. It should only take about five minutes from Carrer de la Princesa down to Plaça del Palau, and not much longer from Via Laietana to Ciutadella Park. However, I have never managed to hurry through these medieval streets, past the fruit and vegetable stalls on Born square, and not get stuck in front of the shop windows of the Galerie Gu, or that curious glass shop in the Carrer Vidrieria. You should allow one or two hours for your tour through the Ribera quarter; there's a lot going on in this barrio.

On Carrer de la Princesa, African peddlers dressed in wide caftans busily run in and out of the countless wholesale stores, trying to flog their cheap electronic goods and jewellery, tacky vases and paperweights. Groups of school kids and camera-laden tourists search for the Picasso museum, and the car boot of an unsuspecting Englishman is being emptied in front of the Pensión Caribe, whose only claim to fame is the entrance.

The quarter's long-forgotten past is being rediscovered. Bar owners are removing ugly plaster from historic walls, and restaurants are putting up new tables in front of ancient stone facades. The best examples for new-old design are the *formatgerias* such as Gades, Al Primer Grit and La Cua Curta: come here for a *copa* of wine or some cheese or paté.

While the fashionable bars of the Eixample still indulge in bare concrete and oxidised metal, in bars like El Nus and El Born the neon has long been removed. You can tell what they once were: a grocer's and a fishmonger's. And it is meant to be noticed.

In the Middle Ages Ribera was the largest settlement outside the city walls and was situated directly on the beach. Barceloneta was settled later. Respectable aristocrats sought addresses in the elegant Carrer de Montcada and used to fight duels in the Passeig del Born. It was here that traders and grocers peddled their wares and people celebrated carnivals. The street name Plateria - today Argenteria - is derived from the silversmiths, and to this day many streets are named after the guilds of the glassblowers *(Vidrieria)*, hoodmakers *(Caputxes)*, swordsmiths *(Espaseria)* and potters *(Olles)*.

R I B E R A

One of the tiny alleys of the Ribera quarter.

At the beginning of the 18th century Felipe V destroyed half of the district to make room for a fortress, today the location of the **Parc de la Ciutadella** (see Sights: Parks). Under Carlos III, traders and nobles moved into nearby barri Mercè, which had new access to the sea, and subsequently Ribera was forgotten for 200 years, and deteriorated.

To this day it is a poor residential area. Those who can't afford the majestic apartments opposite the park and around the Born live in damp hovels in dark alleys like the Flassaders or Bany Vells. Despite its perhaps quixotic appeal, the amount of washing hanging from windows shows just how many people live in these overcrowded conditions - just a few steps from the chic galleries and resplendent museums.

The palaces are lined up one after the other in Carrer de Montcada: Palacio de los Marqueses Llio, 14th century, now the Textile Museum; Palacio Berenguer d'Aguilar, 13th century, today the Picasso Museum; Casa Cervello-Cuidice, 16th century, today the headquarters of Omnio Cultural. Here my pace slows down automatically. Hordes of peeling Europeans in shorts and sandals, carrying all their cash, passports and tickets, scramble for admission and are sized up by skilful pickpockets.

The **Museu Picasso** (Montcada 15, tel. 319-6310. Open Tues.-Sat. 10 a.m.-8 p.m. M: Jaume I. Admission) is housed in three 13th-14th century palaces. Interior patios with palm trees, rising staircases, parquet floors and a café-restaurant in a former stable make this visit a real treat. No first-class works here, but you can study the drawings of 14-year-old Pablito, as well as paintings and drawings given by his long-suffering private secretary, Jaume Sabartes, and works from Picasso's time in Barcelona. The Harlekin and the 50 variations of Velazquez's masterpiece, *Las Meninas*, are interesting, as is the ceramics selection donated by his wife Jacqueline.

Another lovely palace houses the **Museu Textil y de la Indumentaria** (Montcada 12-14, tel. 310-4516. M: Jaume I. Open Tues.-Sat. 9 a.m.-2 p.m. and 4:30-7 p.m., Sun. 9 a.m.- 2 p.m. Admission). Catalonia is famous for its textile industry, and this museum displays wonderful handwoven and richly embroidered silk and shawls from the world exhibitions of 1888 and 1929, with curious bullfighting and floral motifs. The first floor contains the Fashion Museum with finely pleated turn-of-the-century Fortuny outfits and a collection of perfectly dressed dolls. Ladies evening wear of the Spanish

RIBERA

aristocracy from the 70s and 80s is also on display.

At number 18 the black habits of nuns from the Niño Jesús kindergarten begin to mingle in the picture, and at the end of Montcada the cobbler El Rápido fills the *placeta* with fiery flamenco. On the right is the **Santa Maria del Mar** (Passeig del Born 1. M: Jaume I. Bus: 16, 17, 45, T 100. Open daily 10 a.m.–12:15 p.m. and 5-7 p.m.), the most beautiful pure Gothic church in the city. This spartan 14th-century church fascinates me precisely because of the simplicity of its lines. A glass rosette shines beautifully above the entrance. There is no admission during mass: you'll have to sit through all of it, so it is advisable to visit during the week. There are always weddings here, but you can also hear jazz concerts or classical music on special fiesta days throughout the year.

Ribera suddenly boomed in the 1970s. The palaces of the Montcada, up to now used as warehouses, were turned into museums, avant-garde exhibitions opened at the Metronom, formerly an old sugar depot, and all Barcelona sipped cocktails in Miramelindo and Gimlet. After a long night, the 'in thing' was breakfast in the main market. The iron construction dates back to the year 1873. When the market closed its doors, the surroundings slipped back into village life. At the baker's you knew everyone, and at the butcher's you gossiped about them.

Today, artists are rediscovering Ribera. Sculptors and writers are looking for accommodation, gallery owners for whom the Consell de Cents has become too conventional are hunting for warehouses and vaulted cellars (see *The Arts* for gallery listings). Bars display works by painters who now and then settle their tab with a painting. Rising numbers of private view visitors frequent the restaurants.

Yet again my walk in Barcelona's most Catalan quarter has taken a long time, but it has also been a little melancholic. No matter how beautiful the new galleries and bars are, the old man that scooped olives for me from a barrel no longer stands in front of the basement steps, and transvestites no longer meet on Plaça de les Olles.

Take the four steps along Carrer Anisadeta, the shortest street in the city, named after an old dear with a taste for anise. Get lost in the maze of little alleys behind the Santa Maria de Mar and have a last look at Ribera before it becomes too 'in', or before it turns again into a sleeping beauty.

CAFES AND BARS

Café del Museu. Montcada 15, tel. 315-0102. Café open Tues.-Sat. 10 a.m.-7 p.m.; restaurant open Tues.-Sat. 1-4 p.m.

The cool café-restaurant in the Picasso Museum has an international clientele. Try a *brazo de gitano* (gypsy's arm) and cream cakes with your coffee. The set lunch costs 1,500 pesetas.

Café de la Ribera. Plaça de les Olles 6, tel. 319-5072. Bar: Mon.-Fri. 9 a.m.-4 p.m. and 8 p.m.-12 mid.; Meals: 1-3 p.m. and 8-11 p.m.

At lunchtime stockbrokers and office workers patiently wait at the bar for a free table in the colourfully tiled Ribera. In the evening the neighbours get together for a communal *cena*. Good quality fresh fish is *a la plancha*, and huge salads. For dessert, crunchy *carquinyolis*, a nutty cake, and Moscatel. Sensational prices: the set menu for 700 pesetas.

El Xampanyet. Montcada 22. tel. 319-7003. Mon.-Sat. 11 a.m.-4 p.m. and 6:30-11 p.m.

The sign above the door, '*Hay Sidra Fresca*' has been up since 1929, and motley folk from nearby galleries and museums drink this fresh sweet cider, accompanied by mussels and anchovies on bread with tomato. Colourful ceramic tiles and wooden ice boxes (!) create a great atomosphere.

La Campana. Princesa 36, tel. 319-7296.

In the summer a favourite for *grandizados,* iced coffee and lemon drinks, and in the winter *turró,* a marzipan-like calorie bomb made from almonds and honey.

Local. Fossar de los Moreres 7, tel. 310-0438. Mon.-Thurs. 10 a.m.-2 a.m., Fri.-Sat. 10 a.m.-2:30 a.m., Sun. 12-4 p.m. and 6 p.m.-2 a.m.

This minimalist bar where you can also have breakfast is located right on the holy square of Catalan martyrs and has uninterrupted views of the Gothic church Santa Maria del Mar. In the evening local waiters and bar owners meet here for their last *copa* and Spanish rock.

Pastisseria Güell. Plaça de los Olles 7, tel. 319-3883.

RIBERA

In my view this beautifully renovated shop dating from 1878, is the city's best patisserie. Not as grandiose as the Farga and Mauri in Eixample, but the tarts and cream slices in Güell are softer and fluffier than anywhere else. The teacakes made of filled puff pastry and the *carquinyolis* are also tempting. Through the window you can see the bakery where José fills cream puffs.

Rodrigo. Argenteria 67, tel. 310-7814. Fri.-Tues. 8 a.m.-1 p.m., Wed. 5 p.m.-1 a.m.

Rodri is what his friends and clients call him, and Rodri is the name of his famous anise which he and his gang serve all day, and always with a smile. The premises are new and functional, but what counts is the mix of people. Housewives for breakfast, domino-playing pensioners in the afternoon and globe-trotting students from all over the world in the evening. The Cava or sangria is potent. Eat a precautionary hot bocadillo.

The fabulously friendly owner of the Vinoteca in Ribera.

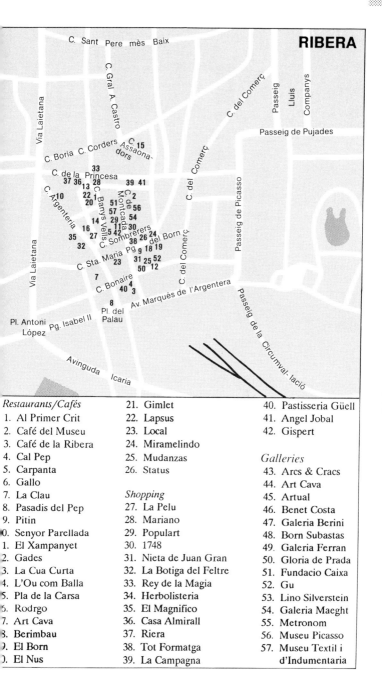

RIBERA

Restaurants/Cafés
1. Al Primer Crit
2. Café del Museu
3. Café de la Ribera
4. Cal Pep
5. Carpanta
6. Gallo
7. La Clau
8. Pasadis del Pep
9. Pitin
10. Senyor Parellada
11. El Xampanyet
12. Gades
13. La Cua Curta
14. L'Ou com Balla
15. Pla de la Carsa
16. Rodrgo
17. Art Cava
18. Berimbau
19. El Born
20. El Nus

21. Gimlet
22. Lapsus
23. Local
24. Miramelindo
25. Mudanzas
26. Status

Shopping
27. La Pelu
28. Mariano
29. Populart
30. 1748
31. Nieta de Juan Gran
32. La Botiga del Feltre
33. Rey de la Magia
34. Herbolisteria
35. El Magnifico
36. Casa Almirall
37. Riera
38. Tot Formatga
39. La Campagna

40. Pastisseria Güell
41. Angel Jobal
42. Gispert

Galleries
43. Arcs & Cracs
44. Art Cava
45. Artual
46. Benet Costa
47. Galeria Berini
48. Born Subastas
49. Galeria Ferran
50. Gloria de Prada
51. Fundacio Caixa
52. Gu
53. Lino Silverstein
54. Galeria Maeght
55. Metronom
56. Museu Picasso
57. Museu Textil i
    d'Indumentaria

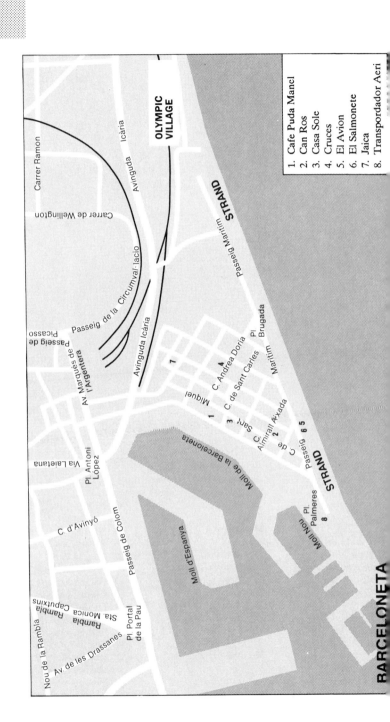

1. Cafe Puda Manel
2. Can Ros
3. Casa Sole
4. Cruces
5. El Avion
6. El Salmonete
7. Jaica
8. Transpordador Aeri

BARCELONETA

BARCELONETA

Barcelona memories are made of this. Barceloneta is the waterfront area where restaurants serve spicy gambas by moonlight on tables that stretch across the beach to the very edge of the sea. Some of the locals complain that Barceloneta has been annexed by Catalan high society and wealthy tourists. But if you happen to be a visitor yourself, it is hard not to fall in love with Barceloneta.

Barceloneta is a small prolongation on the southeastern fringe of Barcelona. It came to life on the drawing board in 1753 as an artificial district outside the city walls. Large numbers of poor migrant workers from southern Spain arrived in the booming Mediterranean city and found a new home in the tiny houses of this suburb, laid out at right angles. For the most part they worked as fishermen or in the port just around the corner, the sea right at their doorstep. Proximity to the sea was the only positive aspect in these narrow alleys which offered hardly any spaces.

At this time Barcelona was still living with its back to the sea. It was only much later, towards the end of the 19th century, that increasing numbers started to discover sun and water for recreation and leisure. While the wealthier classes went to the playgrounds of the Costa Brava and Costa Dorada, the more modest were drawn to Barceloneta.

Sea baths like the Bays de Sant Sebastiá were built: a delightfully decorated complex with seawater basin, casino and beach huts, an airy oasis on the edge of the industrial city. Fish restaurants, bars and beach huts sprang up in no time and the zone of the three M's was born, as coined by the writer Mànuel Vàzquez Montalban: Musica, Marine, Molusco - music, sea and shellfish. It became Barcelona's new advertisement. However, industrial effluence increasingly polluted the city's beach, fewer and fewer people came to bathe and Barceloneta was faced with grave problems.

The small flats in the narrow alleys offered little light and fresh air, hardly any sanitation and were plagued by rats. Work opportunities became scarcer with the decrease in fishing in the Mediterranean, and people got poorer. In Barcelona, where 90% of all drugs are smuggled in by sea, Barceloneta became the refuge of drug dealers and users: a problem area on the one hand, picturesque on the other.

And then the transition. Since Barcelona has been on course for the Olympics, everything began to change. The Catalan capital has recognised the advantages of its location on the Mediterranean, and suddenly Barceloneta, ignored by its municipality over many years, has found itself surrounded by expensive neighbours. To its left rises the **Moll de la Fusta**, the elegant promenade with post-modernist bars, where a cocktail costs as much as a month's rent in the 35-square-metre lodgings of the former fisherman's quarter. On the right, in Poble Nou, the Olympic village is under construction, which will be converted into an exclusive residential development after the games.

Consequently, many foreign investors are speculating for the 'little ugly doll', and the inhabitants, who feel attached to their barrio in spite of its many negative aspects, are getting anxious. Which houses will remain and which will be pulled down? No one in Barceloneta really knows. Everyone agrees that the quality of housing should improve. But, "please for us, and not only for the rich who suddenly want to live by the sea", says Antoni Miquel, restaurant owner and singer of the legendary band Los Sirex. His restaurant Catalunya is one of the few beachfront restaurants in Barceloneta that has not yet been pulled down by the municipality. The romantic pleasure of eating with views of the sea and with sand between your toes is probably soon going to be a thing of the past when the remaining *chiringuitos* - the little fish bars - have to make room for more profitable developments.

Although the municipality has achieved much, such as La Maquinista, an airy housing scheme on old factory land where 250 families from Barceloneta have found pleasant living space, many of those whose houses were pulled down could not move there. Many families had to move into depressing high-rise flats in the suburbs, and many are still anxious about their future in their dilapidated but beloved barrio, where in the evening they sit on folding chairs by their front doors or chat on the Plaça Barceloneta.

Meanwhile, there's a lot of construction everywhere. The rundown yet picturesque harbour is earmarked to become a 'tertiary zone with shopping facilities along the lines of Marseilles, Toronto and Boston'.

BARCELONETA

On the beach the Banys de Sant Sebastiá, this decaying nostalgic colossus, has had to make way for a building site. Palms and showers are springing up on sand which is cleaned daily. Barceloneta is becoming 'Euroepan'; it is winning - and at the same time losing.

If you get lost in the narrow alleys there is still much to discover. No artistic monuments, no key historical sites, but a little world of ordinary people, a piece of Barcelona's everyday culture with its dark and bright sides: the laid-back petanque players on what used to be the railway, a tray of fish in a battered beach bar, a *carajillo* among the residents of the Plaça Barceloneta. Walks through streets which are still scarred from the bombing by German fascists during the Spanish civil war, or evenings spent in bars listening to the unspeakable songs of a toothless busker, all these things are lasting memories. Again and again you can glimpse that Mediterranean blue between the linear streets. It tempers the picture of daily misery in this little world with its scars, wounds and yesterday's charm. According to the government's Ley de Costas, which ended private ownership of Spain's beaches in 1988, the sea ought to belong to everyone. Hopefully the didn't only have in mind those who are going to make a fortune out of 'Barcelona 92'.

CAFES AND BARS

Cafe Puda Manel. Passcig Nacional 60, tel. 319-3013. Tues.-Sun. 1-4 p.m. and 8 p.m.-12 mid.
Opposite the harbour right next the the Metro station, you'll find one restaurant after the other. This bodega is one of the most pleasant, and the fried baby octopus, *pulpitos*, is delicious.

Cruces. Andrea Dòria 39. Mon.-Sat. 8 a.m.-10 p.m. Closed in August.
This tiny tapas bar has existed since 1880. Not an architectural masterpiece, but here the barrio's more modest people and sailors meet. This restaurant resembles a bathroom because of its tiles on walls and floors. The advantage of this is that it doesn't attract tourists.

BARCELONETA

El Avion. Platja Sant Miquel 38. Daily 1-4 p.m. and 8 p.m.–12 mid.
Simple *chiringuito*. That is to say, a beach bar with all kinds of fish at
low prices. The views of the sea are simply great.

Jaica. Ginebra 11, tel. 319-5002. Daily 8 a.m.–1 a.m.
One of my favourite tapas bars and bodegas. There is always something
going on around the wine barrel that is the bar. During the summer
you can sit outside at a few tables, but the ambience is rougher inside.
A truly local bar. Joan the landlord pours excellent beer from the
barrel, also Cava and Rioja at low prices. Order mussels (*musclos*) or
bacallà sec, the traditional Catalan cod dish.

POBLE NOU

The 'new village' was only built some one hundred years ago to house migrant workers arriving in Catalonia from Andalusia, Extremadura and other parts of Spain. Here the textile, silk, shoe and service industries offered opportunities for men and women.

The plan for the Villa Olímpica on the beach at Poble Nou reminded many in Barcelona of the existence of this forgotten district. Because the Olympic village is going to be turned into a residential area of exclusive flats once the games are over (indeed, most of them were already sold in 1990), the property value of Poble Nou rose, and the dilapidated workshops and industrial plants were converted into white yuppie lofts. Here, freelance designers like Javier Mariscal have opened their workshops, and the infrastructure of this revitalised district is also beginning to take shape. New restaurants are opening, and on the poor man's Rambla, the Rambla Poblenou, more and more cafés are being smartened up.

But not even the Olympics are able to change the petit bourgeois and Andalusian atmosphere of this quarter overnight. Time seems to stand still on some corners and squares. Take a stroll from the Metro station Poble Nou up the Ramblas. Have a look at the side streets or criss-cross the tree-lined streets by bus.

If you have time, you should also visit the **Cementiri de l'Est** (Avinguda Icària, tel. 309-8433. M: Llacuna). In the summer it is open daily until 8 p.m., but mind the long siesta: the grounds are closed 1-4 p.m. Flocks of fat pigeons are at home in this forgotten old cemetery, designed in 1819. The departed rest in tall, dilapidated and ghostlike walls, separated by their small tin compartments: a city for the dead, overflowing with flowers, photos and enamelled portraits.

A new beach which replaces old railroad tracks, opens in 1992, stretching in a soft white line from Barceloneta to Poble Nou. The seven-kilometre long **Parc de Mar** has changing cabins and showers, and the municipality promises to introduce special beach vehicles to keep it clean. Unfortunately, Barceloneta's beaches are still littered with Coke cans, beer bottles and picnic leftovers.

POBLE NOU

Information about the annual summertime Festival de Poble Nou can be obtained from the tourist office on the Ramblas or in the publication *Guia de Ocio*

CAFES AND BARS

La Mar Bella. Taulat 81, tel. 300-7913. Mon.-Sat. 12 noon-4 p.m. and   8 p.m.-mid., Sun. 12 noon-4 p.m.

Simple fish restaurant with friendly service. Here the neighbourhood celebrates weddings and first communions.

BARRIO CHINO

Barrio Chino has that romantic ring of Chinatown, invoking visions of Peking duck and street traders. However, you will hardly come across any Chinese in Barrio Chino. Sailors gave the district its name because it reminded them of the bustle, bars and striptease joints they encountered in Hong Kong, Macao and New York's Chinatown. If you approach it from the harbour you'll find the Barrio Chino left of the Ramblas and the Gothic quarter on the right.

The Ramblas divide Barcelona's Soho, which is located between the streets Sant Pau, Hospital, Nou de la Rambla and Cadena. This Bermuda triangle has been the undoing of many a sailor and foolish tourist. The cheapest hookers parade for their clients in Carrer Robador and, appropriately, the condom factory and a hospital are just around the corner. Even Doctor Fleming, the inventor of penicillin, has a monument there.

But the Barrio Chino is not all misery and squalor. At Carrer Hospital 56, you can step through a small door in the huge wooden portal onto the grounds of the **Antic Hospital de Santa Creu** (M: Liceu), an alms hospital for the poor dating from the 15th century. Gaudi died here in 1926. You can wander through the spacious courtyard and examine the fine *azulejos* (glazed tiles) depicting religious scenes. Today the complex houses the national Catalan library and an art school that sometimes organises interesting exhibitions in the chapel.

The **Palau Güell** (Nou de la Rambla 3-5, tel. 317-3974. M: Liceu, Drassanes) is one of the least known but most beautiful buildings by Antoni Gaudí. Today a theatre museum, the **Museu de les Arts de l'Espectacle** (Open Mon.-Fri. 4-8 p.m. Admission) is my favourite museum in Barcelona.

Gaudi built it as a city residence for his patron, Count Eusebi Güell. The textile millionaire wanted a sumptuous neo-Gothic palace for celebrations and as a suitable background for his antique collections. This new house was connected with his two palacios on the Ramblas by a passage. (Today one of these is the Centro Gallego).

The central, three-storey high chamber, with its star cupola, is grandiose and resembles a chapel. Once, in fact, there was an altar hidden in a cupboard, and the organ pipes in the galleries offered great acoustics during mass and concerts in this hall. Daylight shines through tiny round skylights in the conical cupola with its cobalt blue tiles. The wrought-iron entrance gates and window grating, hearths and banisters, are also fascinating. There are over 40 pillar and capital designs in this building. Everything is finished with the greatest craftsmanship in wood, stone, iron, varnish and stained glass. The real exhibition objects, such as posters and books on show business, are outshone by the background of this magnificent architecture.

The **Hotel Espanya** (Carrer Sant Pau 9. M: Liceu) is another modernist masterpiece, built in 1903 by Lluis Domènech i Montaner. It is worth a visit for a view of the turquoise lobby, the grandiose marble hearth in the bar, and the wonderful murals of mermaids and sea creatures on the walls of the dining room.

Follow this same street to the **Monestir de Sant Pau del Camp** (Sant Pau 101. M: Paral-lel. Usually open Mon.-Sat. 10 a.m.-1 p.m.) This monastery with its romantic cloister has been sensitively restored, but you'll find it in one of the saddest areas, right in the middle of the red light district. Parts of the church, such as the tomb of Wilfredo II, dating from 911, and the facade are Roman, while the convent and chapel are Gothic, dating from approximately 1300. Amazingly, the masonry work on columns in the cloister, portraying knights fighting dragons, is over 600 years old.

If you go, leave your cameras in the hotel, and don't wear shorts. Because the Spanish don't even wear shorts in the sweltering heat, you would expose yourself as a tourist and therefore be easy prey for local pickpockets.

But do take Eurocheques and/or cash and credit cards because you'll find some of Barcelona's best and cheapests restaurants in the many little streets (see Restaurants). It's the food that counts, so don't be put off by a few files, faded wallpaper and similar flaws. I am fascinated by this barrio, and hope you will be, too.

CAFES AND BARS

La Rivolta. Hospital 116. M: Liceu. Tues.-Sat. 1-4 p.m. and 8 p.m.-1 a.m.

Anarchists run this small pizzaria. Cheap and fun.

Bar Marsella. Sant Pau 65. Wed.-Mon. 9 a.m.-12 mid. Closed September.

This authentic and rough corner bar is also known by the name Pastis, because here they serve the deathly, absinth-like anise that Picasso and Van Gogh so loved.

Egipte. Jerusalem 3, tel. 317-7480. M: Liceu. Tues.-Sat. 1-4 p.m. and 8:30 p.m.-mid.

Great for tortillas. Good menu del dia.

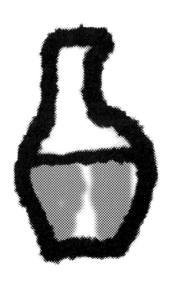

MONTJUIC

The Montjuïc, the 215-metre-high 'Mountain of the Jews', lies between the old town and the sea. The mountain offers something for everyone, but it has to be said that opinions differ about Montjuïc.

This year the focus of the area will be the **Estadi Anillo Olímpico** (Avinguda de l'Estadi, tel. 490-1992. M: Espanya. Bus: 61). The stadium, rashly built for the 1936 Olympics which subsequently took place in Berlin, has been converted for the 1992 Olympic games. It is considered an architectural masterpiece.

Aficionados of design and architecture love the city's most elegant building, the **Pavello d'Alemanya** (Avinguda de Marques de Comillas, tel. 423-4016. Open daily 10 a.m.-6 p.m in winter; 10 a.m.-7:30 p.m. in summer). Built by Mies van der Rohe for the 1929 world exhibition, its stunning features include an all-glass wall; green marble; the master's furniture; the Barcelona chair with its X-shaped frame and Georg Kolbe's beautiful sculpture of a naked woman.

At the foot of the mountain housed in the Palau Nacional, is the **Museu d'Art de Catalunya** (Montjuïc Park, tel. 423-1824. M: Espanya. Open Tues.-Sun. 9 a.m.-2 p.m. Admission). The national palace was built for the 1929 world exhibition, and the museum was recently renovated by the Italian architect Gae Aulenti. Especially worth seeing are the wonderful 11th and 12th-century Roman frescoes recovered from the remote mountain chapels in the Catalan Pyrenees, along with statues and wooden and stone busts of Christ. The Gothic Art section displays artifacts from other Spanish provinces. The Museu de Ceramica is hidden on the first floor with a selection of Spanish tiles and other medieval earthenware pots, olive urns and oil casks.

To the right is a street leading to the **Museu Arqueologic** (Montjuïc Park, Plaça Santa Madrona, tel. 423-2149. M: Espanya. Open Tues.-Sat. 9:30 a.m.-1 p.m. and 4-7 p.m.; Sun. 10 a.m.-2 p.m. Admission, free on Sun.). This magnificent archaeological museum is located in the former graphics palace of the 1929 world exhibition. The classical building resembles a Greek temple, and the Etruscan artifacts in the lobby reinforce this impression. Particularly interesting are the excavations from the coast at Empuries, Ibiza, Formentera and other Balaeric islands.

Another gem from the 1929 world exhibition is the **Fonts Illuminoses de Montjuïc** (Plaça de la Font Màgica. M: Espanya. June-Sept., weekends and holidays 9 p.m.-12 mid., with music 10-11 p.m.; winter, weekends 8-p.m.-11 p.m., with music 9-10 p.m.). This gigantic and colourfully illuminated fountain, surrounded by jets, is a favourite spot for both tourists and young locals.

The **Teatre Grec**, near the Catalan Arts Museum and Plaça Espanya, is well-known for its experimental plays. Information on the Festival Grec in the summer, which brings together theatre companies from all over the world, is available from the tourist office or the Guía de Ocio, and at Palau de la Virreina Rambla 99, tel. 301-7775.

Parents with kids looking for kitsch and carousels should visit the Parc d'Atraccions and the Spanish village, **Poble Espanyol** (Avinguda Marqués de Comillas, tel. 325-7866. M: Espanya and from there a free shuttle bus. Bus: 13, 61, 100. Open daily 9 a.m.-2 a.m. Admission). I don't like this artificial, sterile village built by the city for the 1929 world exhibition. But tastes differ. The 18 reconstructions of village squares, churches and alleys from all the provinces do not give you the real feel of Spain. The admission alone is enough to deter many locals. Tourists from all over the world converge here for overpriced drinks and the souvenir shops. Children like it, as do those who like to impress the folks back home with their pictures of 'traditional' Spain.

If you like gliding through the air, take the cable railway from Avinguda de Miramar: **Montjuïc Funicular** (M: Paral-lel. Summer, daily 11 a.m.-9 p.m.; weekends and holidays 11:30 a.m.-7 p.m.; winter 12 noon- 5:45 p.m.), Montjuïc Teleferic (from above the Montjuïc Funicular station. Summer, daily 12 noon-8:30 p.m., winter, weekends and holidays 11 a.m.- 2:45 p.m. and 4-7:30 p.m.). A round trip is worth it, as the views of the harbour, the sea and the city are impressive.

On your way up to the peak is the colourful **Parc d'Atraccions** (tel. 241-7024. Bus: 61. Open 24 June-11 Sept., Tues.-Sat. 6 p.m.-12 mid., Sun. 12 noon-12 mid.; winter, weekends and holidays 12 noon-8 p.m. Admission), with 40 carousels and rides. Younger kids who are still afraid of white knuckle rides enjoy this lovely 1950s atmosphere.

Parents can console themselves at the café and wine bar.

The fortress up on the hill is home to the **Museu Militar** (Castell de Montjuïc, tel. 329-8613. Bus: 61, 100. Open Tues.-Sat. 10 a.m.-2 p.m. and 3:30-8 p.m., Sun. and holidays 10 a.m.-7 p.m. Admission), for those who love weapons, suits of armour and torture instruments.

The **Fundació Miró** (Plaça Neptu, tel. 329-1908. M: Paral-lel and then the funicular. Bus: 100. Open Tues.-Sat. 11 a.m.-7 p.m., Thurs. until 9:30 p.m.; Sun. and holidays 10:30 a.m.-2:30 p.m. Admission) is a sheer delight and a quiet haven for contemplation high above the hectic city. This light, white building, designed by Joseph Lluís Sert in 1974, excels in pure design. As a close friend of Miró, Sert created the ideal exhibition centre for the artist's colourful sculptures and paintings. Temporary exhibitions of international artists are also held here. The impressive view of the city and the excellent restaurant with tables in the courtyard are in themselves worth the admission.

CAFES AND BARS

Las Cascadas. Passeig de les Cascades. M: Espanya. Mon.-Fri. 8 a.m.-9 p.m., Sat.-Sun. 10 a.m.-10 p.m. Closed in November.

This little self-service bar is as old as the Palau Nacional and the surrounding majestic buildings. It offers coffee, beer and juices as well as well bocadillos, tortillas and small salads. Good views of the thundering fountains and the city.

Miramar. Terassa del Morsot, Miramar, tel. 242-3100. Bus: 61, 201, 101 or the Transbordador Aeri from the port, the Torre Sant Jaume station or from Barceloneta, Torre de Sant Sebastià. Thurs.-Tues. 10 a.m.-12 mid. Closed in November.

Only the great views of the harbour and the Columbus monument makes this large restaurant next to the gondola station worth mentioning - not the food.

Gaudi's Casa Calvet in Eixample is very restrained compared to his Casa Battló

EIXAMPLE

A bird's eye view of Barcelona or a look at a map for the first time reveals a geometric city, as if designed by computer. North of the old town, Barcelona is laid out just like a chessboard. There was uproar in city hall when in 1859 the town planner Idelfons Cerdà submitted his 'Plan Cerdà' to the mayor, who suffered a nervous breakdown as a result. The hapless mayor quit when the radical plan was accepted by central government in Madrid against the will of Barcelona's city council. The city even declared itself bankrupt and had to borrow millions from Madrid for cement and tiles.

Today most self-respecting citizens would like to live in Eixample, even though the houses and streets are barely distinguishable. However, the designs of new champagne bars, restaurants, nightclubs and shops compensate for this unimaginative layout. The Diagonal, until some years ago known as Avenida de Generalísimo Franco, offers the best shopping in the city's most futuristic shops. It is easy to lose your orientation in this experimental geometry, but a walk through the wide streets of Eixample will give you an idea of everyday life in Barcelona.

The district's first block was built in 1863 on the corner of Carrer Roger de Llúria and Consell de Cent, and boasts Art Nouveau pastel murals. Recently some astute civil servant at city hall designated Eixample as the 'Golden Quarter' because here between Gran Via de les Corts Catalans and Diagonal, Plaça Catalunya, Plaça Francesc Macia, Carrer del Comte Sarrià and Passeig de Sant Joan, you can marvel at glorious Art Nouveau architecture.

Passeig de Gràcia alone is a monument to modernism, and walking north up this street you can see some of the finest buildings of Barcelona's three greatest architects of that era. The municipal tourism office building at number 35 is Domènech i Montaner's **Casa Lleo Morera**. **Casa Amatller**, by Puig i Cadafalch, is at number 41, next door to Gaudí's **Casa Batllo**, number 43. The undulating **La Pedrera** (Casa Mila), one of Gaudí's best-known creations; lies further up at number 92. The **Casa Fuster** apartment block at number 132 is typical Domènech, while the **Museu de la Música** (Casa Quadras) at

EIXAMPLE

the corner on Diagonal is a Puig masterpiece. (See chapters on Gaudí and Modernism).

It's here where the middle-classes live their quiet life, and it's here where the image-conscious eat, shop and go to a cafe. Many residents of this part of Barcelona have not ventured down to the old town for many years. Of course, the tourist should not take this attitude. To me, Eixample is a spaceship from a mythical land somewhere between Europe and America, which has landed right in the middle of ancient Barcelona. The tall, even facades could easily be Brussels, Berlin or Rome, the chrome and neon bars could be New York or Tokyo, and today's boutiques are the same the world over. The 'Plan Cerdà', however, was uniquely Barcelona!

CAFES AND BARS

Amarcord. Passeig de Gràcia, Provença 261 La Pedrera building, tel. 215-7249. M: Passeig de Gràcia.

This comfortable cafe-bar is located right under Gaudí's surrealist La Pedrera. In summer there are tables on the pavement. Open daily.

Balmoral. Diagonal 500. M: Diagonal.

Entirely in 1960s style. Mosaics on the floor, and a mammoth bar where you can have a pleasant breakfast on your own. Sandwiches, omelettes and milk shakes are the specialities. Unusually cool and quiet for Barcelona.

Bracafe. Casp 4, tel. 302-3082. Daily 7 a.m.–12 mid. M: Passeig de Gràcia.

My favourite! Ancient waiters linger in this café, where it smells of Havana cigars and excellent coffee, ground on the premises. Frequented by grandpa and grandma who sit for hours on the dark leather wall benches. Tables on the pavement are taken by youngsters, but regulars of this traditional café only sit indoors. Definitely not renovated since opening in 1932. Art Deco with patina.

Cafe del Centro. Girona 69. M: Girona. Mon.-Sat. 6 a.m.-10 p.m. Closed Aug.

Wonderful sleepy coffee house which reminds me of Viennese cafés. Marble columns and black and white tiled floor recreate turn-of-the-century charm.

La Jijonenca. Rambla de Catalunya 35, tel. 301-9196. M: Passeig de Gràcia. Daily 10 a.m.-1 a.m.

My favourite open-air bar! You can sit under undulating, white iron bars to the right and left of the boulevard, where you can watch the passers-by. If you want to escape the heat and traffic, you can relax on the futuristic, white leather benches in the narrow interior. You must try the homemade hazelnut ice cream and the enormous milkshakes. Sandwiches are rather expensive, but the lunch special is popular and recommendable.

Mana Mana. Passeig de Gracia 78, tel. 215-6387. M: Passeig de Gràcia. Mon.-Sat. 10 a.m.-12 mid.

Of the many street cafés on the Passeig, this is the least touristy. But if you're prepared to walk a bit further, go on to the Rambla de Catalunya, which runs parallel. It's more serene and civilised there.

Mauri. Rambla de Catalunya 102, tel. 215-1020. M: Diagonal. Mon.-Sat. 9 a.m.-9 p.m., Sun. 9 a.m.-3 p.m.

This *saló de te* is Barcelona's oldest and most exclusive coffee and teahouse. The rococo-style establishment, founded in 1870, is still frequented by the best families, who eye each other over tea and sandwiches.

Oller. Passeig de Sant Joan 146, tel. 257-8159. M: Verdaguer. Mon.-Fri. 9 a.m.-10 p.m., Sat.-Sun. 9 a.m.-2 p.m.

Neither the décor nor the location of the café is unusual. But the atmosphere is conducive to contemplation. A true neighbourhood café where housewives pop in for a coke, a croissant and the latest gossip.

Sandor. Placa Francesc Macià 5 corner at Diagonal, tel. 200-8913. Only by bus or after a long walk from M: Hospital Clínic.

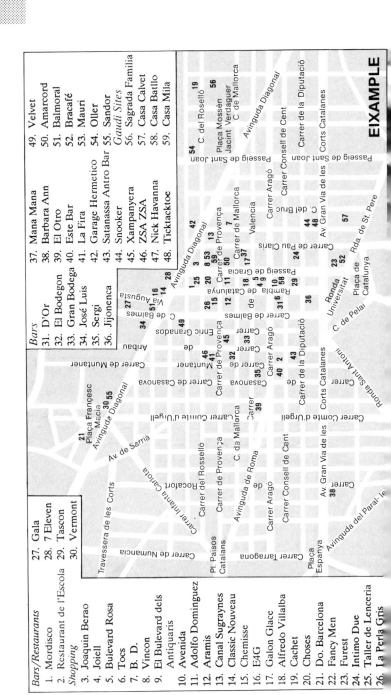

Bars/Restaurants
1. Mordisco
2. Restaurant de l'Escola

Shopping
3. Joaquin Berao
4. Joiell
5. Bulevard Rosa
6. Tocs
7. B. D.
8. Vincon
9. El Bulevard dels Antiquaris
10. Avenida
11. Adolfo Dominguez
12. Aramis
13. Canal Sugraynes
14. Classic Nouveau
15. Chemisse
16. E4G
17. Galon Glace
18. Alfredo Villalba
19. Cachet
20. Choses
21. Do. Barcelona
22. Fancy Men
23. Furest
24. Intimo Due
25. Taller de Lenceria
26. La Perla Gris
27. Gala
28. 7 Eleven
29. Tascon
30. Vermont

Bars
31. D'Or
32. El Bodegon
33. Gran Bodega
34. José Luis
35. Sergi
36. Jijonenca
37. Mana Mana
38. Barbara Ann
39. El Otro
40. Este Bar
41. La Fira
42. Garage Hermetico
43. Satanassa Antro Bar
44. Snooker
45. Xampanyera
46. ZSA ZSA
47. Nick Havanna
48. Ticktacktoe
49. Velvet
50. Amarcord
51. Balmoral
52. Bracafé
53. Mauri
54. Oller
55. Sandor

Gaudi Sites
56. Sagrada Familia
57. Casa Calvet
58. Casa Batllo
59. Casa Mila

EIXAMPLE

In the finest shopping and residential area, though amid the exhaust fumes of the eight-lane Diagonal. This café is renowned for its fruit tarts and moneyed clientele.

Velodromo. Muntaner 213, tel. 230-6022. FFCC: Muntaner. Mon.-Sat. 6 a.m.- 1 a.m. Closed Aug.

Yet another panelled café with wicker chairs in Thonet style, three pool tables in the corner, and super coffee. Time has stood still since 1900. The sweet delicacies are always fresh and Señor and Señora Llaras are always happy to serve you.

Zurich. Plaça de Catalunya 35. M: Catalunya. Daily until 12:30 p.m.; Sun. until 11:30 p.m.

Fantastic central location for a rendezvous with friends. Too loud for romantics, always surrounded by roaring traffic. Quite touristy at the street tables with the enormous sunshades, but surprisingly, in the white salon, there is always a quiet corner. Old men play chess and dominos, and even the waiters take their time. Why is this café named after a Swiss city? The former owner worked as a waiter in Zurich at the turn of the century, and in 1920 named his café after his beloved city.

Casa Vicens in Gracia was built for a tile manufacturer by Gaudí in 1885

GRACIA

Thank God for this graceful little village, right in the middle of mighty Barcelona with its 1.7 million inhabitants. Many tourists never come all the way up here. I love the quiet atmosphere of the **Plaça del Sol**, where on summer weekends bands play and the whole quarter dances under colourful lanterns. On the square of the Sun you'll find one café after another, and the tapas bars are run by families, ecologists and students, so everything is less expensive than in nearby Sarrià or Pedralbes.

A curiosity worth seeing is the colossal **Venetian** tower below Gràcia's city hall on Plaça Rius i Taulet, named after turn-of-the-century megalomaniac mayor.

Unfortunately, the Plaça del Diamant is rather sad and grey and surrounded by dilapidated houses with plaster falling from the facades. Nothing remains of the charm portrayed by Merce Rodoreda in her wonderful novel *On the Plaça del Diamant*.

Gracia is home to students and artists, layabouts and workers, basket weavers and cobblers, young families with little money and, more recently, the fashionable.

Get off at Metro stations Diagonal or Fontana, stroll along streets and squares at random, have a cerveza or a copa at the bar, or simply observe how the day takes shape on the Plaça del Sol from the morning into the small hours. People have written whole books like this...

On the outskirts of Gràcia lies the fabulous **Parc Güell**, one of Gaudí's most famous creations. It was originally conceived as a private residential estate, with plans for 60 villas, recreation areas and a market square. However, enthusiasm for this suburban utopia never caught fire, and the public inherited the decorative, meandering pathways, twisted stone columns, giant lizards and undulating ceramic benches as a surrealist park (see also Gaudí and Parks).

I enjoy walking from Parc Güell down Gran de Gràcia and Passeig de Gràcia to the Ramblas and down to the port. Only then can you really say: I know Barcelona. Take suitable footwear for this marathon. Have fun!

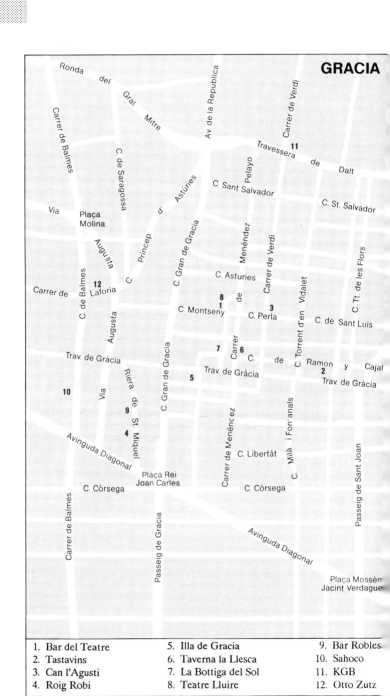

GRACIA

1. Bar del Teatre
2. Tastavins
3. Can l'Agusti
4. Roig Robi
5. Illa de Gracia
6. Taverna la Llesca
7. La Bottiga del Sol
8. Teàtre Lluire
9. Bar Robles
10. Sahoco
11. KGB
12. Otto Zutz

CAFES AND BARS

Bar del Teatre. Montseny 47, tel. 218-6738. Tues.-Sat. 1-4 p.m. and 8 p.m.-1 a.m.

The restaurant-bar of the Teatre Lluire is a dark little place with wooden blinds, and the only decorations are photos of actors. Cheap snacks and Spanish specialities such as *paella*.

Tastavins. Ramon i Cajal 12, tel. 213-6031. Mon.-Sat. 1-4 p.m. and 9 p.m.-12 mid. Closed Aug.

Neighbourhood bar with a surprisingly good menu, mainly steaks with unusual chese and pepper sauces.

Can l'Agusti. Verdi 28, tel. 218-5396. Thurs.-Tues. 1-4 p.m. and 8 p.m.-12 mid.

Come early, especially for lunch, otherwise the extremely cheap daily special will be sold out.

Taverna la Llesca. Terol 6. Tues.-Sun. 1-4 p.m. and 9 p.m.-1 a.m. Closed Aug.

Good value taverna, where you can have all kinds of tostadas au gratin, bocadillos and kebabs.

A radiant bride in Gaudi's Parc Güell, where wedding parties often meet for a drink.

The whimsical Gaudí villa Bellesguard, in the mountains near Tibidabo, is worth a trek.

SANT GERVASI, SARRIA, PEDRALBES AND TIBIDABO

If you're taking a little more time in Barcelona, and if you enjoy a cosmopolitan environment where the air is clean and the people rich, take the ultramodern, fully air-conditioned Ferrocarils de Catalunya train from Plaça de Catalunya and whiz up to **Sant Gervasi**, where at Plaça de Molina you'll be tempted by flashy bars with first-class tapas. Richer still are the people who live near the Reina Elisanda and Plaça Sarrià stations in the district of the same name. This is Mercedes and BMW territory and you can stroll without fear of pickpockets, though perhaps uninspired, along the spotless wide streets of this expensive residential area at the foot of Tibidabo.

Carry on all the way up to one of Gaudí's most original houses, **Villa Bellesguard** (Bellesguard 16-20), nestling in the hills. Built between 1900 and 1902, the house is today owned by a family of doctors, and although you cannot enter, the trip is well worth it as this villa is wonderfully located and resembles a fairy-tale castle. To the left of the entrance you can still see the ruins of King Marti's Gothic castle.

The tenor José Carreras lives in **Sarrià**, and above, in Valvidrera, which you can reach from the FFCC station Peu Funicular by an antiquated rack railway, lives the hero of Vàzquez Montalbàn's thrillers, the gourmet Pepe Carvalhó, cooking his celebrated duck goulash into the early hours.

If you're a good walker, then continue all the way up the Carrer Major de Sarrià and left into **Parc l'Orenata** where you can enjoy a beautiful panorama from the old castle. Many excellent restaurants, mostly with garden or terrace, have opened all the way up here near their moneyed clientele.

SANT GERVASI, SARRIA, PEDRALBES AND TIBIDABO

TIBIDABO

You should set aside at least half a day for a visit to Tibidabo. In the summer, walking up the steep streets is less arduous in the late afternoon, and in the evening you can stop off at one of the many fantastic garden restaurants, expensive on the Plaça Tibidabo, or, more hidden though still rather expensive, adjacent to Carrer Teodor Roviralta and Avinguda del Tibidabo.

If you can get off at the FFCC station Tibidabo at the Plaça John Kennedy or arrive on the tourist bus 100, you'll see the blue tram **Tramvia Blau**, opposite. You can rattle up the Avinguda del Tibidabo seated on 90-year-old wooden benches past grandiose turn-of-the-century modernist villas.

Located in the suburbs at the foot of Tibidano is **Casa Muntadas** (Avinguda del Doctor Andreu 48). Dating from 1901, it is one of the simpler villas designed by Puig i Cadafalch, as it is based on the ground plan of a *masia,* a Catalan farmhouse.

Another modernist building, designed by Joan Rubio i Bellver, is **Casa Roviralta** (Avinguda del Tibidabo 31). This 1913 building is nicknamed 'the white monk', as it used to be a Dominican monastery. Rubio's last project, another unusual building on the same street, can be seen from the Tramvia Blau.

Then you can change on the Funicular for the best views of Barcelona! On the **Plaça Tibidabo**, the white church and modern statue of Jesus, as equally atrocious as its counterpart on Rio's Sugarloaf Mountain, are disappointing. Here children and their tormented parents can move on to La Muntanya Magica (Cumbre del Tibidabo, tel. 211-7942, free information number 900-300-466. Bus: 100. Open Apr.-11 Sept., daily 11 a.m.-8, 9 or 10 p.m. according to season; 12 Sept.-Mar., weekends 11 a.m.-8 p.m.; open daily during Christmas and Easter holidays. Admission). The amusement park has a scurrilous museum of automaton dolls. I have to admit that the roller coaster on the magic mountain was a hair-raising experience. Buy the *Pase Libre,* because with this pass you can go on all the rides until you're dizzy. From the merry-go-round there is an excellent view of the city.

It is a tradition in Barcelona for lovers to spend hours in the car up here on the slopes of El Tibi and in the Parc de Collserola. But don't worry, you don't have to witness the Spanish art of making out, as the young at heart only indulge in these pleasures after dark.

CAFES AND BARS

Bar de la Plaça. Plaça de Sarrià 1, tel. 203-1082. FFCC: Reina Elisanda or bus: 66, 94, 64, 34. Sun.-Fri. 8:30 a.m.-10 p.m. Closed Aug.

Café and tapas bar - the anchovies and *pan con tomate* are particularly delicious. Two pooltables.

Can Pau. Plaça de Sant Vicenc de Sarrià 1, tel. 203-1052. FFCC: Sarrià. Mon.-Sat. 8 a.m.-1 a.m. Closed Aug.

Simple Spanish bar, with few tables but excellent food.

Tomas. Major de Sarrià 49, tel. 203-1077. FFCC: Sarrià. Daily 8 a.m.- 10 p.m. Closed Aug.

Café and tapas bar. Speciality *patates braves*.

El Café de la Republica. República Argentina 83, (Tibidabo), tel. 210-2393. M: Vallcarca. Open Mon.-Sat.; Fri. and Sat. until 3 a.m. Closed holidays.

More of a bar than a café, uptown and with uptown clientele.

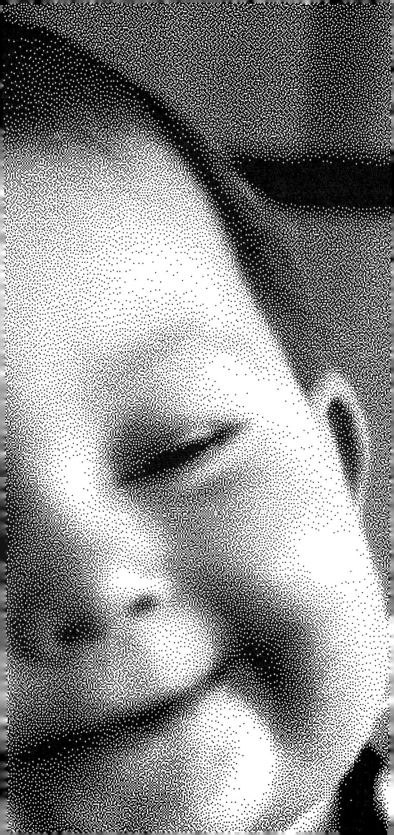

CHILDREN IN BARCELONA

Children of all ages just love Barcelona. Where else would you find a city with two amusement parks? And they're not miles out of town either, but always in sight on the city's two mountains! Where else can you glide in gondolas or a cable car above the harbour, the old town and up into the mountains? Only in Barcelona!

Although it might sound a cliché about Mediterranean people, it's a simple truth that the Spanish love and respect their children more than we northerners. Offspring, be they babies or teenagers, sit with their parents in restaurants until midnight as if it were the most natural thing in the world. You will hardly hear a single reprimand. There seem to be fewer conflicts within these larger families than in our standard northern trio of mum, dad and kiddie. Surprisingly, in Barcelona you'll never find shy, sulking or difficult children. The attitude that children are part of daily life, even late into the night, and in many respects are to be treated just like adults, seems to work. No angry stares from uptight waiters if baby chucks a spoon on the floor or torpedoes the next table with carrots. Barcelona is a paradise for young parents.

The city offers a never-ending supply of fun so that the little ones can't possibly get bored. Apart from the Magic Mountain on Tibidabo and the amusement park on Montjuïc, children will be enticed by the Spanish village, the beaches in Barceloneta, the museums, and boats trips around the harbour or on lakes in some of the parks. And if you've had enough of the little rascals for a day, you can take them to a special children's hotel or hire the rather expensive services of a 24-hour babysitter. But wouldn't you give up some filthy lucre for a few hours of peace?

BABYSITTERS

You will hardly ever need a babysitter in Barcelona, as children also come out at night. The early evening siesta after school is an old tradition and the *niños* are therefore quite bouncy until after midnight.

CHILDREN IN BARCELONA

Even small hostales can often put you in touch with young women or elderly ladies who are happy to earn a little pocket money babysitting. Otherwise, turn to the following rather expensive agency:

Baby and Home. Tel. 411-1877. Appointments 9:30 a.m.-1:30 p.m. and 4-7 p.m.

Most of the young girls at this agency speak English. Minimum fee 2,000 ptas. At night you will have to pay the girl's cab fare home.

CHILDREN'S HOTEL

Parvulario y Hotel Para Niños. Avinguda Pearson 40, tel. 203-7627. Mon.-Fri. only, 4,000 ptas.

I don't quite understand why this children's hotel looks after kids and serves breakfast and dinner only during the week. I'm told it's for school kids who only see their mum and dad at the weekend and eat lunch at school. Expensive day-home!

CARNET JOVE

The Spanish introduced the **Carnet Jove** for young people between the ages of 14 and 25. This card entitles you to concessions of up to 50% in cinemas, museums, youth hostels and even in shops, restaurants, bars, discos, music clubs and concerts. It's well worth the outlay! Look for the sign '*Carnet Jove, aquí, sí!*' and you'll save money!

You can obtain this youth card at many branches of the savings banks, the *caixas,* for 300 pesetas. By the way, they are also valid in France, Portugal and some other European countries.

If you need more information, contact the **Youth Department**: **Direccio General de Joventut.** Generalitat de Catalunya Viladomat 319, tel. 322-9061.

AMUSEMENT PARKS

La Muntanya Magica. See Tibidabo.

Parc des Atraccions. See Montjuïc.

CHILDREN IN
BARCELONA

MUSEUMS

Museu Maritim. See Ramblas.

Museu Militar. See Montjuïc.

Museu de la Música. See Museums.

ENTERTAINMENT

Futbol Club Barcelona. See Museums.

Fonts Illuminoses. See Montjuïc.

Poble Espanyol. See Montjuïc.

Centre Cultural del Caixa de Pensions. Laietana 56, M: Urquinaoana. Mon.-Fri. 11 a.m.-2 p.m. and 4-8 p.m., Sat. 10 p.m.-8 p.m.

   This cultural centre, belonging to the savings bank offers free use of computers, games, videos, drawing and art materials.

Ludoteca Casa Golferichs. Gran Via, corner with Viladomat. Telephone information 010. M: Espanya.

   Ludotecas are games houses for children and youths. The Casa Golferichs, a modernist building, was recently converted into one: four floors packed with computers, comics, videos, Lego, board games and an activity room. For 12- to 21-year-olds. (Of course, older computer freaks can also come along.)

Ludoteca Centro Civic de Sants. Olzinelles 113. Telephone information 010. M: Sants.

   Public games house with supervisors for the very youngest aged 1-6.

Kinos Florida. Floridablanca 135, tel. 423-2118. M: Urgell.
You can leave the little devils in the creches of these three new cinemas if you want to watch the latest Woody Allen in peace. Unfortunately

they run fewer art films than US box office hits - dubbed into Spanish.

Filmoteca. Travessera de Gràcia 63, tel. 201-2906. Kids programme at 12 noon every Sunday.

Cheapest cinema in town. Children get in half price, and young people (14-25) pay half on producing the Carnet Jove.

MILKBARS, ICE CREAM AND RESTAURANTS

Granja Santa Clara. Llibreteria. M: Jaume I.

Granja Viader. Xuclà 4. M: Liceu.

Granja Xador. Argenteria 61. M: Jaume I.

Granja Llaras. Nou de la Rambla 36.

In Spain, *granjas* are farms with dairy cows. Barcelona's granjas are milkbars offering milkshakes, yoghurt, hot chocolate, rice pudding, puddings and Danish pastries. Cheap and ideal for the kids.

La Jijonenca. Rambla de Catalunya 35, tel. 301-9196. M: Catalunya. Daily 9 a.m.-1:30 a.m.

The white, soft leather benches on the walls make this cool ice cream bar even icier. The thick milkshakes, sandwiches, horchata and the famous ice cream make this a Mecca for ice cream gourmets, but it's not cheap.

Baffi. Ferran 59. M: Jaume I. Daily 10 a.m.–8 p.m.

The colouring of the ice cream looks rather synthetic.

Heladeria Gatti. Urgell 290, corner with Diagonal. M: Diagonal and then a long walk, or bus: 15 and 41.

The ice cream is obviously good in this smart area.

Glaco. Gran Via 518, corner with Urgell. M: Urgell.

Only if you're passing by. The extra trip is hardly worth it. You're better off in Jijonenca for the best ice cream in town.

Hollywood. Diagonal 493, corner on Plaça Francesc Macià, tel. 322-1015. M: Diagonal and then a long walk, or bus 15 and 41. Daily 1 p.m.–1.15 a.m., Sat.–Sun. 'til 2:15 a.m.

American food, hamburgers, fries, BBQ, hot dogs, milkshakes. Special kids menu for *niños*.

MARKETS

You'll discover the most interesting and colourful markets of this port city in market halls in each of the districts. Mostly housed in turn-of-the-century iron structures, these *mercats* mirror the character of the Catalan metropolis.

All Barcelona mingles between pyramids of oysters and shrimps, dates and olives, fennel and aubergines. Housewives in pinafores and worn out slippers haggle as hard over the best piece of loin and fresh fish as their sisters in Chanel outfits and pumps. Chefs and hotel managers eagerly shop around for their dinner menu. At market bars, hungry office workers perch on uncomfortable stools next to students and doctors. They pick from tapas or gorge black octopus risotto and *gambas a la plancha*. Here you'll get a better idea of the real Barcelona than in the cathedral or the Sagrada Familia. Just follow your senses, not only in the Boqueria on the Ramblas, packed with tourists, but also in the markets in Ribera, Gràcia or Sarrià. Study the Catalan and Spanish way of life! And don't just visit the flea markets. The honey and natural produce markets on Plaça Pi or the artisans in Parc Turó are more original.

FLEA MARKETS

Antiques Mercat. Plaça del Pi, tel. 317-1996. M: Jaume I. Thurs. 9 a.m.-8 p.m.. Dec. 8 a.m.-11 p.m., closed Aug.

Dealers display their trinkets on Thursdays in the little square behind Mare de Déu del Pi church. The patient collector will mostly find jewellery, old fans, hats, lace tablecloths and shawls, silver, old postcards and photo albums. The market was larger when it was still located on Plaça de Déu. It will return to its home in front of the cathedral once the works on the subterranean car park for tourist buses are completed in 1992 or 1993.

Els Encants. Plaça de les Glories, tel. 246-3030. M: Glories. Mon., Wed., Fri., Sat. 8 a.m.-8 p.m.; in winter 8 a.m.-7 p.m.

MARKETS

More of a hub for rag-and-bone men than a true flea market as in London or Paris. Cheap furniture and rare bargains in second-hand clothes lure the masses, mainly on Saturdays, to this desolate square between the motorway and the building site of the new concert hall.

MARKET HALLS

Opening hours: Mon.-Sat. 8 a.m.-3 p.m. and 5-8 p m.

Mercat Abaceria Central. Travessera de Gràcia, corner at Torrijos. M: Joanic.
Central market in the student and workers district of Gràcia.

Mercat de la Concepcio. Between València and Arragó, corner at Bruc. M: Girona.
A market for the fastidious shopper in the quiet residential area of Eixample. Many flower stalls and delicatessens.

Mercat Galvany. Santaló, corner at Madrazo. FFCC: Muntaner.
Interesting old market in a smart district.

Mercat Lesseps. Verdi 214. M: Lesseps.
Small market near Parc Güell.

Mercat Sant Antoni. Comte d'Urgell and Mansó. M: Poble Sec.

Large market where you can get cheap clothes, kitsch, souvenirs, and on Sundays, new and second-hand books, magazines, postcards and coins.

Mercat Santa Caterina. Plaça Santa Caterina. M: Jaume I.

This is where people from the popular districts of Ribera and Sant Pere go shopping.

Mercat Sant Josep, Boqueria. Ramblas. M: Liceu.

Because of the tourists, many traders in the Boqueria don't take a siesta, but of course the atmosphere is more authentic during normal Spanish hours. No true Catalan goes shopping in the midday heat, they have lunch, *basta*!

Mercat Sarrià. Passeig Reina Elisanda de Montcada and Major de Sarrià. FFCC: Reina Elisanda.

SPECIALIST MARKETS

Fira d'Art. Sants 79. M: Plaça de Sants. First Sunday of the month, 10 a.m.-3 p.m.

In the Cotxeres cultural centre, old and young offer handicrafts, ceramics, bric a brac, pictures and toys.

Fira del Col.lectiu d'Artesans de l'Alimentacio. Plaça del Pi. M: Liceu. First Friday and Saturday of the month, 10 a.m.-8 p.m.

Honey and natural products.

Fira Nova Artesania. Rambla Santa Mònica. M: Drassanes. Sat.-Sun. 11 a.m.-7 p.m.

Cheap handicrafts, souvenirs, belts, shawls, T-shirts and accessories.

Fira del Productes Naturals. Plaça Sagrada Familia. M: Sagrada Familia. On the second weekend of each month, 10 a.m.-3 p.m.

Organic fruit and vegetables, natural honey, nougat, cheese, quark and cakes, as well as honey products such as honey bread and bonbons.

MARKETS

Mercat Numismatic i Filatelia. Plaça Reial. M: Liceu. Sun. 9:30 a.m.–2:30 p.m.

Stamp and coin market near the Ramblas.

Mercat Numismatic i del Llibre. Mercat de Sant Antoni, Comte d'Urgell, corner at Mansó. M: Poble Sec. Sun. 10 a.m.–2 p.m.

Dealers trade in coins, stamps, new and used books, comics, magazines, old postcards and photo albums.

Mercat Pintura. Plaça Sagrada Familia. M: Sagrada Familia. Weekends and holidays, 10 a.m.–3 p.m.

The right place to look for oil paintings of raging bulls and fiery flamenco dancers.

Mostra d'Art. Plaça Sant Joseph Oriol. M: Liceu. Sat. 11 a.m.–8:30 p.m., Sun. 11 a.m.–2:30 p.m. Closed Aug.

Mainly amateur artists and tourist junk, but a few stands belonging to art students.

Mostra d'Art. Plaça del Roser. FFCC: Reina Elisanda. Last Sunday of the month, 10 a.m.–3 p.m., apart from July and August.

Naive art and retail kitsch. Creative wallpaper.

SHOPPING

Shopping in Barcelona is fun, above all during the sales, as prices plummet here like in no other town. Towards the end of the sales, designer clothes are reduced by up to 75%, and Spanish T-shirts and jeans can be had for 10% of their original price. Strolling around the shopping malls of Bulevard Rosa and Avenida, and Galeries Turó and Malda, will give you a quick insight into Barcelona's fashion. Leather jackets, shoes, handbags, ceramics and porcelain as well as wine, whiskey, cigarettes, cigars and some electronic goods can be more economical than back home.

You'll find the most interesting new designers and shops in Diagonal, Rambla de Catalunya, Passeig de Gràcia, and the side streets Rossello, Consell de Cent and Mallorca in Eixample, while the shops near Portal de l'Angel, Portaferrissa and Pelai in Barri Gòtic and around the Sant Antoni market offer cheaper clothes and sportswear.

Most shops are open from 9 a.m. until 1 or 2 p.m. and from 4-8 p.m. Department stores are open from 10 a.m.-8 p.m.

DEPARTMENT STORES

El Corte Ingles. Plaça de Catalunya 14 (Eixample), tel. 302-1212. M: Catalunya; and Diagonal 617 (Pedralbes), tel 419-5206. M: Maria Cristina. Mon.-Sat. 10 a.m.-9 p.m.

What the English has to do with it is a mystery to me, but I presume the name is meant to sound inviting. Strangely, a plastic bag from El Corte is a status symbol in Spain, like a bag from Harrods in London. Why? Perhaps because you can find everything under one roof at unashamedly high prices, and because of its wide selection. However, if you know the cheap electronic shops in the harbour, the large shopping malls of Bulevard Rosa and the market halls, you won't need to visit this ugly concrete building on Plaça de Catalunya. Only the view from the terrace of the roof cafeteria is worth the sprint through this otherwise boring department store.

SHOPPING

Galerias Preciados. Portal de l'Angel 19-20 (Eixample), tel. 317-0000. M: Catalunya; and Diagonal 471-473 (Eixample), tel. 322-3011. M: Diagonal. Mon.-Sat. 10 a.m.-9 p.m.

For years this second department store chain has been trying desperately to compete with the Corte. They have not quite succeeded despite their almost identical products and slightly lower prices. Barcelona's department stores are well behind their counterparts in Europe, Japan and the U.S.

SHOPPING MALLS

Avenida. Rambla de Catalunya 121 (Eixample), tel. 317-1398. M: Passeig de Gràcia. Mon.-Sat. 10:30 a.m.-2 p.m. and 4:30-8:30 p.m.

This fashion centre contains 48 shops and a café.

Bulevard Rosa. Passeig de Gràcia 55 (Eixample), tel. 309-0650. M: Passeig de Gràcia; Diagonal 474 (Eixample), M: Diagonal; Diagonal 609-615 (Pedralbes), tel. 419-1280. M: Maria Christina.

The name Bulevard Rosa has been synonymous with this beehive of boutiques since 1978. Over 100 shops in the oldest mall on Passeig de Gràcia, and 88 in the newest mall high up in the smart residential and office district, Zona Alta.

Galeries Malda. Portaferrissa 22 (Barri Gòtic), tel. 318-8940. Mon.-Sat. 10:30 a.m.-1:30 p.m. and 4-8:30 p.m.. **Mercadillo.** Portaferrissa 17 (Barri Gòtic), tel. 317-3192. Mon.-Sat. 11 a.m.-8:30 p.m. **Galleries Ferrissa.** Portaferrissa 23 (Barri Gotic), tel. 317-1398. M: Liceu. Mon.-Fri. 10:30 a.m.-2 p.m. and 4:30-8:30 p.m., Sat. 10:30 a.m.-8:30 p.m.

Fashionable and even slightly cheaper than the above malls. Fewer brand names and more Catalan products. The odd punk and goth also shops here. There is a pleasant rooftop café in Mercadillo.

Galleries Turo. Tenor Viñas 12 (Sant Gervais), tel. 317-1398. FFCC: Muntaner. Mon.-Sat. 11 a.m.-2 p.m. and 4:30-9 p.m.

In the most unmarket residential area: 33 boutiques for the

expensive and more conservative taste.

Via Wagner. Placa Wagner (Les Corts), tel. 200-1646 FFCC: Muntaner. Mon.-Sat. 10:30 a.m.-2 p.m. and 4:30-9 p.m.

One hundred shops near Diagonal, souvenirs and cafés, as well as fashion.

FASHION FOR MEN AND WOMEN

Adolfo Domminguez. Passeig de Gràcia 89 (Eixample), tel. 215-1339. M: Passeig de Gràcia.

Dominguez is Spain's most successful designer with boutiques in London, New York, Milan and Paris. His baggy dresses and costumes in subdued El Greco colours radiate urbane simplicity. Excellent materials. Men's trenchcoats are made of finest cotton mixed with silk, and flow dramatically behind the body. A must for the fashionably vain.

Aramis. Rambla de Catalunya 103 (Eixample, tel. 215-1669. M: Diagonal.

Men upstairs, women downstairs, classic style is predominant. Shirts can be made to measure. Wide selection of colours and materials. Designers such as Valentino and Ungaro guarantee high prices.

Canal Sugraynes. Roger de Llúria 129 (Eixample), tel. 210-1774. M: Verdaguer.

Rather more extravagant fashion by interesting young Spanish designers - many so new that they are still unknown in their own country.

Casual Junior. Bulevard Rosa, Passeig de Gràcia 55 and València 266 (Eixample), tel. 215-3461. M: Passeig de Gràcia.

Multicoloured clothes for those in their teens, cheap jeans, Benetton-stype jumpers and sweatshirts.

Classic Nouveau. Bulevard Rosa, Diagonal 474 (Eixample), tel. 234-0930. M: Diagonal.

SHOPPING

Modern branch of the Fiorucci chain. Everything in 1950s college style. Striped T-shirts, colourful sweatshirts, jumpers with embroidery, wide jeans and khaki trousers.

Chemisse. Ramblas de Catalunya 117, tel. 237-6734. M: Catalunya.
Shirts and blouses in any shape and colour, all patterns and materials, arranged on shelves according to tone and size.

E4G. Diagonal 490 (Eixample), tel. 218-3544. M: Diagonal; and Tenor Viñas 7, tel. 209-0822. FFCC: Muntaner; and Bulevard Rosa (Pedralbes), Diagonal 609-615, tel. 419-0022. M: Maria Cristina.
Trendies only buy their clothes in E4G. Black Levi 501s hang next to outrageous creations from Paris, Madrid, Milan or New York. Skin-tight Lycra catsuits, embroidered with sequins attract models and advertising copywriters. Pop music, matching the trendy club fashion, blares from huge speakers.

Emporio Armani. Via Augusta 10 (Gracia), tel. 218-7679. M: Diagonal.
The good-value Diffusion line from Giorgio Armani, whose more exclusive designs can be admired in his shop on Diagonal. Casual cuts, the fabulous Armani blazers for *señoras* and *señores*, leather jackets made of soft nappa, curious Panama hats, sporty underwear, tracksuits and accessories such as bags, shoes and belts.

Franel-La. Tenor Viñas 1 (Sant Gervasi), tel. 201-8479. FFCC: Muntaner.
For those who want to dress in the latest collections from designers such as Marithe et Francois Girbaud, Closed, Junior Gaultier and Chipie. Take a fat chequebook.

Galon Glace. Passeig de Gràcia 76 (Eixample), tel. 215-6972. M: Passeig de Gràcia.
Avant-garde shop stocking designs from Gigli, Yorke & Cole from Paris and Armand Basi from Barcelona. The basement is full of chairs, tables and sofas from the 1950s and 1960s. Matching vases, lamps and china are placed everywhere in the shop, to great effect.

Giorgio Armani. Diagonal 624 (Les Corts), tel. 200-9901. M: Maria Cristina.

The grand master, Soft cuts, classic materials and unbelievable prices. But if you want to know who is top designer for the end of the 20th century, have a good look around this very cool boutique.

Groc. Munaner 385 (Sant Gervasi), tel. 202-3077. FFCC: Muntaner.

Antonio Miró is said to be Barcelona's best designer. His inspired costumes and suits reveal humour and love of detail. In order to really appreciate Miró's style you must try the jackets and dresses on. Understatement with a certain twist.

WOMEN'S FASHION

Alfredo Villalba. Rambla de Catalunya 88 (Eixample), tel. 215-0542. M: Diagonal.

Young Barcelonesas love the fashion of this Catalan designer. He creates a feminine look, new outfits each month, and the materials are from Italy and therefore the best.

Cachet. Rosselló 415 and València 265 (Eixample), tel. 215-9233. M: Diagonal.

Naf Naf-style fashion, but also less expensive Spanish brands. Young girls love the colourful waistcoats, shorts, overalls and patchwork dresses.

Choses. Passeig de Gràcia 97, tel. 215-0746. M: Diagonal and Ferran Agulló 3, tel. 209-0732. FFCC: Muntaner.

These elegant shops are packed with designer names from France, Japan and Italy. But you'll have to splash out if you want pieces by Claude Barthelemy, Kenzo, Chloe or younger designers such as Corinne Cobson.

Do.Barcelona. Mestre Nicolao 14 (Les Corts), tel. 209-8013. M: Hospital Clínic.

This is the place for you if you're after a crazy bikini or a body-hugging glittery dress, multicoloured sequinned blouses or dresses made by the trendy Spanish brands Daniel G. and Bamboo.

Don Carlos. Mallorca 236 (Eixample), tel. 216-0407. FFCC: Provenca.

Rather more classic gear for the career conscious woman. The favourite colours on the shelves are navy blue and flannel grey. Tidy white blouses galore.

Eugenio Sein. Ferran Agulló 2 (Les Corts), tel. 200-0385. FFCC: Muntaner.

Eugenio is not famous yet, but that's what his clients like. Soft, flattering dresses made of silk, cotton and linen, wide trouser suits and well-cut Torero-style blouses bring to mind Karl Lagerfield, Martine Sitbon and Romeo Gigli.

MEN'S FASHION

Calco Tets. Bulevard Rosa, Passeig de Gràcia 55 (Eixample), tel. 487-0527. M: Passeig de Gràcia.

Underwear for the all-out fashion conscious man. The best names, the best cuts and colours, but, watch it, prices to match. Bodysuits and swimwear from Nikos, flared boxer shorts from l'Homme Invisible and risqué T-shirts that will bring out the best in your bulging muscles.

Fancy Men. Diagonal 463 (Eixample), tel. 230-6420. M: Diagonal.

Looking for brand names? No problem. As the name implies, a place for elegant tastes. Browse through the shelves full of Valentino, Missoni, Armani...

F.G. & Compania. Bulevard Rosa, Passeig de Gràcia 55 (Eixample), tel. 216-0299. M: Passeig de Gràcia.

Good-value classic men's fashion is hard to find, but in this glass cabin there is row upon row of suits in natural fabrics in navy, grey and black, next to more trendy styles of large checks and jackets in unsual colours.

Furest. Passeig de Gràcia 12 and 14 (Eixample), tel. 301-2000. M:

Catalunya; and Diagonal 468 (Eixample), tel. 218-2665. M: Diagonal.

The branch on Passeig de Gràcia is sheer bliss. The latest fashions are displayed on three floors, from swimwear and sunglasses to elegant evening dress in silk. If you buy a suit here, you can have the trousers taken up in 24 hours.

LINGERIE AND SWIMWEAR

Intimo Due. Pau Claris 113 (Eixample), tel. 302-5105. M: Passeig de Gràcia.

Underwear for Carmen and Pablo from the best international designers, presented in a bright post-modern cube. Bodysuits made of lace, cotton, lycra, satin and silk, from the extravagant to the romantic.

La Perla Gris. Rosselló 220 (Eixample), tel. 215-2991. M: Diagonal.

I found my favourite swimsuit in the Grey Pearl: frilled and conservatively cut, like the swimwear fashion in my mother's old photos. Elegant underwear from La Perla, Dior and Occhi, but also more risqué models.

Taller de Lencerai. Rosselló 271 (Eixample), tel. 415-3952. M: Passeig de Gràcia. Branch on Bulevard Rosa, Pedralbes, Diagonal 605-615, tel. 419-0614. M: Maria Christina.

The speciality of the house in hand-sewn dressing gowns in silk and cotton, embroidered and with lace, tassels or even feather plume. However, the selection of romantic lingerie is enormous, from silk culottes to tiny brassieres and slips. If you want to glide around the house like Claudette Colbert in 1930s Hollywood films, then this is the place for you.

SHOES

Camper. Passeig de Gràcia, corner at Mallorca (Eixample). M: Passeig de Gràcia; and Via Augusta 35 (Gràcia). FFCC: Gràcia.

Very modern chain offering ultra loud designs for teenies and students. You can also find a few interesting canvas lace-ups among the multicoloured plastic soles and Timberland imitations.

SHOPPING

7 Eleven. Diagonal 466 (Eixample), tel. 218-4558. M: Diagonal.

Very modern shop with a steep ramp. The décor and loud music are more interesting than the shoes. Garish, colourful models, very pointed and high. Good cowboy and ankle boots. The young staff are not bothered if you only walk around the shop and admire the interior design.

Gala. Via Augusta 29-31 (Gràcia). FFCC: Gràcia.

Gala not only offers footwear for the gala evening, but also the best Spanish and international brands such as Farrutx, Clergerie and Make-Up.

Make-Up. In the Bulevard Rosa shopping arcade (Eixample), tel. 216-0881. M: Passeig de Gràcia.

Spanish avant-garde shoes. You'll find great glitter sandals and rawhide leather slippers with star embroidery, at surprisingly realistic prices.

La Manual Alpargatera. Avinyó 7 (Barri Gòtic). M: Jaume I.

Who's never heard of canvas espadrilles (*alpargatas*)? I have never seen such variety. In this store you can get simply every model of these super-comfortable canvas shoes. And if you don't find the right kind, four girls will knock up some espadrilles in a couple of hours. You can choose from all the colours of the rainbow, any heel, and cotton or shiny satin ribbons. The most exclusive pair will cost you around £10. Children's sizes are also available.

Tascon. Rambla de Catalunya 42 and Passeig de Gràcia 55, Bulevard Rosa (Eixample). M: Passeig de Gràcia 462, M: Diagonal.

Large selection of mid-range models. Especially beautiful are the handwoven shoes from Mallorca which resemble the rather more expensive Stephane Kelian variety.

Vermont. Plaça Francesc Macià 8, and in the Bulevard Rosa shopping centre, Diagonal 609, Tienda 43 (Pedralbes). M: Maria Cristina.

Exclusive shop for those with a penchant for shoes. The largest selection of original and first-class models by international designers. If the hand-sewn shoes of Robert Clergerie mean anything to you, then you'll know that this shop is the creme de la creme. The ex-model Willy van Rooy sells her elaborate street fashion sandals.

Zambo. Balmes 197 (Gracia). FFCC: Gràcia.

Shoes for men and women, and not only by Zambo. Large selection of sports shoes and boots such as Sebago and New Frontier, the Timberland imitations.

CHILDREN

Carol i Daniel. Balmes 278 (Sant Gervasi), tel. 237-2077. FFCC: Plaça Molina. Mon.-Fri. 10 a.m.-8 p.m.

Beautiful christening robes and everything else for the baby. For the kid with a taste for tradition and style.

Caval de Cartro. Avinguda de Josep Tarradellas 124 (Eixample) M: Entena.

Well-stocked toy shop with wooden toys, and not only that awful plastic stuff.

Chapita. Galerias Halley, Passeig de Gracia 62 (Eixample). M: Passeig de Gràcia. Mon.-Sat. 10:30 a.m.-2 p.m. and 4:30-8:30 p.m.

Funny children's fashion of excellent quality, and cheaper than back home.

Jacadi. Rambla de Catalunya 79 (Eixample), tel. 215-2491. M: Diagonal. Mon.-Sat. 10 a.m.-2 p.m. and 4-8 p.m., Sun. 10 a.m.-2 p.m.

Classic children's wear (to age 16) by this famous French company.

Pass. Rambla de Catalunya 16, corner at Gran Via (Eixample). M: Catalunya. Mon.-Sat. 10 a.m.-2 p.m. and 4-8 p.m.

This centrally located shop offers many good-value and unusual creations and brands. Funny shoes and belts, hats and braces.

SHOPPING

HAIR STYLISTS

La Pelu. Argentería 70-72 (Ribera), tel. 310-4807. M: Jaume I; and Verdi 29 (Gràcia). M: Fontana. Mon.-Wed. 9:30 a.m.-7 p.m., Thurs.-Fri. 9:30 a.m.-9 p.m., Sat. 9:30 a.m.-1 p.m. and 5-9:30 p.m. In summer until 11 p.m.

Fun! Why not have green streaks done for once?

Manolo Diaz. Balmes 133 (Gràcia), tel. 217-7776. M: Diagonal.

Trendies like this chic salon, where young stylists create the latest looks for men and women.

Mariano. Princesa 12 (Ribera), tel. 310-1333. M: Jaume 1. Men only.

Straightforward barber. Clean shave (525 ptas), manicure (650 ptas) and beard dyeing (only 500 ptas). Mariano will also look after your toupee.

Mythes. Roger de Llúria 80 (Eixample), tel. 258-3528. M: Passeig de Gràcia.

Career women visit this elegant salon. Only first-class products used. Realistic prices.

New Look. Muntaner 442-446 (Sant Gervasi), tel. 209-5289. FFCC: Muntaner; and Bulevard Rosa (Pedralbes), Diagonal 609. M: Maria Cristina.

Casual cut and blow-dry for *señoritas* and *señores,* as well as a women's beauty salon.

COSMETICS AND BEAUTY SALONS

Artemisa 2. Gal.la Placídia 4-6 (Eixample), tel. 237-7052; and Aribau 312 (Eixample), tel. 209-6748. M: Passeig de Gràcia.

Perfumery, fashion jewellery, combs, bathroom accessories, as well as hair removal and beauty treatment. A real supermarket of vanity, run by Mercedes Bofill.

Sanelen. Mallorca 136 (Eixample), tel. 253-6935. M: Passeig de Gràcia.

Two floors devoted to beauty. You can spend hours here on hair removal, manicure, hair styling, massage and sauna.

Unas, Etc. Muntaner 415 (Sant Gervasi), tel. 201-7857. FFCC: Muntaner. Mon.-Sat. 9:30 a.m.-8 p.m.

In Spain, hairless legs and armpits are obligatory. You'll be regarded as an oddity if you dare go to the beach without a clean bikini line. Therefore, beauty salons always do good business with waxing. This salon recently won an award from city hall. Take advantage of a manicure, pedicure and massage.

JEWELLERY

Bagues. Passeig de Gràcia 41 (Eixample). M: Passeig de Gr`acia.

Classic jewellery for classic women. Cartier-style, but more economical.

Efectos Especiales. Bulevard Rosa, Passeig de Gràcia 55 (Eixample), tel. 215-9031. M: Passeig de Gràcia; Bulevard Rosa, Diagonal 474 (Eixample), 218-5561. M: Diagonal; and Bulevard Rosa (Pedralbes), Diagonal 609, tel. 419-1034. M: Maria Cristina.

Fashion jewellery for all tastes, from classic Chanel-style pearl necklaces to flowery earings. Wide belts with interesting buckles, hair ribbons and clips, tiny bags and colourful plastic rings.

Enric Majoral. Laforja 19 (Sant-Gervasi), tel. 238-0752. FFCC: Gracia; and Bulevard Rosa, Diagonal 609 (Pedralbes), tel. 419-1880. M: Maria Cristina.

In Majoral's two shops you can browse through the best creations of mainly Spanish jewellery designers, but also a few from Italy and Germany. Mostly genuine products.

Joaquin Berao. Rosselló 227 (Eixample), tel. 218-6187. M: Diagonal.

Spain's most innovative jewellery designer is known on the

SHOPPING

international stage for his sometimes naturalist and often daring creations. His wide, wavy silver rings and heavy patinated bronze earrings are also in demand in New York and London.

Joiell. Passeig de Gràcia 53 (Eixample), tel. 215-9131. M: Passeig de Gràcia; Bulevard Rosa, Diagonal 474 (Eixample), tel. 237-7467. M: Diagonal.
    Small boutique with lots of precious silver pieces.

Oriol. Bori i Fontesta 11 (Les Corts), tel. 201-0377. FFCC: Muntaner.
    Precious stones set in gold and platinum. Only for those with a fat wallet. Beautiful wedding and engagement rings.

The Watch Gallerie. Diagonal 626 (Les Corts), tel. 418-3711. M: Maria Cristina.
    Only the best and most expensive is on offer behind the tall glass windows and in the displays of this exclusive temple of timepieces. Rolex, Jaeger-LeCoultre, International Watch Co., Cartier, Breitling.

CURIOSITIES AND GIFTS

Beardsley. Petrixol 12 (Barri Gòtic). M: Liceu.
    In the cellar, beautiful wrapping and writing paper; above in the little store, lots of ceramics, porcelain figures, small furniture and accessories for the home.

La Botiga del Feltre. Argenteria 78 (Ribera). tel. 319-3900. M: Jaume I.

Here you can buy new baize for the pool or bridge table. This unique boutique has been dealing in felt of all colours since 1795. Worth seeing!

La Caixa de Fang. Freneria 1 (Barri Gòtic). M: Liceu.

Small souvenir shop, situated next to the cathedral, selling ceramic articles, wood carvings for kitchen and home, and curious pâpier mâché figures for kids.

Coses de Casa. Plaça Sant Josep Oriol 5 (Barri Gòtic). M: Liceu.

If you're looking for wildly patterned linen, napkins, tablecloths or extravagant curtains, you will find something in this long established shop.

La Cubana. Boqueria 26 (Barri Gòtic). M: Liceu.

The Cuban lady sells fans, gloves and combs.

Dos i Una. Rosselló 275 (Eixample). M: Diagonal.

This small boutique sells humorous trays and china by Mariscal, T-shirts, desktop accessories, wild sunglasses, plastic jewellery and original postcards.

Fabrica de Peines. Portal de l'Angel 14 (Barri Gòtic). M: Catalunya.

This is the right place for fancy combs, hair clips made of horn and tortoise shell, brushes made of natural bristle, and other unconventional hair accessories.

SHOPPING

Herbolisteria. Flassaders 20 (Ribera), tel. 319-6942. M: Jaume I.

This hidden herbalist shop offers tinctures and essences from essential oils, blossoms, roots, ginseng balsam, rosewater and handmade candles. Mondays, Wednesdays and Fridays, expert advice and personal herbal mixes for illnesses and complaints.

Itaca. Ferran 26 (Barri Gòtic). M: Jaume I.

Not cheap, but the quality of the handmade ceramics from all over Spain is first class. Ask for the especially precious handpainted plates and jugs from Talavera.

Nieta de Juan Gran. Vidrieria 6-8 (Ribera), tel. 319-4046. M: Jaume I.

Vidrieria takes its name from the legendary Barcelona glass of the 14th century. You'll find the last glass shop of its kind here at number 6-8. The old wooden shelving is crammed to the ceiling with bottles, crucibles, wine glasses and fruit bowls. At the back of the shop you can browse for curiosities.

Papirum. Baixada de la Llabreteria 1 (Barri Gòtic). M: Jaume I.

One of my favourite shops specialising in handmade Venetian marbled paper. Maps, notebooks, books, boxes, picture albums, cards and writing paper made from this wonderful but expensive material.

Populart. Montcada 22 (Ribera), tel. 310-7849. M: Jaume I.

Almost everything in Populart is handmade: puppets, brightly painted papier mâché figurines and fans. Somewhere among the art and junk you can find reproductions of Gaudí's door handles.

Rey de la Magia. Princesa 11 (Ribera), tel. 319-7393. M: Jaume I.

Since 1881 the serious magician has bought his wares in the 'King of Magic': numerous signed portraits testify to this. The trick is only revealed behind a black curtain after purchase. What about a magician's basic kit at 12,000 pesetas? Simply magic!

Rosario Puig Casado. Canuda 3 (Barri Gòtic). M: Jaume I.

Old-fashioned flamenco dresses, torero jackets, hats, fans and swords, also for children.

1748. Placeta de Montcada 2 (Ribera), tel. 319-5413. M: Jaume I.

Earthenware jugs, crockery and traditional blue-yellow painted tiles.

Sharper Image. Bulevard Rosa, Diagonal 609 (Pedralbes), tel. 419-4925. M: Maria Cristina.

An American import. This high-tech chain has at least one branch in every town. The place for electronic and technical gadgets. CDs and the best binoculars, spacesuits, transparent telephones, the tiniest halogen lamps, replica 1950s toasters.

Zabriskie. Mallorca 198 (Eixample), tel. 323-1247. M: Diagonal; Galerías Via Wagner, Bori i Fontesa 17 (Les Corts), tel. 200-9920; La Avenida Rambla de Catalunya 121 (Eixample), tel. 237-2318. M: Passeig de Gràcia.

Toys for executives and children. Everything you never really needed but still wanted to look at. Desktop accessories, silver, chrome, glass and plastic brooches. Furniture by the latest designers.

RECORDS

Discos Castellos. Tallers 3 and 7 and Nou de la Rambla 15 and 44 (Barrio Chino). M: Liceu.

This record chain offers music for all tastes. Rap, House and Metal fans will be at home in the Carrer Tallers, while in the other locations you'll find modern Spanish bands and Flamenco.

Edison's. Riera Baixa 4 and 10 (Barrio Chino). M: Liceu.

Not one but two record shops in a tiny alley of the Sant Antoni quarter. CDs, records and tapes from independent American and British labels. In one of the shops you can also buy second hand. But watch out for scratches on records: CDs sound as good as new and are much cheaper.

Flag. Joaquín Costa 2 (Barrio Chino). M: Liceu.

Newton. Riera Alta 8 (Barrio Chino). M: Liceu.

TLF. Joaquín Costa 51 (Barrio Chino). M: Liceu.

Shops with interesting imports, but also new Spanish bands, such as Pata Negra. A few shelves with music from Latin America, salsa and flamenco.

BOOKS

Altair Forca. Balmes 69 (Barrio Chino), tel. 254-0134. M: Universitat.

Travel bookshop with a fantastic selection of rambling maps and sailing charts. Very helpful and competent staff. Señor Pedrol speaks English and other staff French.

Casa Almirall. Princesa 16 (Ribera), tel. 319-8006.

The Casa Almirall offers books on symbolism and religion. Half bookshop, half gallery, the former paper factory, dating from 1733 is worth seeing if only for its stone floor and wooden beams.

Makoki Comix. Plaça Sant Joseph Oriol (Barrio Chino). M: Jaume I.

Great shop for comic book fans. Also badges, games and T-shirts with comic characters.

Norma Comics. Passeig de Sant Joan (Eixample), tel. 245-4526. M: Arc de Triomf.

Lots of comics, a paradise for the aficionado of cartoons and sketches. Everything from modern Spanish to American Ninja-turtles. Also books, T-shirts and postcards.

Tartessos. Canuda 35 (Raval), tel. 301-8181. M: Liceu.

This friendly and chaotic shop specialises in photography books and exhibitions. Interesting picture postcards and receptive staff.

Tocs. Consell de Cent 341 (Eixample), tel. 215-3121. M: Passeig de Gracia. Mon.-Sat. 10 a.m.-9 p.m. in summer closed at 8 pm.

One of my favourite bookshops, as you can find English and French publications in Spain, as well as Spanish books and magazines and foreign press. No one is bothered if you leaf through them.

DESIGN AND FURNITURE

B.D. Ediciones de Diseño, Mallorca 291 (Eixample), tel. 258-6909. M: Passeig de Gràcia.

This listed Art Nouveau villa is worth a visit in itself. The top Spanish designers all exhibit here, from Oscar Tusquets' Gaudí-inspired chair to replica Gaudí furniture. In contrast to the Italian, Spanish design is surprisingly good value. Overseas delivery can be arranged, for a price.

Vinçon. Passeig de Gràcia 96 (Eixample). M: Diagonal.

Barcelona's biggest and best design shop where you can spend hours looking around. Everything from a shiny silver Cobi (Mariscal's Olympic mascot) to carpets, wardrobes, and halogen lamps, all with delivery and instalment service. Take a look at the fabulously tiled inner patio and the stylish upper floor.

ANTIQUES

Arkupe. Plaça de Montcada 1-3 (Ribera), tel. 319-1572. M: Jaume I. Mon.-Fri. 11 a.m.-2 p.m. and 4-8 p.m., Sat. 11 a.m.-2 p.m. and 6-8 p.m.

This pleasant and elegant antique shop, situated behind an impressive Gothic portal in one of the 16th-century palaces near the Picasso museum, offers figurines from Benin and Gabon as well as marble statuettes, neo-Gothic cupboards and other eclectic pieces.

Camilla Hamm. Rosselló 197 (Eixample), tel. 218-2211. M: Diagonal. Mon.-Fri. 10:30 a.m.-1:30 p.m. and 4:30-8 p.m., Sat. 10:30 a.m.-2 p.m.

Amiable Camilla has lived in her adopted homeland, Barcelona, for over 20 years, and earns her crust with interior decoration (the Hotel Rivoli). In this shop she sells Art Deco and Art Nouveau furniture, as well as silver and brilliant designer jewellery from famous names, such as Schiaparelli or Trifari.

Centre d'Antiquaris. Passeig de Gràcia 55 (Eixample), tel. 215-4499. M: Passeig de Gràcia.

Collectors with ample means will find most of what their hearts desire in this two-storey market, from African wooden figures to 18th-century Talavera ceramics, Art Nouveau jewellery to Baroque furniture. Many dealers rent tiny glass cabins only to be present on this elegant boulevard, but they will also show prospective buyers their depots and shops crammed with precious goods located in the outer districts.

Miriam Sans Martinez. Banys Nous (Barrio Chino), tel. 317-2013. M: Jaume I.

An Ali-Baba cavern full of Venetian and rococo mirrors, lace tablecloths, silk robes, and the finest china, all run by the mysterious Miriam.

Novecento. Passeig de Gràcia 75 (Eixample), tel. 215-1183. M: Passeig de Gràcia.

As the name implies, the year 1900 is of special interest in this small shop which mainly specialises in Art Nouveau jewellery.

Teresa Bausili. Alfons XII 63 (Sant Gervasi), tel. 201-4689. FFCC: Sant Gervasi.

A small shop in the upper part of town dealing in antique jewellery, silver-plated candelabras, gold-plated mirrors, crystal chandeliers and wafer-thin hand-painted china: all you need for the luxury household.

FOOD AND WINE

Angel Jobal. Princesa 38 (Ribera), tel. 319-7806.

You can smell the shop from far off. All kinds of spices are piled on big wooden shelves, even pepper and paprika by the kilo. Mr Jobal exports every variety of saffron all over the world. On closer inspection, saffron brought back from India might well turn out to have originated from Calle Princesa 38.

E&A Gispert. Sombreres 23 (Ribera), tel. 319-7535.

Tea, marmalade and mustard are the specialities of this traditional house. But the nuts and almonds, which you can get by the kilo freshly roasted and still warm, are unbeatable. The oven is already 125 years old, but still works great.

Fargas. Pi 16, corner at Plaça Cucurulla (Barrio Chino), tel. 302-0342. M: Liceu.

Beautifully packaged chocolates, pralines and bonbons, handmade from an old recipe for almost 200 years.

El Magnifico. Argenteria 64 or Grunyi 10 (Ribera), tel. 319-6081, 310-3361. M: Liceu.

Salvador Sans and his family have been roasting and blending coffee from Costa Rica, Nicaragua, Tanzania and Papua New Guinea since 1919. The Mezcla Real was created for the King, or would you prefer a Kilimanjaro?

R. Riera. Princesa 14 (Ribera). M: Jaume I.

Senor Riera stocks every Cava, wine and liqueur from Catalonia. He is very friendly and sometimes offers samples. Wines from the barrel!

Tot Formatga. Passeig del Born 13 (Ribera). M: Jaume I.

Literally 'all cheese'. The medium Manchego is very good.

SHOPPING

La Botiga del Sol. Xiquets de Valls (Gràcia), on the Plaça del Sol.
FFCC: Gracia.

Barcelona's biggest bio-store with natural foods, organic juices,
wine, fruit and vegetables, wholemeal bread, records, books, and
magazines on healthy living.

ROUND-THE-CLOCK

Drugstore. Passeig de Gràcia 71 (Eixample), tel. 215-7074. M:
Passeig de Gràcia. Open daily 24 hours.

Though slightly scruffy in appearance, there are 12 branches where
you can find everything you could possibly
want at 5 a.m. from a supermarket to books,
photographic equipment to perfume.
Even pool tables and video games to lure
the insomniac.

Drugstore David. Tuset 19-21
(Eixample). Tel. 209-6957. M:
Diagonal. Daily 9 a.m.-5 a.m.

Fifty-three small shops in cold 1970s style, including bookshop,
tobacco kiosk, mini-supermarket, cafés and restaurants.

VIP's. Rambla de Catalunya 7 (Eixample), tel. 301-4805. M: Plaça de
Catalunya. Mon.-Thurs. and Sun. 9 a.m.-2 a.m., Sat. and holidays 9
a.m.- 3 a.m.

For nightowls who at 2 a.m. still want to buy the *Best of Frank
Sinatra*, grab a quick hamburger or omelette, or rent the latest video. I
used to enjoy it here, browsing through books, records and magazines at
night.

FOOD AND DRINK

Spanish cuisine has nothing in common with Latin American. Chili, tacos and enchiladas are as exotic in Barcelona or Madrid as in London. Spanish cuisine is authentic and rather down-to-earth. You can taste the ingredients, which are not overwhelmed by spices or sauces. The base is olive oil, garlic and peppers.

All over Spain you can find golden *tortillas*, 'round like the sun'; rich *paella*, a classic dish of saffron rice, seafood and chicken; *gazpacho*, a cold vegetable soup; and the fantastic jamon serrano, cured ham. And, of course, the famous *tapas*: snacks and starters of every kind, from olives to stuffed squid.

Spanish cuisine as such is a cliché, as each region of the Iberian peninsular does its own thing. Each of the nine regions takes equal pride in its recipes, dialect, history and culture.

Gourmets rave about Basque cuisine: lavish fish with creamy sauces; *cazuela*, a Spanish bouillabaisse; and dried cod with garlic, paprika and bread crumbs. Baby eels, no bigger than worms, are a delicacy but an acquired taste. Also unique are the cooking clubs where, unfortunately, only male members are admitted to cook and eat, and as a  consequence many a Basque marriage has been left on the rocks. This passion for cooking has even inspired Basques to venture abroad. The best and most expensive restaurants in Catalonia are sure to be Basque.

Catalan cuisine is particularly innovative and unusual. In Barcelona you can even find dishes such as lobster with chicken in hazelnut sauce or duck in chocolate sauce on set menus. Catalans swear by *pan con tomate*, toasted country bread with olive oil, garlic and tomato, and they're especially proud of *oca con peras,* baby goose with pears.

For Spaniards, fresh ingredients are a must. This is why you will

Supermarket window

find less fish than lamb, suckling pig, beans and the traditional *chorizo* (sausage) in barren, mountainous Castile. From Castile - or, to be precise, Madrid - comes a Spanish favourite: *cocido*, a stew with chicken, beef, bacon fat, black pudding, garlic sausage and chick peas. Yet another Castilian speciality is *ajo blanco*, a white garlic soup with a slice of toast. Restaurants specialising in roast or grilled meat are called *asadores*.

Travellers must adapt their eating habits when in Spain. Meals are eaten here at least two hours later than in central Europe. A typical Spaniard's day could look like this:

8 a.m. - breakfast with churros, fried doughnuts, and coffee; 11 a.m. - tapas; 2 p.m. - *comida* (lunch with no less than three courses); 6 p.m. - *merienda* (tea and pastries); 8 p.m.-10 p.m. - tapas and sherry; 10 p.m.-1 a.m. - *cena* (dinner).

Despite this heavy programme, you can see few overweight Spaniards - perhaps all their talking, laughing and gesticulating doesn't give them time enough to eat when they are out in groups! Barcelona is empty between 2 and 5 p.m., when only the tourists linger in the streets. Spaniards have their siesta then and work late until 8 p.m. In the humid and unbearably hot summer months, work starts at 8 a.m. and ends at 3 p.m. with a very short break around midday. No wonder most restaurants are closed in August. Who would want a lengthy meal in this heat? And the vast number of small, family-run restaurants in the residential and shopping areas can hardly survive on tourists alone.

A little tip: don't always go into the tapas bars and tavernas near large squares, museums, sights or boulevards like the Passeig de Gràcia. Rather, look in small side streets and away from tourist traps. You will find recommendations here and chapters on each individual district. You could even consult the locals. In Spain it's quite normal and often very good to lunch in one of the local tavernas. In this country, eating out is not considered a luxury.

FOOD AND DRINK

The following gourmet glossary should help you understand Catalan and Spanish menus:

GOURMET GLOSSARY

breakfast *desdejuni; desayuno*
lunch *esmorzar; almuerzo*
dinner *sopar; cena*
waiter *cambrer; camarero*
dining room *menjador; comedor*
meal *àpat; comida*
glass *got; vaso*
bottle *ampolla; botella*
cup *tassa; taza*
cutlery *cobert; cubierto*
fork *forquilla; tenedor*
spoon *cullera; cuchara*
knife *ganivet; cuchillo*
starters *entremès; entremeés*
main course *plat principal; plato principal*
dessert *postres; postre*
guest house *fonda; fonda*
table *taula; mesa*
toothpick *escuradent; palillo*
bread *pa; pan*
roll *panet; panecillo*
patisserie *pastisseria; pastelería*
plate *plat; plato*
complaint *reclamació; reclamación*
sauce *salsa; salsa*
service *servei; servicio*
bill *compte; cuenta*
WC *lavabo; lavabo*

DRINKS

aperitif *aperitiu; aparetivo*
mineral water carbonated/still *aigua amb/sense gas; agua con/sin gas*
mineral water *aigua mineral; agua mineral*

drinking chocolate *cacau; cacao*
coffee *cafè; café*
white coffee *cafè amb llet; café con leche*
black coffee *cafè sol; café solo*
tea *te; té*
beer *cervesa; cerveza*
chocolate *xocalata; chocolate*
cognac *conyac; coñac*
lemonade *llimonada; limonada*
orangeade *taronjada; naranjada*
cider *sidra; sidra*
white wine *vi blanc; vino blanco*
rosé wine *vi rosat; vino rosado*
red wine *vi negre; vino tinto*

FOOD AND DRINK

SALAD AND VEGETABLES

oil *oli*; *aceite*

garlic *all*; *ajo*

basil *alfàbrega*; *albahaca*

sugar *sucre*; *azúcar*

cinnamon *canyella*; *canela*

onion *ceba*; *cebolla*

laural *llorer*; *laurel*

mustard *mostassa*; *mostaza*

oregana *orenga*; *orégano*

paprika *pebre vermell*; *pimentón*

pepper *pebre*; *pimienta*

salt *sal*; *sal*

sage *salvia*; *salvia*

thyme *farigola, timó*; *tomillo*

vinegar *vinagre*; *vinagre*

vegetables *verdura*; *verdura*

carrots *pastanagues*; *zanahorias*

olives *olives*; *aceitunas*

artichokes *carxofes*; *alcachofas*

aubergines *alberginies*; *berenjenas*

mushrooms *xampinyons*; *champiñones*

salad *amanida*; *ensalada*

peas *pèsols*; *guisantes*

green beans *mongetes verdes*; *judías verdes*

pulses *llegums*; *legumbres*

potatoes *patates*; *patatas*

cucumbers *cogombres*; *pepinos*

paprika *pebrots*; *pimientos*

SOUPS

stock *brou*; *caledo*

consomme *consomé*; *consomé*

bean stew *fabada*; *fabada*

stew *menestra*; *potaje*

soup *sopa*; *sopa*

SIDE DISHES

creamed potatoes *puré de patates*; *puré de patatas*

rice *arròs*; *arroz*

cannelloni *canelons*; *canelones*

croquettes *croquetes*; *croquetas*

noodles *fideus*; *fideos*

EGGS

fried eggs *ous al plat*; *huevos al plato*

hard boiled egg *ou dur*; *huevo duro*

poached egg *ou passat per aigua*; *huevo pasado por agua*

scrambled eggs *ou remenat*; *huevos revueltos*

omelette *truita*; *tortilla*

MEAT

meatballs *mandonguilles*; *albóndigas*

roast *rostit*; *asado*

steak *bistec*; *bistec*

FOOD AND DRINK

white pork sausage *botifarra;*
    butifarra
tripe *tripes; callos*
snails *cargols; caracoles*
meat *carn; carne*
pork *porc; cerdo*
rabbit *conill; conejo*
lamb *xai, be; cordero*
spicy sausage *xoriço; chorizo*
cutlets *costella; chuleta*
schnitzel *escalopa; escalopa*
ragout *estofat; estofado*
pheasant *faisà; faisán*
broiler *gallina; gallina*
liver *fetge; hígado*
wild boar *porc senglar; jabalí*
ham *pernil; jamón*
hare *llebre; liebre*
pork loin *llom; lomo*
goose *oca; oca*
duck *ànec; pato*
turkey *gall dindi; pavo*
breast *pit; pechuga*
partridge *perdiu; perdiz*
fried chicken *pollastre; pollo*
kidney *ronyons; riñones*
sausages *salsitxes; salchichas*
saucisson *llonganissa; salchichón*
brains *cervells; sesos*
fillet *filet; lomillo*
veal *vedella; ternera*
beef *vaca; vaca*
venison *cérvol; venado*

FISH

clams *cloïsses; almejas*
anchovies *anxoves; anchoas*
conger eel *anguila; anguila*
baby eel *angules; angulas*
herring *areng; arenque*
tuna *tonyina; atún*

cod *bacallà; bacalao*
sea bream *besuc; besugo*
mackerel *verat; caballa*
squid *calamars; calamar*
crab *cranc; cangrejo*
scampi *cigales; cigalas*
shellfish *crustacis; crustàceos*
dentex *dentol; dentón*
gilthead *daurada; dorada*
shrimps *gambes; gambas*
sole *llenguado; lenguada*
bass *llobarro; lubina*
fruits de mer *marisc; marisco*
mussels *musclos; mejillones*
hake *lluç; merluza*
grouper *mero; mero*

oysters *ostres*; *ostras*
fish *peix*; *pescado*
octopus *pop*; *pulpo*
monkfish *rap*; *rape*
turbot *remol*; *rodaballo*
salmon *salmó*; *salmón*
barbel *moll*; *salmonete*
sardines *sardines*; *sardinas*
cuttlefish *sípia*; *sepia*
trout *truita*; *trucha*

FRUIT AND DESSERT

apricots *albercocs*; *albaricoques*
almonds *ametlles*; *almendres*
hazelnuts *avellanes*; *avellanas*
cherries *cireres*; *cerezas*
plums *prunes*; *ciruelas*
flat *flam*; *flan*
raspberries *gerdons*; *frambuesas*
strawberries *maduixes, maduixots*;
    fresas, fresones
fruit *fruita*; *fruta*
ice cream *gelat*; *helado*
lemon *llimona*; *limón*
mandarins *mandarines*; *mandarinas*
apples *pomes*; *manzanas*
peaches *préssecs*; *melocotones*
melon *meló*; *melón*
honey *mel*; *miel*
oranges *taronges*; *naranjas*
cream *nata*; *nata*
walnuts *nous*; *nueces*
cake *pastís*; *pastel*
pears *peres*; *peras*
pineapple *pinya*; *piña*
pine seeds *pinyons*; *piñones*

bananas *plàtans*; *plátanos*
grapefruit *naronja*; *pomelo*
cheese *formatge*; *queso*
quark *mató*; *requesón*
watermelon *síndria*; *sandía*
grapes *raïm*; *uvas*
juice *suc*; *zumo*

PREPARATION

charcoal grill *a la brasa*; *a la brasa*
grilled *a la graella*; *a la parrilla*
baked *al forn*; *al horno*
steamed *al vapor*; *al vapor*
gratiné *gratinat*; *gratinado*

FOOD AND DRINK

RESTAURANTS

Meal times are somewhat later in Spain. Generally, restaurants are open for lunch from 1:30 until 4 or 4:30 and in the evening from 9 until midnight. Cafes serve meals from 9:30 a.m. till 9 p.m., but you can usually get snacks until midnight. When no specific times are listed below, normal opening hours usually apply.

The Cheap and Cheerful section deals with restaurants which charge up to 2,000 ptas; Good Value, between 2,000 and 4,500 ptas; Chic and Gourmet, 4,500 ptas and above. The prices given are per person for a three-course meal, without wine but including service and tip. But be sure to check out the menu del dia, which is often much cheaper than the price bracket indicates. These are usually only offered at lunchtime on weekdays.

CHEAP AND CHEERFUL

Agut d'Avignon. Trinitat 3 (Barrio Chino), tel. 317-3693. M: Liceu, Daily 1-3 p.m. and 9-11:30 p.m. Closed Easter week.

Picasso painted his *Demoiselles d'Avignon*, inspired by a long-gone brothel, in this street. Country atmosphere with rustic cuisine and surprisingly low prices.

Amaya. Ramblas 20-24 (Barrio Chino), tel. 302-1037. M: Drassanes. Daily 1:30 p.m.-12:30 a.m.

Though the dried cod stew is not what it used to be, for a quick lunch in the old town the Amaya is still one of the better options. Don't eat at the counter, but look for a table in the back room.

Cal Pep. Plaça de les Olles 49 (Ribera), tel. 315-4937. M: Jaume I. Mon.-Sat. 12 noon-5 p.m. and 7:30 p.m.-12 mid.

It's always full here in enterprising Pep's third restaurant, with everything market fresh. The fried squid, sardines and calamares are simply delicious. Unique giant table in the rustic back room. A bristly boar's head hangs from the wall.

Can Culleretes. Quintana 15 (Barrio Chino), tel. 317-6485. M: Liceu. Tues.-Sun. 1-4 p.m. and 9-11 p.m. Closed Sunday evenings.

This restaurant, with its colourful wall tiles already has 200 years under its belt, yet the good Catalan cooking is as fresh as on the first day. Friendly service and good wine list. Set lunch for around £8.

Carballera. Reina Cristina 3, (Ribera), tel. 310-1006. M: Barceloneta. Daily 7 p.m.-12 mid.

There is always a cheerful, noisy atmosphere in this huge harbour pub. Whole families sit at big tables and munch shrimps, mussels and other seafood. The managers are from Galicia and their house wine goes down well with the fish.

Casimiro. Londres 84 (Eixample), tel. 410-3093. M: Hospital Clinic. Mon.-Sat. 1-4 p.m. and 8 p.m.-12 mid.

Señor Casimiro López specialises in pasta and cakes. I start to long for Barcelona when I think of his cheesecake with wild strawberries, for which I willingly pay £2. The hot peppers stuffed with dried cod at around £3 are also good value. The lunch special is outstanding and much cheaper than eating a la carte in the evening.

Catalunya. Playa de Sant Miquel 34 (Barceloneta), tel. 319-5136 or 310-5708. M: Barceloneta. Daily 1-4:30 p.m. and 8 p.m.-12 mid.

A small *chiringuito* or beach bar soon to be relocated in the alleys behind, as a consequence of the new beach legislation. Family-run restaurant with all kinds of good value fish, unfortunately a little oily. The owner Antoni Miguel sings with veteran rock group, Los Sirex.

El Centollo. Rossello 204 (Eixample), tel. 215-8367. M: Diagonal. Mon.-Fri. 1:30-4 p.m. and 8:30-11 p.m. Closed August.

Very central tapas bar with a small restaurant serving freshly prepared market produce. Good price/value ratio.

Centro Galego. Ramblas 37 (Ramblas), tel. 302-6165. Mon.-Sat. 10 a.m.-11 p.m.

Modest restaurant on the first floor of the Galician centre. Friendly service and low prices. A hundred years ago, this rather dilapidated building, annexed to the Palau Güell on Nou de la Rambla, used to be the city residence of Count Güell, Gaudì's benefactor.

La Clau. Agullers 18 (Ribera). M: Jaume I. Mon.-Fri. 2-4 p.m. and 9-11:30 p.m.

Friendly six-table restaurant with lots of wood and an open kitchen in the same room. Lawyers, civil servants and flashy chic secretaries look on while the hare with wild onions simmers on the stove. Set lunch for 900 pesetas.

La Finiestra. Sant Gervasi de Cassoles 22 (Sant Gervasi), tel. 212-5443. FFCC: Putget. Mon.-Sat. 1:30-4 p.m. and 9 p.m.-1 a.m. Closed two weeks in August.

Catalan cuisine in three small rooms, the prettiest is right at the back. Very economical lunch special from 1,000 pesetas.

Quatre Barres. Quintana 6 (Barrio Chino), tel. 302-5060. ML Liceu. Tues.-Sat. 1:30-4 p.m. and 9-11:30 p.m.

This fish restaurant is a pleasant surprise in the middle of the Barrio Chino. Impeccable interior and friendly owner, who even greets newcomers as though they were regulars. Two rooms full of local business people and craftsmen. Excellent value.

Madrid-Barcelona. Aragó 282 (Eixample), tel. 215-7026. M: Passeig de Gracia. Mon.-Sat. 1:30-4 p.m. and 8:30 p.m.-12 mid. Closed August.

Renowned Spanish home-cooking, which always goes down well with local managers, bankers and business people.

Don Jabugo. Muntaner 270 (Sant Gervasi), tel. 202-2220; and Descartes 30, tel. 201-0505. FFCC: Muntaner. Also Figols 47-49, tel. 330-6856. M: Les Corts. Mon.-Sat. 1-4 p.m. and 8 p.m.-1 a.m.

The best ham bars, where you can eat all kinds of cured ham, small salads, steaks and other sausage and cheese dishes with *pan con tomate* in a bodega atmosphere. Not exactly cheap, as these bars are located in the better districts.

Pitarra. Avinyó 56 (Barrio Chino), tel. 301-1647. M: Liceu. Mon.-Sat. 1-4 p.m. and 8:30-11 p.m. Closed Aug.

The poet eats here! Praised by Eduardo Mendoza (see interview), this unpretentious pub serves everyday dishes such as fish stew, grilled seafood or lamb, beef and pork. Delicious *pan con tomate* and *jambón de jabugo* (cured ham).

Pitin. Passeig del Born (Ribera), tel. 319-5087. M: Jaume I. Mon.-Sat. 7:30 a.m.-8 p.m.

Lovely home cooking in the tiny Pinin is easy on your pocket. Beef fricassee for only 500 pesetas. In the summer you can eat outside under a sun shade.

Ponsa. Enric Granados 89 (Eixample), tel. 253-1037. FFCC: Provenca. Mon.-Fri. 1-4 p.m. and 9 p.m.-12 mid., Sat. 1-4 p.m. Closed mid-July - mid-Aug.

Since 1907 this traditional restaurant has prepared classic Catalan dishes such as *estofado de toro* (roast beef), light omelettes with wild mushrooms or fresh sardines. Fair prices, particularly for lunch.

Puda Manuel. Passeig Nacional 60, tel. 319-3013. M: Barceloneta. Tues.-Sun. 1-4 p.m. and 8 p.m.-1 a.m.

Visit this simple harbour restaurant before the dilapidated docks in front of the terrace change into a sterile mall. City hall's plan to 'beautify' the waterfront is a nightmare for many local people. Hopefully the faded charm of this fish bar, with its plastic furniture, chequered tablecloths and huge portions of grilled fish will not disappear.

La Rivolta. Hospital 116 (Barrio Chino). Closed Aug.

Pizzeria frequented by students of the nearby university. Interesting music, also salads, tortillas and sandwiches.

GOOD VALUE

Agut. Gigñas 16 (Barrio Chino), tel. 315-1709. M: Jaume I. Tues.-Sat. 1-4 p.m and 9 p.m.-12 mid. Closed July.

FOOD AND DRINK

Agut is always fully booked, particularly around 2 p.m. when hungry customers crowd the front door of this rustic restaurant. Cheerful and very comfortable. Try the Catalan speciality *pollo con gambas*, chicken with shrimps. Tastes great, despite the unlikely mixture! The lunch special is particularly good value, dinner is more expensive.

Aitor. Carbonell 5, tel. 319-9488. M: Barceloneta. Mon.-Sat. 1:30-4 p.m. and 9-11:30 p.m. Closed Easter week, Christmas and 15 Aug.-15 Sept.

Another first-class Basque restaurant. Naturally fish is the speciality. Try the fresh tuna pie *marmitako* or *fruits de mer*. Excellent wine list, even the house wine is a good Rioja.

Al Primer Crit. Baynes Vells 2 (Ribera), tel. 319-1097. M: Jaume I. Tues.-Sun. 8 p.m.-1:30 a.m.

It's worth hunting in the maze of little alleys for this pretty restaurant. On the terrace couples enjoy their crab salad with Roquefort sauce and chicken in *salsa verde*. The house Cava costs 900 ptas. Jordi with the pigtail only plays jazz. Wonderful wooden bar in front of the bare stone wall in the cellar

La Balsa. Infanta Isabel 4 (Tibidabo), tel. 211-5048. FFCC: Tibidabo. Mon.-Sat. 2-3:30 p.m. and 9-11:30 p.m. Closed Mon. lunchtime.

Oscar Tusquets's glass pavilion is hidden high in the hills around Barcelona. Light cuisine with a touch a California, especially imposing in the summer when you can help yourself from a buffet in the garden or terrace. Surprisingly good value for its exclusive location and quality.

Can Ros. Almirante Aixada 7, tel. 319-5049. M: Barceloneta. Mon.-Sat. 1-4 p.m. and 8 p.m.-mid.

Far away from the always noisy Passeig Nacional on the corner with Sant Miquel, the Can Ros is ideal for a romantic rendezvous. Like everywhere in the beach area the menu consists of fish, mussels, shrimps, octopus, oysters, lobster, crabs and eels - all first class.

Casa Sole. Sant Carles 4, tel. 319-5012. M: Barceloneta. Mon.-Fri. 1-4 p.m. and 8 p.m.-12 mid., Sat. 1-4 p.m.

One of the oldest and most authentic restaurants. The elegant blonde with the tall hair is the proprietor, who will take you to your table in this two-floor restaurant. First class Catalan cuisine, naturally specialising in fish and *fruits de mer*. Surprisingly realistic prices for the quality and ambience.

Carpanta. Sombreres 13 (Ribera), tel. 319-9999. M: Jaume I. 1-4 p.m. and 9 p.m.-12 mid. Closed Sun. evenings.

He wears brilliantine and a dinner jacket, she curly hair and a feather plume. Everything surrounding these two 1920s full-size portraits is pure Art Nouveau: from the stained-glass windows and the wall mosaic, to the chairs. So the steak tartar with baby eel, and fillet steak in almond sauce with anchovies costs that bit more. Stick to the set menu and the splendid Penedés and Rioja wines.

La Cua Curta. Carassa (Ribera), tel. 315-3002. M: Jaume I. Tues.-Mon. 8:30 p.m.-1 a.m.

Young people sit at marble tables, with paté, cheese, fondues and the wine of the day. The old stone walls are only partly plastered, and sculptures, dolls and baskets from Southeast Asia stand on wooden commodes. Very comfortable and chatty atmosphere.

L'Ou Com Balla. Banys Vells 20 (Ribera), tel. 310-5378. M: Jaume I. Tues.-Sun. 8 p.m.-1:30 a..m.

Teresa offers quiet tones, soft colours and classical music in her little *formatgeria*. Surrounded by antique paraphernalia, romantics pick from salads and cheese and read tarot.

Pla de la Carsa. Assaonadors 13 (Ribera), tel. 315-2413. M: Jaume I. Daily 7 p.m.-2 a.m. Closed New Year's Eve.

An institution among *formatgerias*. A wrought-iron spiral staircase interlocks two floors: old Barcelona in every nook and cranny. Forty different cheeses from all over Europe, guaranteed from fresh milk. Taste the Catalan goat's cheese Montsec, and Urbasa ewe's cheese from the Basque country. In the winter there are even Raclette. The wine

FOOD AND DRINK

list is also impressive: from nouveau Beaujolais to the excellent house wine Sajazarra 1983. Young clientele from all over Catalonia.

Los Caracoles. Escudellers 14 (Barrio Chino), tel. 302-3185. M: Liceu. Daily 1:30-4 p.m. and 8:30 p.m.-12 mid.

Snails (*caracoles*) are the main attraction of this restaurant. Outside chicken on a spit, and inside the many small rooms reverberate with many languages like the tower of Babel. Still a favourite with the locals despite the many tourists, who don't seem to be put off by the location: in a dark alley in a rougher part of the Gothic quarter.

La Cuineta. Paradis 4 (Ribera), tel. 315-0111. M: Jaume I. Daily 1:30-4 p.m. and 8:30 p.m.-12 mid.

This restaurant, right next to city hall is a favourite with the mayor and his pen pushers, and packed with antiques and golden mirrors. Make a note of the *palacio*, as many interesting restaurants are closed Sundays.

Can Pescallunes. Magdalenese 23 (Barrio Chino), tel. 318-5483. M: Urquinaona. Mon.-Fri. 1:30-3:30 p.m. and 8:30 p.m.-12 mid.

Looks like a mountain chalet with its huge hearth and beams. Catalan specialities such as asparagus en croute, monkfish with plums. Good selection of wines from Penedés and Lleida.

Casa Isidro. Carrer de les Flores 12 (Poble Sec), tel. 241-1139. M: Paral-lel. Mon.-Sat. 1:30-4 p.m and 8:30 p.m.-12 mid.

The elegant lady of the house is the daughter of the great chef Isidro. Even the King of Spain loves to eat here when visiting friends in Barcelona. Very french grande cuisine in turn-of-the-century décor and silky pastel tones.

Casa Leopoldo. Sant Rafael 24 (Barrio Chino), tel. 241-3014. M: Liceu. Tues.-Sat. 1-4 p.m. and 9 p.m.-12 mid.; Sun. 1-4 p.m. Closed Aug. and Easter.

Father and daughter do the cooking in this wonderfully old-fashioned restaurant. This establishment with its excellent Catalan cuisine opened its doors in 1939. The Leopoldo is famous for its giant *degustación de pescados y mariscos* seafood dish, Catalan rustic cooking such as oxtail ragout and meatballs in octopus sauce.

La Cupula. Teodoro Roviralta 37 (Tibidabo), tel. 212-4888. FFCC: Avinguda Tibidabo. Daily 1:30 p.m.-1 a.m.

A smaller, more intimate *asador*. The smell of roast meat fills the three small rooms. Delicious fish and lamb dishes and suckling pig from the spit. You can eat here non-stop from lunch into the early hours.

Restaurant de l'Escola. Muntaner 70-72 (Eixample), tel. 253-2903. Mon.-Fri. 1-3 p.m. and 8 p.m.-12 mid.

In this chic restaurant which belongs to a famous catering college you can enjoy students' and teachers' exquisite gastronomic experiments at reasonable prices.

Gades. L'Esparteria 10 (Ribera), tel. 315-3884. Mon.-Thurs. 8 p.m.-1 a.m. Fri.-Sat. 8 p.m.-2 a.m.

The beautiful stone vault is said to date from the 14th century when the beach still reached the door. The Gades, carefully renovated, offers idyllic surroundings for fondues and light fare. The three pretty owners serve first class wine from all over Spain. Uptown clientele from the better parts of town.

Gallo. Passeig Picasso 38 (Ribera), tel. 319-7013. M: Jaume I. Tues.-Sat. 1:30-4 p.m. and 9-11:30 p.m. Closed Sun. evenings.

From the outside, the Gallo looks like an old beer cellar, but inside you can sit very comfortably at well set tables and have juicy salmon with dill sauce as an appetizer. Manu the chef loves Basque cuisine. His fillet steak with marrow sauce and hake in herb sauce are sheer poetry. With it a bottle of Ermita d'Espinells is a must. My tip: on Monday mornings go for a cold buffet to the exhibition openings. Invitations can be found in bars in Ribera.

Gambrinus. Moll de la Fusta. M: Drassanes. Daily 12 noon-4 a.m.

Extravagant establishment: glass walls and a characteristic red lobster on the roof. Designed by Javier Mariscal who wanted to evoke the sinking of the Titanic. The iron chairs on the terrace and the rusty

FOOD AND DRINK

tables are meant to resemble flotsam and jetsam. Drinks okay, but the paella could do with more fish and shrimps. Because of its location, very touristy. Best after midnight.

La Glorieta de Sant Gervasi. Hurtado 25 (Tibidabo), tel. 211-6646. FFCC: Avinguda Tibidabo. Reserve evenings.

Romantic restaurant with several small rooms and a quiet garden behind the house. Specialities are dried cod and squid *risotto arros negre*.

Gran Colmado. Consell de Cent 318 (Eixample), tel. 318-8577. M: Universitat. Mon.-Sat. 1:30-4 p.m. and 8.30 p.m.-12 mid.

In this chic restaurant, where you can eat Catalan food with the Barcelonese at an incredibly long table, it's not just the ice boxes full of champagne and the deli that create the cool atmosphere, but also the stern, geometric, high-tech decor. You can also shop here, but spirits and cold-pressed olive oil are rather pricey.

La Mercantil Peixatera. Aribau 117 (Eixample), tel. 253-3599. FFCC: Provenca. Daily 1:30-4 p.m. and 8 p.m.-1:30 a.m. Closed Mon. lunch.

Nomen est omen, and so the fishmonger is an outstanding seafood restaurant. Lunch special from approximately £8.

Mordisco. Rosselló 265, corner of Passeig de Gràcia (Eixample), tel. 218-3314. Daily 8 p.m.-2 a.m.

This popular meeting point is bar, café and pub in one. Small and not exactly cheap. This is where the boutique owner meets her lover and the banker meets the girl from the chemist next door.

Muffins. València 210 (Eixample), tel. 254-0221. FFCC: Provenca. Tues.-Sat. 1:30-3:30 p.m. and 8:30 p.m.-12 mid.

Opened by the owners of the Chicoa (see Expensive). The curious name fits this place: plastic atmosphere with plastic lamps, plastic plants and plastic flowers. Menu similar to sister establishment. Speciality: dried cod, in seven varieties.

L'Olive. Montaner 171 (Eixample), tel. 230-9027. M: Hospital

Clinic. Daily 1:30-3:30 p.m. and 8 p.m.-1 a.m.

Bright rooms, white tablecloths, this place feels like an Italian temple. Architects, designers, TV presenters, and actors jostle for tables here.

L'Oliana. Santaló 54 (Gracia), tel. 201-0647. FFCC: Gràcia. Daily 1-4 p.m. and 9 p.m.-1 a.m.

A sister restaurant of L'Olive. Same décor and same excellent dishes. Even more chic clientele, particularly in the evenings, as Carrer Santaló is in the top nightlife area. Reservations essential, especially in summer and on weekends.

Passadis del Pep. Plaça de Palau 2 (Ribera), tel. 310-1021. M: Barceloneta. Daily 1-4 p.m. and 9 p.m.-12 mid. Closed Mon. for lunch and in Aug. Reservations essential.

This fish restaurant is hidden near the stock exchange and the main post office, a mecca for seafood fans. Unfortunately, there is no menu, but the waiter will put together different meals of around ten courses: everything edible in a shell, prepared every possible way. Allow three or four hours for your meal. This was an absolute orgy, but I'll never regret one bite, or one peseta of the hefty bill!

Els Pescadors. Plaça Prim, tel. 309-2018. M: Poblenou. Daily 1-4 p.m. and 8 p.m.-1 a.m. Reservations essential.

Tranquil little place in Poble Nou, where you can relax in the summer on the sun terrace with some Rioja or Cava. Good menu for snacks with tapas and cheese. Not cheap, but first class Catalan cuisine.

El Raco d'en Freixa. Sant Elies 22 (Sant Gervasi), tel. 209-5759. FFCC: Sant Gervasi. Tues.-Sat. 1-4 p.m. and 8:30-11 p.m.

Chef and owner Joseph Maria Freixa really proves that he has worked in France for many years. Try the duck with figs, *magret de pato con higos*, and don't forget the desserts. Surprisingly good value lunch special.

Sal i Pebre. Alfambra 14 (Pedralbes), tel. 205-3658. M: Zona Universitat. Mon.-Sat. 1-4 p.m. and 8 p.m.-12 mid.

FOOD AND DRINK

A restaurant in honour of Gaudí right next to the university. In the entrance there is a ceramic and mosaic bench which calls to mind the serpent benches in Parc Güell. For those who can't do without meat, but also a large selection of grilled seafood.

Senyor Parellada. Argenteria 37 (Ribera), tel. 315-4010. M: Jaume I. Mon.-Sat. 1-3 p.m. and 9 p.m.-12 mid. Closed Aug.

Sit comfortably between columns in the big, bright room with an overhead ventilator. The Catalan/French cuisine is good, service friendly, the clientele young and congenial. Be safe and make a reservation.

Set Portes. Passeig Isabel II 14 (Ribera), tel. 319-3046. M: Barceloneta. Daily 1 p.m.-1 a.m.

Not one of my favourites, but Barcelona experts swear by this giant restaurant. My opinion: too many tourist buses, and too expensive for the rather ordinary quality of a rather ordinary Spanish menu.

El Túnel. Ample 33 or Gignas 12 (Barrio Chino), tel. 315-2759. M: Drassanes. Tues.-Sat. 1-4 p.m. and 9 p.m.-12 mid. Closed Mon. and Aug.
And:
El Túnel de Montaner. Sant Màrius 22 (Sant Gervasi), tel. 212-6074. FFCC: Putget. Mon.-Sat. 1:30-4 p.m. and 9 p.m.-12 mid. Closed Aug. and Sat. lunchtime.

Both 'tunnels' are very long rooms. The restaurant in the old town resembles a train compartment. Curiously, you can enter from two narrow streets of the Barri Gòtic, as it occupies the ground floor of two houses. The turn-of-the-century décor is very atmospheric. Gourmets recommend pasta and rice dishes. The old pictures and engravings of Barcelona are remarkable, as is the classic Catalan cuisine. The newer restaurant up in the Zona Alta is very similar: excellent price/value ratio and superb wine list and Catalan cuisine.

Zure-Etxea Asador. Jordi Girona Salgado 10 (Sant Pere), tel. 203-8390. M: Arc de Triomf. Mon.-Sat. 1:30-4 p.m. and 9-11:30 p.m. Closed Aug.

Jose Alcaíde has been serving Basque specialities to his loyal clientele for many years. Give the *angulas a la bilbaína* a miss if you can't bear the sight of transparent eels in olive oil and garlic. I'm puzzled as to why these baby eels should be so popular with gourmets. They're slimy and almost tasteless. Everything else, however, I can recommend, above all the steaks and roast beef, lamb and the delectable partridge and pheasant dishes.

CHIC AND GOURMET

Azulete. Via Augusta 281 (Sant Gervasi), tel. 203-5943. FFCC: Tres Torres. Mon.-Sat. 1:30-3:30 p.m. and 9-11:30 p.m. Closed Sat. lunch, Easter, 1-15 Aug. and 23 Dec.-7 Jan. Make reservations a few days in advance.

If you want to visit only one elegant restaurant in Barcelona, you must try Victoria Roques's creations. The beautiful chef and owner, always in her white apron, spends her holidays in Peking, Paris, Bangkok or Geneva and studies the art of cooking with the best chefs. Eclectic combinations of Chinese, Japanese and Swiss recipes, mixed with Catalan specialities. Whatever you order is brilliant. Round off your culinary extravaganza with a hot baked apple filled with vanilla ice cream. The modern conservatory is a romantic setting.

El Asador de Aranda. Avinguda Tibidabo 31 (Tibidabo), tel. 417-0115. FFCC: Avinguda Tibidabo or Tramvia Blau. Daily 1-4 p.m. and 8 p.m.-1 a.m. Closed Sun. evenings. Reservations essential.

This restaurant is superbly located in an Art Nouveau villa at the foot of Tibidabo. You can eat delicious giant portions of *carnes a la brasa* (fried steak) and meat on a skewer and, with it, crunchy salads. You'll find a million-dollar view from the terrace, especially at night. Very romantic.

Botafumeiro. Gran de Gràcia 81 (Gràcia), tel. 218-4230. M: Fontana. Tues.-Sat. 1 p.m.-1 a.m., Sun. lunch. Closed Aug. and Easter. Make reservations a few days in advance.

A paradise for seafood: delicious lobster, prawns, crabs. Heaps of mussels and oysters served by a whole crowd of waiters. However, this splendour has its price: one of the most expensive restaurants in town.

Chicoa. Aribau 71 (Eixample), tel. 253-1123. FFCC: Provenca. Mon.-Sat. lunch. Closed Aug. and holidays. Reservations absolutely essential.

One of the best restaurants in the city. Rustic and authentic ambience, first-class service. Especially good are the fish cannelloni and *suquets de langosta*, a kind of lobster stew. A three-course meal with house wine will cost around 4,000 ptas.

Club Maritimo. Moll d'Espanya (Harbour), tel. 315-0256. M: Barceloneta. Mon.-Sat. 1-4 p.m. and 9 p.m.-1 a.m. Reservations essential.

City hall plans to pull down this wonderful restaurant as part of the harbour redevelopment scheme. Gourmets as well as sailors and members of this exclusive yacht club eat here. One of the brothers is maitre d'hotel, the other cooks traditional Catalan dishes such as *sequets de pescado* (a kind of fish stew), prawns on a spit au gratin, and fresh pasta with spinach and Roquefort.

Finisterre. Diagonal 469 (Eixample), tel. 239-5576. M: Hospital Clinic. Daily 1-5 p.m. and 8 p.m.-12 mid. Be safe and make reservations.

The owner of the Finisterre is also one of the directors of the restaurant guild. If you want to see how Barcelona's high society eats, book one of the sought-after tables. Excellent French cuisine.

Florian. Bertrand i Serra 20 (Sant Gervasi), tel. 212-4627. FFCC: Bonanova. Mon.-Sat. 1:30-4 p.m. and 9-11:30 p.m. Closed Sun., Easter and two weeks in Aug. Reservations essential.

Cool ambience for writers, journalists and Catalan 'Sloane Rangers' who enjoy Rosa Grau's creative Mediterranean cuisine. Try *ensalada de alcachofas con marinado de pescado*, artichokes in piquant fish sauce, or baby eels with garlic and parsley. Rather expensive.

Freiduria Sant Gervasi. Craywinckel 30 (Tibidabo). FFCC: Avinguda Tibidabo. Tues.-Sat. 1-4 p.m. and 8:30 p.m.-12 mid.

Great fresh fish in this neighbourhood pub. Andalusian owners cook their national dishes. Terrace and garden.

Guria. Casanova 97 (Eixample), tel. 253-6325. M: Urgell. Daily 1-4 p.m. and 9-11 p.m. Closed two weeks in Aug. and Easter. Reservations recommended.

It is well known that Basques make Spain's best chefs. This is the place if you like lobster stew in saffron sauce. Don't leave home without your gold card!

Hans Bar. Muntaner 473 (Sant Gervasi), tel. 211-1713. FFCC: Muntaner. Daily 1:30-4 p.m. and 9:30 p.m.-1 a.m. Reservations at weekends.

This 'in' restaurant combines classic Catalan cuisine with nouvelle cuisine. Particularly delicious are the spinach and salmon cannelloni, marinated smoked salmon, peppers with bacalao and prawn sauce. Terrace in the summer, minimalist décor: black and white photos on white walls.

Jaume de Provenca. Provenca 88 (Eixample), tel. 230-0029. M: Hospital Clínic. Tues.-Sun. 1-4 p.m. and 9-11:30 p.m. Closed Aug. Reservations essential.

Without doubt, Don Jaume de Bargues is one of the best chefs in Spain. Book one of the elegant tables in his gourmet restaurant at least one week in advance. The cannelones, filled with treats such as lobster, lamb or cheese, and the fish risottos are all famous. Great wines from the best Spanish bodegas in Rioja and Penedés. Spoil yourself with a complete meal for around £25 (cheaper at lunchtime) - you won't regret it.

Neichel. Avinguda Pedralbes 16 bis (Pedralbes), tel. 203-8408. M: Palau Reial. Mon.-Sat. 1-4 p.m. and 8:30 p.m.-12 mid. Closed Easter, Christmas and Aug. Reservations recommended in summer.

The undisputed star of Spain's chefs. El magnifico! Although Jean Louis Neichel is Swiss, his Spanish *gran cocina* displays great creativity. Wafer-thin salmon filets, pigeon breast with asparagus, huge selection of cheeses. The menu degustación is a must - around £35.

FOOD AND DRINK

Reno. Tuset 27 (Gràcia), tel. 200-1390. FFCC: Gràcia. Daily 1-4 p.m and 8:30 p.m.-12 mid. Closed Sat. in June, July and Sept.

1960s atmosphere with black leather benches. Polite and experienced waiters will help you select from the extensive wine list. Catalan cuisine with a touch of Escoffier.

Roig Robi. Seneca 20 (Gràcia), tel. 218-9222. Mon.-Sat. 1:30-4 p.m. and 9 p.m.-12 mid. Closed holidays. Reservations essential.

The patio is ideal for mild summer nights in this smart restaurant, with Catalan and French cuisine.

La Venta. Plaça Doctor Andreu (Zona Alta), tel. 212-6455. FFCC: Avinguda Tibidabo or Tramvia Blau. Mon.-Sat. 1:30-4 p.m. and 8:30 p.m.-mid. Reservations essential.

This restaurant with superb Catalan cuisine is especially famous for its fantastic location at the foot of the Tibidabo and its pretty terrace with views of the city. Waiters are arrogant to customers not suitably dressed, so do as the Barcelonese do and dress up for a night on the town.

FRENCH

Brasserie Flo. Jonqueras 110 (Sant Pere), tel. 317 8037. M: Urquinaona. Daily 1-4 p.m. and 9:30 p.m.-1:30 a.m.

This is a place for those who love the 'Flo' and 'La Coupole' in Paris. Gigantic hall with corner benches and bistro tables where there is always at least one rowdy birthday celebration. For the Catalans, Paris is nearer than Madrid, so their cooking is more French than Castilian or Andalusian. Ideal for a snack or steak *frites* after the theatre or cinema. Great value, extensive selection of food and wine.

La Souple a l'Oignon. Padua 60 (Zona Alta), tel. 212-7742. M: Lesseps. Mon.-Sat. 1:30-4 p.m. and 9 a.m.-12 mid.

Unpretentious but excellent cuisine *grande-mère*. As the name implies, Monsieur Martini serves French classics such as Burgundy snails, steak frites, fondue bourguignon, soup de mer or grilled shrimps, and for dessert delicious crème brulée or profiteroles.

FOOD AND DRINK

ITALIAN

Il Florino. Cornet i Mas 45 (Sarrià), tel. 205-3017. FFCC: Sarrià. Tues.-Sat. 1-4 p.m. and 8:30 p.m.-12 mid., Sun. 1-4 p.m.

Best Italian in town. Two menus: one with pizza, pasta and small meat dishes such as *scaloppine*, the other with Italian nouvelle cuisine. Not expensive.

Tramonti 1980. Diagonal 501 (Eixample), tel. 410-1535. M: Diagonal and then bus.

Franco Lombardi is, as the name suggests, from Milan, capital of Lombardy. Treat yourself to wafer-thin *carpaccio*, tender veal in piquant tomato and anchovy sauce, and other Italian dishes.

JAPANESE

Kiyokata. Muntaner 231 (Eixample), tel. 200-5126. M. Hospital Clinic. Tues.-Sat. 1:30-4 p.m. and 8:30 p.m.-12 mid. Sun.-Mon. open half-day. Closed Aug.

Barcelona's Japanese twiddle their chopsticks and enjoy their *sushi*, fresh raw fish on a bed of rice. Japanese interior and rice paper screens like in Tokyo.

Tokyo. Comtal 20 (Barrio Chino), tel. 317-6180. M: Catalunya. Mon.-Sat. 1-4 p.m. and 8-11:30 p.m. Closed holidays.

Simple Japanese without much fuss. Spinach in sesame sauce or chicken teriyaki (chicken from the spit) are equally authentic. The tuna and eel are best.

Yamadori. Aribao 68 (Eixample), tel. 253-9264. FFCC: Provenca. Mon.-Sat. 1-4 p.m. and 8:30 p.m.-12 mid.

Simpler menu and décor than the elegant Kiyokata. Try the noodle dishes or shabu-shabu, a kind of meat fondue prepared before you on the table.

FOOD AND DRINK

CHINESE AND INDONESIAN

Pekin. Rosselló 202 (Eixample), tel. 215-0177. FFCC: Provenca. Mon.-Sat. 1-4 p.m. and 9 p.m.-12 mid., Sun. 1-4 p.m.

The best-designed Chinese restaurant in Europe. Everything sparkles and shines under marble lamps. The dark mahogany, the Nile-green windows, the black octagonal porcelain plates and the attentive service make a visit to this gourmet temple an aesthetic treat.

Sin Chow. Villirana 74 (Sant Gervasi), tel. 218-1041. FFCC: Padua.

Pretty neighbourhood Chinese with economical menu. Lunch special from 600 ptas.

Ta-Tung Chino. Marià Cubí (Sant Gervasi), tel. 201-0095. FFCC: Gràcia. And Madrazo 54 (Sant Gervasi), tel. 200-9986. FFCC: Plaça Molina.

Helpful staff, red silk lampshades and the black varnished paravents give these restaurants a more pleasant atmosphere. However, authentic cuisine has given way to Spanish tastes. Not quite Peking, but the locals enjoy the somewhat toned-down food.

Bunga Raya. Assaonadors 7 (Sant Pere), tel. 319-3169. M: Jaume I. Tues.-Sun. 1-4 p.m. and 8 p.m.-12 mid.

This Indonesian restaurant in the Gothic quarter near the Picasso museum, serves Malaysian specialities, such as *satay* (kebabs in peanut sauce), a *roti,* a kind of pancake eaten with curries or meat dishes. You can eat here for a fiver, if you can't take any more tapas.

INDIAN

Shalimar. Carme 71 (Barrio Chino), tel. 329-3496. M: Liceu. Daily 1-11:30 p.m.

Very economical Pakistani cuisine in the Barrio Chino. I really liked the tandoori chicken. If you don't like it hot, the friendly owner will recommend a mild dish such as chicken kashmir or beef curry with bananas, almonds and pineapple in cream sauce.

FOOD AND DRINK

Rajah. Sant Pau 39 (Barrio Chino), tel. 329-2303. M: Liceu. Fri.-Wed. 1-4 p.m. and 7 p.m.-12 mid.

Same owners as the Shalimar and similar menu. This economical Pakistani restaurant with eight tables attracts mostly youngsters. Family-run place where no one gets uptight if you sit for hours over a gamba curry and a beer.

MEXICAN AND CUBAN

Cantina Mexicana. Encarnació 51 (Gràcia), tel. 210-6805. M: Fontana. Mon.-Sat. 1-4 p.m. and 9 p.m.-1 a.m.

A lot of extremely potent Tequila Sunrise goes down here, and you can even look at the awful worm in its bottle of Mezcal. The patio is very comfortable in the summer, and the tortillas, as well as cheese and chilli enchiladas, are not too mushy.

Zurracapote. Arístides Maillol 21 (Les Corts), Tel. 334-2930. M: Palau Reial. Mon.-Sat. 1-4 p.m. and 8:30-11:30 p.m.

Cuban cuisine can be infernally hot and full of chilli. But this cantina near the university and the Boulevard Rosa shopping centre offers something for the milder taste. For example, grilled plantain-bananas and fried chicken with refried beans. Good value, like many other exotic restaurants.

VEGETARIAN

Biocentre. Pintor Fortuny 24 (Barrio Chino), tel. 302-3567. M: Liceu. Mon.-Sat. 12:30-4 p.m. Closed holidays.

A bio-store with small restaurant. The three-course special is very good value, and the salad buffet is ideal in the summer. For picnics, packed lunches including rice dishes, cakes and salads, are also available.

Les Corts Catalanes. Gran Via de les Corts Catalanes 603 (Eixample), tel. 301-0376. M: Catalunya. Mon.-Sat. 1-4 p.m. and 8-11 p.m.

The most extensive vegetarian selection in town is proud of its salad bar, wide ranging cereals and tea selection. You can even have a beer or wine with your mozzarella pizza or cauliflower gratinée.

Govinda. Plaça Vila de Madrid 4 (Barri Gòtic), tel. 318-7729. M: Catalunya. Mon.-Sat. 1-4 p.m. and 8 p.m.-12 mid. Closed Aug.

Indian restaurants are a rarity in Spain - in London, New York and, above all, India they are very popular, as many Indians are vegetarian by religion. Lassi, the yoghurt drink with rosewater or mango, is very refreshing.

L'Hortet. Pintor Fortuny 32 (Barrio Chino), tel 317-6189. M: Liceu. Mon.-Sat. 1-4 p.m. Closed holidays.

Health Freaks form a queue at 1 p.m. in front of this unpretentious restaurant with pine tables. There is hardly any selection; everyone is happy with the two three-course menus at 600 pesetas. Try the gazpacho, it's wonderfully refreshing and piquant.

Illa de Gràcia. Sant Domènech 19 (Gràcia), tel. 238-0229. M: Fontana. Tues.-Sun. 1-4 p.m. and 8-11 p.m. Closed 15-31 Aug.

My favourite vegetarian restaurant. Cool black and white surrounds the bright wooden tables, young artists display their latest works, and the broccoli noodles and spaghetti spinach are formidable.

Macrobiotica Zen. Muntaner 12 (Eixample), tel. 254-6023. M: Universitat. Mon-Fri: 12:30-4 p.m.

You can eat the daily vegetable special, sometimes with tempeh of tofu, and fabulous yoghurt desserts. Fantastic wholemeal breads, tea and seaweed for the macrobiotic kitchen are also available.

Self Naturista. Santa Anna 15-17 (Ravoli), tel. 302-2130. M: Catalunya. Mon.-Sat. 1:30-4 p.m. and 8:30-11 p.m.

Not an especially pleasant place, but central and ideal for cheap and quick snacks such as lentil soup, cheese and salad sandwiches or apple cake. Self service.

NIGHTLIFE

The Catalan capital is famous all over the world for its nightlife. When it comes to nightlife even old favourites like New York, Paris and London cannot compete with Barcelona. This city is indisputably la crème de la crème for round-the-clock fun, from dusk to dawn.

As the name implies, Bar-celona is a city of bars. Post-modern bars like the Zsa Zsa, Velvet and TickTackToe, or mega-cool clubs such as Nick Havanna and Universal, dazzle even bored jet-set tourists. Chrome sparkles, waterfalls cascade down algae-green glass walls, 48 screens flick image-bites from cult films into the crowd, neon cases invite you to buy the latest paperbacks, and a lone iguana lurks behind bulletproof glass in his own desert. Bowling alleys await you in the back and you can even amuse yourself with mini-golf and pool. In Barcelona you'll disappear into a Bermuda triangle of nightclubs, only to re-emerge the following morning. Nights here seem twice as long as anywhere else.

Do as the locals do and go to bed between 7 p.m. and 11 p.m. before diving into the nightlife with the hedonist masses. You can pick at titbits in tapas bars, but if you feel like haute cuisine, let me assure you that even renowned gourmet restaurants serve opulent five-course meals long after midnight.

While some establishments list general opening and closing times, the Spanish take a laissez-faire attitude towards such matters, and times vary according to the day, the season or the whim of the owner. In general, bars are open 10 a.m.-midnight, and club hours are 10 p.m.-3 a.m. weekdays, 10 p.m.-5 a.m. weekends, closed Sundays. If in doubt, phone ahead or check the latest edition of *Guia de Ocio*.

TAPAS BARS

Nightlife in Barcelona begins with tapas. It's just a way of life. But tapas are not quite as commonplace here as in Madrid or Andalusia. Many Spaniards joke about this: 'No wonder Catalans don't go in for tapas in a big way. These cheapskates don't give anything for free'.

NIGHTLIFE

Tapa is Spanish for lid; in times gone by it was usual to cover your glass of wine with a free slice of ham. Today it's tradition to put a small plate of sardines, anchovies, olives or chips on the bar with your glass of beer, vino or Cava. Although in Barcelona's tapas bars the portions of cured ham, grilled crab, fried potatoes, squid or tortilla are slightly larger, they hardly ever come free. You'll find the most atmospheric tapas bars in the port district near the main post office, around the Plaça del Sol in Gràcia and in Barceloneta.

Bodega Quimet. Poeta Cabanyes 25 (Poble Sec), tel. 242-3142. M: Paral-lel. Thurs.-Tues. 9 a.m.-11 p.m. Closed Aug.

The tapas bars are legendary in this popular district around the rundown nightlife area of Paral-lel near Barrio Chino. Bodega Quimet is my favourite; the many olive stones, toothpicks and crumpled-up serviettes on the floor are proof of this.

Can Maralletes. Cuenca 35 (El Clot; Guinardo). M: Camp de l'Arpa. Daily 11 a.m.-11 p.m.

This curious ancient bar resembling a half-ruined castle, has an authentic Catalan ambience. Here you can get an idea of life in Barcelona before mass tourism. Off the beaten track, but worth a trip into the unknown.

Casa Fernandez. Santaló 46 (Sant Gervasi), tel. 201-9308. Daily 12 noon-1 a.m. Closed Aug.

This elegant beer and tapas bar is the latest effort from the creator of Nick Havanna and Gimlet. The house even prides itself on its own beer. Apart from excellent tapas they serve international dishes like *gnocchi* with pesto, or apple pie tarte *tatin*. Especailly busy during the weekend.

Casa Tejada. Tenor Viñas 3 (Sant Gervasi). M: Zona Universitario. Mon.-Sat. 11 a.m.-12 mid.

This extremely charming bodega serves giant portions of simple tapas such as tortilla, sardines, grilled prawns and chorizos, or piquant sausage, as well as hot fried potatoes. It is located around the corner from the technical university in the university zone across Diagonal.

D'Or. Consell de Cent 339 (Eixample), tel. 215-6439. M: Passeig de Gràcia. Mon.-Sat. 12 noon-12 mid.

The name of this beer cellar derives from the frothy golden beers served here from a wide selection. Spanish beers on tap include Voll-Damm and Tartan, beer connoisseurs drink Guinness or Belgian Chimay. Hearty tapas are the ideal compliment.

El Bodegon. Mallorca 197 (Eixample), tel. 253-1017. M: Passeig de Gràcia. Mon.-Fri. 8 a.m.-1 a.m.

Not only tapas but also small dishes. They are proud here of their *cocina mercado*, simple home-cooking with market-fresh ingredients.

Gran Bodega. València 201 (Eixample). M: Passeig de Gràcia. Mon.-Sat. 12 noon-1 a.m.

Students and young married couples with crying babies frequent this very economical bar. First you can look along the bar where different salads and tapas, fish specialities and meat salads are displayed, and then order from the extensive menu. Go early in the evening, otherwise all the tables in the street will be taken. It's not much fun to eat in the narrow bar. Not for romantics, as trucks constantly thunder past, and the customers are on the loud side, too.

La Jarra. Mercè, corner at Somó Oller (Barri Gòthic). M: Drassanes. Daily 10 a.m.-12 mid. Closed on the occasional Sunday.

A bar straight out of *Star Wars*. Wild and long-haired blokes, mosaic floor scattered with toothpicks and serviettes: not for hygiene fanatics. But Spaniards measure the success of a tapas bar by the heaps of litter under the bar. The speciality is *jamón canario*, the spicy cooked ham from the Canaries, where the stoical owner was born. Enjoy a portion, without bread, with your beer or wine, or order another portion of *patatas bravas*, hot potatoes with piquant tomato sauce.

Jose Luis. Diagonal 520 (Eixample), tel. 200-8312. M: Diagonal. Daily 10 a.m.-12 mid.

The best tapas bar for gourmets. Unfortunately, the modern atmosphere of this cool bar with two floors, large windows, bright parquet floor and lightning waiters, could equally be Paris or Munich.

NIGHTLIFE

Yuppies and posh people love to sip a glass of Cava here and savour fillet steak or crab tapas. The constant supply of titbits from the kitchen really teases my appetite. I could gobble tapas here every day of the week.

Bar Robles. Riera de Sant Miquel 51 (Gràcia). M: Diagonal. Mon.-Sat. 9:30 a.m.–12 mid.

This small tapas bar in Gràcia is frequented by local workers and artisans. A bit rough, but very realistic prices.

Cafeteria Santa Anna. Santa Anna 8 (Raval). M: Catalunya. Mon.-Sat. 9 a.m.–9 p.m.

More of a self-service snack bar than a genuine bar. This plastic cafeteria, in a constantly bustling pedestrian zone, is very popular with shoppers from nearby Plaça de Catalunya and Portal de l'Angel.

Sergi. València 194 (Eixample). M: Passeig de Gràcia. Mon.-Sat. 11 a.m.–12 mid.

Sergi is the proprietor of this bodega and the Gran Bodega, in the same street. But here everything is more serene and civilized. The selection is not as extensive, but the quality of food is higher and the cook seems to take more care and use less oil.

Los Tilos. Passeig dels Til.lers 1 (Pedralbes), tel. 203-7546. M: Palau Reial. Mon.-Sat. 6 p.m.-3 a.m., Sun. 12 noon-3 a.m.

In 1985 Manuel Boyano and Andrés Sune opened this super bar in the university district across Diagonal. The best thing about this place is the great selection of tapas and the garden behind the house, where you can find yourself talking to the locals at round tables under sun shades.

La Vinateria Delcall. Sant Domènec del Call 9 (Gràcia), tel. 302-6092. FFCC: Gràcia. Mon.-Sat. 6:30 p.m.–1:30 a.m.

Good Cava, tapas and Rioja.

TERRACE BARS

Bar del Pi. Sant Josep 1. M: Liceu. Daily 9:30 a.m.–12 p.m.

More cafe than bar near the cathedral in the heart of the Gothic quarter. It's especially peaceful to sit in this square during summer, ideal to escape the hustle and bustle and constant traffic chaos of the Ramblas.

Bar Hidalgo. Balmes 396 (Sant Gervasi). FFCC: Putget. Mon.–Sat. 10 a.m.–12 p.m.

You can linger here all day and into the early hours drinking coffee or a glass of Cava while you watch 'Uptown Barcelona'. A real neighbourhood pub.

Dos Torres. Via Augusta 300 (Sant Gervasi), tel. 203-9899. FFCC: Tres Torres or bus 16, 70, 66. Daily 1 p.m.–2:30 a.m.

Sleek high-tech bar by Francesc Amat, owner of Vincon design shop. Yuppies meet on the terrace for sandwiches, Cava and loud pop before they go clubbing.

Gambrinus. Moll de la Fusta (Barri Gòtic). M: Drassanes. Daily 12 p.m.–4 a.m.

Yet another establishment designed by Mariscal. Apparently you can't escape this man in Barcelona's nightlife. This bar/restaurant was inspired by the sinking of the Titanic. The furniture was supposed to look like flotsam. 'A total mess, good eh?' The cocktails are recommendable, but the *paella* is plain and overpriced. It gets really busy here at 2 a.m. and people stay until dawn.

Marcel. Santaló 44 (Sant Gervasi), tel. 209-8948. FFCC: Muntaner. Daily 9:30 a.m.–2 a.m.

Very popular with young people, who grab a tortilla and *cafe con leche* on their way to the nearby Universal nightclub. The tapas are not breathtaking, but the clientele is. I like to breakfast here, although on weekends it's often difficult to nab a table on the pavement.

Merbeye. Plaça Dr. Andreu (Sant Gervasi). FFCC: Avinguda

NIGHTLIFE

Tibidabo and the Tramvia Blau. Mon.-Sat. 5 p.m.- 2 or 3 a.m.

Mariscal really let himself go with the interior of this trendy bar. Wonderful views, expensive drinks. There is always a slight breeze on the sun terrace.

Mirablau. Plaça del Funicular, Final Avinguda Tibidabo (Tibidabo), tel. 418-5879. FFCC: Avinguda Tibidabo and the Tramvia Blau. Tues.-Sun. 12 p.m.-5 a.m., Mon. 5 p.m.-5 a.m.

Tipsy guests had better not lean too far back on their stools near the glass window directly on the precipice. In the night there is a right rave-up on the dance floor below, but during the day you can have the bright bar all to yourself and pore over an interesting magazine.

Partycular. Avinguda Tibidabo 61, Les Torres (Sant Gervasi), tel. 211-6261. FFCC: Avinguda Tibidabo and the Tramvia Blau. Mon.-Sat. 7 p.m.-2:30 a.m.

As the name implies, this bar with garden was not made for wallflowers. The neon entrance alone is enough to put off the timid. Masses of loud young people born with an Amex Gold Card.

BAR-CELONA BARS

Alkimia. Amigo 35 (Sant Gervasi), tel. 202-3544. FFCC: Muntaner. Daily 8 p.m.-2 a.m.

Something for quieter souls. Just like a private library; you can read esoteric and philosophical literature, leaf through art books and read the future in tea leaves. You can pop in for a cup of coffee and a glass of Cava as from 8 p.m.

Art Cava. Fusina 4 (Ribera), tel. 315-2571. M: Jaume I. Daily 6 p.m.-2 a.m.

Spacious Cava bar with modern design in bright colours and varnished columns. The pool table in the back room is always occupied. Here you can regularly visit art exhibitions accompanied by jazz. Clientele: city people.

Barbara Ann. Gran Via 454 (Sant Antoni), tel. 425-3990. M: Rocafort. Tues.-Sat. 8 p.m.-2 a.m.

Psychedelic rock bar for goths and sixties fans, who stagger around on the tiny dance floor to Jimi Hendrix from the juke box.

Bauhaus. Praga 3 (Gràcia), tel. 256-9716. M: Alfons X.

Small rock bar where home-grown bands from the 1970s lift the roof at weekends. Regulars shoot a quiet game of pool in the back.

Berimbau. Passeig del Born (Ribera), tel. 319-5378. M: Jaume I. Daily 6 p.m.-3 a.m.

The furnishing is rather dated, but it's quite dark in here. Smooching couples on creaking rattan chairs listen to Brazilian samba and drink *kaipirinha*, a sugar cane drink with lime peel for 474 ptas.

Boadas. Tallers 1 (Ramblas), tel. 318-9592. M: Plaça de Catalunya. Mon.-Thurs. 12 noon-2 a.m. Fri.-Sun. and holidays 12 noon-3 p.m. and 6 p.m.-2 a.m.

Intellectuals, business people, artists and students have been meeting in this tiny bar near the Ramblas since 1933: in other words, all Barcelona. Best cocktail bar in the city.

El Born. Passeig del Born 26 (Ribera), tel. 319-5333. M: Jaume I. Mon.-Sat. 6 p.m.-2 a.m.

This used to be a bacallanería, where *bacallà*, dried cod, was soaked in the marble basins. Today they are covered with glass, where Gregorio serves the El Born cocktail, a tasty mixture of Tequila, lemon and banana liqueur. Cream walls and red upholstered 1930s chairs look good on the old tile floor. A tiny spiral staircase leads to the first-floor balcony and views of the square, with the only remaining masonry dating from equestrian tournaments to the 14th and 15th centuries.

Calypso. Rec 59 (Ribera). M: Barceloneta. Mon.-Sat. 6 p.m.-2 a.m.

Tiny, dim bar where you can really get it together to calypso sounds. Ideal for lovers.

NIGHTLIFE

Caos Mil. Berlines 17 (Sant Gervasi). FFCC: Putget. Tues.-Sat. 7 p.m.-1 a.m.

This bar celebrates 1930s and 1950s music. Glenn Miller, Elvis and Frank Sinatra are probably proprietor Carles Mir's idols. The television set on the ceiling shows old Hollywood films or Disney cartoons. Very congenial atmosphere.

El Otro. Valencia 166 (Eixample). M: Urgell. Sun.-Thurs. until 2:30 a.m., Fri.-Sat. until 3 a.m.

Young nightowls sit around a wavy mosaic bar and drink their copa or whiskey sour before setting off clubbing.

The End. Santalo 34 (Sant Gervasi). FFCC: Muntaner. Mon.-Sat. 9 p.m.-4 a.m.

For the very early hours. The Porsches, BMW cabrios and snow-white Mercedes limousines of the *jeunesse doree* are stacked outside.

Este Bar. Consell de Cent 257 (Eixample), tel. 323-6406. M: Universitat. Mon.-Sat. 6 p.m.-2 a.m.

The Spanish painter Miquel Barceló designed the interior, and many of his young and not-yet famous friends display their latest pictures here. People dance, clap and drink into the small hours. A touch of underground.

La Fira. Provenca 171 (Eixample), tel. 323-7271. M: Hospital Clínic. Mon.-Sat. 12 a.m.-2 a.m.

Decorated with old-fashioned slot machines, carousel horses and trick mirrors from the fairground, it's very agreeable despite the loud décor. Students and bons vivants meet with golden girls and career women. You must see this!

Garage Hermetico. Diagonal 442 (Eixample), tel. 415-2231. M: Hospital Clìnic. Mon.-Sat. 6 p.m.-2 a.m.

Classical marble columns contrast with computer games and video monitors that show football or Spanish pop. More people in their thirties than teenagers.

Gimlet. Rec 24 (Ribera), tel. 310-1027. M: Barceloneta. Daily 7 p.m.-2:30 a.m. Weekends until 3 a.m.

Classic bar designed like a 1930s ocean liner. Light wood, mirrors and flashy cocktails to quiet songs. Gimlet launched Barcelona's bar boom. Still popular with intellectuals, journalists and artists.

Gimlet. Santaló 46 (Sant Gervasi), tel. 310-1027. FFCC: Gràcia. Daily 6 p.m.-3 a.m. Weekends longer.

The bar of all bars' latest offshoot. Magnificent design: amber-coloured marble, lit from within, shiny bronze plaques on the walls, soft leather benches and a few tables on the street. In a better part of town and just around the corner from Universal and Otto Zutz.

Jeu de Paume. Marià Cubí (Sant Gervasi). FFCC: Gràcia. Tues.-Sat. 6 p.m.-3 a.m.

This bar in the smart club district north of Diagonal attracts a trendy clientele for the last drink of the night.

Lapsus. Vigatanas 4, corner of Carcassa (Ribera), tel. 319-9440. M: Jaume I. Daily 7 p.m.-2:30 a.m.

One of the most pleasant bars in Ribera. You can watch videos at the bar and the pool tables attract a lot of young people.

London. Nou de la Rambla 45 (Barrio Chino), tel. 302-3102. M: Paral-lel. Wed.-Mon. 6:30 p.m.-3 a.m. Closed Aug.

Jazz bar with pool tables and pub games like darts. Hence the name.

Marienbad. Gran Via 583 (Eixample). M: Urgell. Daily 12 a.m.-1 a.m.

Students and would-be students drink buckets of Pilsener Urquell.

Miramelindo. Passeig del Born 15 (Ribera), tel. 319-5376. M: Jaume I. Mon.-Sat. 8 p.m.-2 a.m., Sun. 7 p.m.-1:30 a.m.

Brazilian drinks or a Mojito (a rum and mint drink) hit even the hardest cocktail lover. Peach-coloured walls, leather seats, with whirring fans hanging from the ceiling, leather armchairs and palms everywhere. Generous measures are served here.

Mudanzas. Vidriera 15 (Ribera), tel. 319-1137. M: Arc de Triomf. Daily 6 p.m.-2:30 a.m.

Mudanzas is all in black and white: chequered floor, varnished black gallery and Tomás Gómez pictures on white walls. The three lads behind the bar work as seamen, hence the wide range of high-grade spirits: 35 whiskies, 23 vodkas, 15 rums, and rarities such as Chinese brandy or French absinth. Here you can hire a captain for a weekend excusion or charter a 23-metre motor yacht over a cuba libre.

El Nus. Miralles 5 (Ribera), tel. 319-5355. M: Jaume I. Thurs.-Tues. 7 p.m.-2 a.m.

Fourteen years ago rice and beans were stored in the red drawers, and hams hung from the ceiling; today it's all bottles of gin, and above the beer tap hangs a giant paper bird. Lluis with the long white hair used to be a painter and adores Juliette Greco, Edith Piaf and the great Oum Koulsoum from Morocco.

Sahoco. Balmes 187 (Eixample), tel. 218-7677. M: Diagonal. Tues.-Sat. 8 p.m.-3 a.m., Sat. often longer

Carlos Dumé knows how to run a successful bar: loud, dark, and with it the most potent cocktails in town. Sahoco is a permanent Brazilian carnival. You can dance to salsa, merengue, cumba and steel drums. Sometimes Caribbean bands play live.

Santanassa Antro Bar. Aribau 27 (Eixample), tel. 451-0052. M: Passeig de Gràcia. Daily until 4 a.m.

Nocturnal ravers dressed in leather, rubber or Alaia outfits have been celebrating here since the summer of 1989. The rich and beautiful mingle to loud Spanish pop like Alaska, Martirio or Miquel Bosé in superb kitsch-décor by the former shop window designer, Rafa.

Snooker. Roger de Llúria 42 (Eixample), tel. 318-8247. M: Passeig de Gràcia. Mon.-Sat. 6 p.m.-2:30 a.m.

One of Barcelona's favourite bars since 1985. Grandiose and as big as a football pitch, with four large pool tables in the back. Elegant waiters in tails serve Cava and illustrious cocktails.

Soweto. Sòcrates 68 (Sant Andreu), tel. 340-1154. M: Fabra i Puig.

The African and Latin American music is also the inspiration for the décor in this club. Salsa, Caribbean sounds, merengue. Plastic palms, wicker furniture and colourful masks on the walls.

Status. Passeig del Born 30 (Ribera), tel. 319-5079. M: Jaume I. Tues.-Sun. 6 p.m.-2:30 p.m.

The window sills serve as tables in this tiny alcove directly on the Born. Ideal for people watching and for rendezvous.

Torres de Avila. Poble Espanyol (Montjuïc), tel. 426-8174. M: Espanya and the free shuttle bus.

Latest bar by Mariscal and architect Alfredo Arribas: Futuristic baroque according to admirers, dreadful kitsch according to dissenters. A hidden camera checks every visitor at the entrance, lifts take you up to the roof from where you can see the glorious sun set and enjoy fantastic views of the city.

Xampanyera. Provenca 236 (Eixample), tel. 253-7455. FFCC: Provenca. Mon.-Sat. 7 p.m.-3 a.m.

The cool décor of shiny steel chairs and sloping steel tables by Jordi Galli seems rather out-of-date. However, the huge selection of champagne and Cava still entices a clientele from politics, business and academia.

Zsa Zsa. Rosselló 156 (Eixample), tel. 253-8566. M: Hospital Clínic.

Gentle establishment, wafer-thin marble behind the bar illuminating the bottle racks. Asian embroidery creates a striking contrast to the ultra-modern style.

NIGHTCLUBS AND DISCOS

There is really not much difference between nightbars and clubs in Barcelona. Only times vary. Most bars are open from 6 p.m. Some cocktail bars mix their lethal drinks from midday and only close at

3 a.m. Clubs only open around 9 p.m. and mostly have bigger dance floors. Drinks are possibly a bit more expensive, and a bouncer will appear like a guard dog, but in the end you'll get in.

If you want to have a drink in at least four bars, as is customary in Barcelona, you won't have to lay out a lot of money as admission is generally free. Sometimes there is a small cover charge if a band is playing.

Ars Studio. Atenes 27 (Sant Gervasi), tel. 417-7156. FFCC: Padua. Daily 8 p.m.-4:30 a.m.

A disco along the lines of New York's Studio 54. Whole packs of señoritas in miniskirts size up fiery-eyed Julios with their white shirts open to the navel. Pulsating music and mammoth dance floor.

Bella Bestia. Riera Sant Miquel 19. M: Diagonal.

The 'beautiful beast' is a stomping ground for goths, old punks and rockers. Only for those who want to show up in rags or black leather.

KGB. Alegre de Dalt 55 (Gràcia), tel. 210-5906. M: Joanic. Tues.-Sat. 10 p.m.-4 a.m.

Crazy opening times and cold metal architecture are the hallmark of this hard rock and rap club. KGB opens on Friday and Saturday again between 6 a.m.-8 a.m., although the iron blinds only came down around 4 a.m. Video banks and occasional live bands attract teenagers.

Network. Diagonal 616 (Les Corts), tel. 201-7238. M: Maria Cristina. Daily 1 p.m.-4 p.m. and 8 p.m.-2:30 a.m.

What's this? Is it a bar? A restaurant? A disco? Network is everything. It's like New York in Reagan's era: so cool, so high-tech, so affected. 'In people' and would-be 'in people' go in and out.

Nick Havanna. Rosselló 208 (Eixample), tel. 215-6591. FFCC: Provenca. Mon.-Thurs. 6 p.m.-3 a.m., Fri.-Sun. 5:30 p.m.-3 a.m.

Where else in this world can you find something like Nick Havanna? Massive video banks amplify the pictures of pop videos and old cult films such as *Casablanca* or Hitchcock's *The Birds*. You can buy the latest American, Catalan or Spanish paperbacks from vending machines, the WC is the eighth wonder of the world, and the music is formidable. Stock market teleprinters buzz in the corner and an army of reptiles flick their tongues at you. Fortunately, these mini-dinosaurs are behind bullet-proof glass. A must-see!

Otto Zutz. Lincoln 15 (Sant Gervasi), tel. 238-0722. Bus: 7, 14, 15, 16, 27.

From the steel banister and balcony on the first floor there is a good view of the crowded dance floor. The music is too loud for conversation, the power bass penetrates flesh and bone. Just right for dancing.

Psicodromo. Almogàvers 86 (Poble Nou), tel. 485-0582. M: Marina. Daily until 4:30 a.m.

This dark club only established itself recently and is a bit off the beaten track from the usual club circuit. The club only livens up around 2 a.m. Goth décor for Gothic brides and ghosts in the style of Nick Cave, Blixa Bargeld or even Lydia Lunch. Nina Hagen would certainly feel at home here.

Ticktacktoe. Roger de Llúria 40 (Eixample), tel. 318-9947. Passeig de Gràcia.

Great club concept with excellent food, large dance floor, pinball machines, pool tables and snooker competitions. Certainly on your 'must see' list.

Universal. Marià Cubí 182-184 (Sant Gervasi), tel. 200-7470 and 201-4658. Bus: 7, 14, 15, 16, 27, 34. Daily 7 p.m.-3 a.m.

Really, the Universal

consists of two contrasting clubs. Upstairs the former factory is quiet and decorated like a spooky castle: long white curtains, turquoise parquet floor, small tables, candelabra, chandeliers; generous measures of excellent drinks. Downstairs is pandemonium: booming dance music, flickering video banks, live performances, long bar and bustling dance floor.

Up & Down. Numància 179 (Les Corts), tel. 204-8809. M: Maria Cristina. Daily 11 p.m.-4 a.m.

Barcelona's numero uno disco is on two floors, up and down. The restaurant on the upper floor is very 'in' and full of finance wizards, high-profile politicians, actresses and presenters from the nearby TV3 television station, who later pile onto the dance floor for some Latin American music.

Velvet. Balmes 161 (Eixample), tel. 217-6714. FFCC: Provença. Daily until 5 a.m.

My absolutely favourite spot in Barcelona: Inspired by David Lynch's film *Blue Velvet*, it's simply great to sit on one of the soft, heart-shaped bar stools at the boomerang bar and watch the dancers. The silver dance floor is small but beautiful, and the poses of the illustrious clientele never fail to amuse. You must see the toilets: they're just wild.

Yabba Dabba. Avenir 63 (Sant Gervasi). FFCC: Muntaner. Mon.-Sat. until 3:30 a.m.

Stone coffins for tables, zebra-pattern bar stools and cool Egyptian ambience make this club a designer El Dorado. Should be near the top of your hit-list.

Ziz Zag. Plató 13 (Sant Gervasi), tel. 201-6707. FFCC: Mutaner.

Pool, videos, the latest Spanish music and the certainty that you'll feel comfortable here, despite the trendy clientele, has attracted visitors since 1977 to this club, which is really only a bar.

Velvet, my absolutely favourite spot in Barcelona.

NIGHTLIFE

LIVE MUSIC

JAZZ

Articulo 26. Gran de Gràcia 25 (Gràcia), tel. 237-5475. M: Gràcia. Mon.-Thurs. until 4:30 a.m., Fri.-Sat. until 5 a.m. and afternoons 6 p.m.-10 p.m.

Programme director Joana Pijoan often books international jazz bands at this concert hall. Pleasant ambience, apart from weekends when the club becomes a disco. During the week there's not only jazz, but also soul, salsa, pop, and even hard rock.

La Cova del Drac. Tuset 30 (Eixample). M: Diagonal. Mon.-Sat. 11 p.m.-2 a.m. No live music Mon. Closed July-Sept.

Indisputably Barcelona's best jazz club. Somewhat hidden behind a plastic cafeteria, but once you've climbed the steep staircase you'll find the *templo del jazz* behind an inconspicuous-looking door.

Harlem. Comtessa de Sobradiel 8 (Barrio Chino), tel. 310-0755. M: Jaume I. Daily 7 p.m.-3 a.m.

This fairly new jazz bar tries to imitate the sombre style of the jazz clubs of Harlem and Paris. Recorded blues and jazz, and often young international bands not yet as famous as the stars that play the Cova del Drac.

Sam's. Plaça Aragonesa 4, Poble Espanyol (Montjuïc), tel. 426-3845. M: Espanya.

Although I'm bored by the touristy Poble Espanyol, this jazz bar is fun. Spanish jazz musicians play this small room every night around 1 a.m. Pleasant in the summer, when you can still hear the music on the terrace under the moonlight.

CAFE CONCERTS

El Molino. Vilà y Vilà 99 (Poble Sec), tel. 241-6383. M: Paral-lel. Tues.-Sun. until 6 p.m. and nights at 11 p.m., Sat. 11:15 p.m.-1 a.m. Holidays open Mon.

NIGHTLIFE

There is pandemonium every night in this tacky neon 'windmill'. An extravaganza in the style of *La Cage aux Folles*. Transvestites in splendid feather costumes, can-can dancers, obscene gestures, vulgar comic acts, and much more. The audience is especially crazy and gets carried away! A real gas.

Scala. Passeig de Sant Joan 47 (Eixample), tel. 232-6363. M: Arc de Triomf.

A compromise between restaurant, ballet and floor show, with long-legged girls in glitter bikinis. Not exactly young Spaniards and tourists with a taste for this kind of entertainment crowd in front of the lavishly decorated stage.

Bodega Bohemia. Làncaster 2 (Barrio Chino), tel. 302-5081. M: Drassanes. Tues.-Sun. 9 p.m.-3 a.m. Closed Wed.

A really nostalgic experience! Nothing seems to have changed in this dusty joint for the last 50 years. Even the singers and dancers are the same. Ancient transvestites with touchingly smudged make-up still give it all they've got on the tiny stage. Go along, as without an audience these glamour figures will soon die out.

BALLROOMS

La Paloma. Tigre 27 (Sant Antoni), tel. 301-6897. M: Universitat. Thurs.-Sun. 6 p.m.-9:30 p.m. Night sessions; Thurs. 11 p.m.-3 a.m., Fri.-Sat. 11:30 p.m.-3:30 a.m., Sun. 11:30 p.m.-2:30 a.m.

Wonderful old dance hall (See La Paloma).

Sutton. Tuset 13, tel. 209-0537. M: Diagonal. Daily 7 p.m.-4 a.m.

Luxurious and elegant casino/ballroom with *gran orquesta*. The clientele? Middle-age bourgeois, men in their prime, greying temples and cashmere jackets, accompanied by their second or third wife or mistress. Also popular with young women looking for a sugar daddy or some fun with their girlfriends on a hen night. Naturally, the Sutton is more interesting at the weekend.

NIGHTLIFE

Cibeles. Còrsega 363 (Eixample), tel. 257-3877. M: Diagonal.
Thurs.-Sun. 11:15 p.m.-4 a.m.

Barcelona's young scene swings in this kitschy dance hall on Fridays
after midnight to 'chucuchucu' and Benny Goodman Big Band sounds.
During the week it's more of a second-rate nightclub. Very
entertaining.

FLAMENCO

Barcelona is not a town for flamenco, which is the music of Andalusians
and Spanish gypsies. Sevilla, Granada, Valencia and Madrid are the
centres for these music and dance shows. In Catalonia you'll find
inferior flamenco establishments. The following are the best:

Los Tarantos. Plaça Reial 17 (Barrio Chino), tel. 317-8098. M:
Liceu. Wed.-Sun., shows at 10 p.m. and midnight.

This flamenco hall hidden under the arches of the Royal Square, is
rather unappealing from the outside. But do venture into the cellar
because it's Barcelona's top flamenco establishment. Top stars make
guest appearances here, particularly at weekends and in the autumn.
You will also be spared the tourist buses which unload at the miserable
El Cordobés or in the equally pitiful El Patio Andaluz.

El Tablao de Carmen. Arcos 9, Poble Espanyol (Montjuïc), tel. 325-
6895. M: Espanya. Tues.-Sun. 9 p.m.-4 a.m., shows at 10:30 and 1:30
p.m. Sun. also at 7 p.m., reduced admission 500 ptas. Dinner show
3,700 ptas. Show and drink 2,200 ptas.

Good Andalusian cuisine and friendly atmosphere. Although the
Spanish village is too sterile and touristy for my taste, I can safely
recommend this show.

LA PALOMA -
BARCELONA'S GOLDEN
BALLROOM

Fanfare. Joseph Pafs, most senior member of the orchestra Malibú, reaches for his violin. An old tango. *La Mariposa*, fills the room. The enormous dance floor is still almost empty under the red spotlights, but the first brave dancers take to the parquet floor. A nimble, middle-aged couple follow through the most difficult steps, two elderly ladies try a simpler two-step, a musing lone dancer sways to the beat of the music. If it wasn't for the fashionable suits, miniskirts and jeans on the younger dancers, you could be forgiven for thinking you were back in the 1920s. But it's 1992 and we are in a relic of times gone by.

Barcelona's oldest ballroom is not just any pleasure dome, it's an institution. It has been pulling in dancers since 1903, and they still love it. La Paloma - a *baile popular* (people's ball) of the first order.

La Paloma is a melting pot that attracts all sorts - workers and unemployed, students and wasters, young and old. It reflects the turbulent past of this Mediterranean city which has experienced four forms of government in the 20th century: monarchy, anarchy, fascism and democracy.

Where today people dance, there was once a factory. The building used to house the Comas forgery. The surrounding neighbourhood, El Raval, was the cradle of Barcelona's industrialisation. Catalonia's textile industry converged on this former suburb in the 19th century, and the many migrant workers from southern Spain, driven to the Catalan capital in search of work, settled in the narrow alleys of this quarter. Social inequality, sad factory buildings and exotic bars together created the microcosm that exists in this triangle between the legendary Ramblas and the Rondas de Sant Antoni and Sant Pau, streets which were built in 1854. This quarter experienced a first boom in the 1880s. The world exhibition of 1888 created employment, and the Comas forgery manufactured the metal components for the Columbus statue erected in the port - one of Barcelona's hallmarks.

LA PALOMA

Public dancing had long been fashionable at the time of the world exhibition. Although Catholic Spain had always tried to suppress this sensuous fun, in 1814 the first *bailes de salón* were taking place. These indoor balls were mostly organised in warehouses by workers' leisure clubs. Balls for the middle classes took place in cafés. The takings had to be donated to good causes as penance for this immoral activity, and the beneficiaries were often orphanages and hospitals.

Over and over again these balls were banned on moral grounds, but in 1863 the time had come: the opening of public ballrooms was approved, and establishments like Apolo, Bohemia, and Iris Park sprang up. They were partly meant for a bourgeois clientele, partly *de patacada*, for those who would otherwise only be dancing in street parties. La Paloma fell into the latter category, the last surviving reminder of the great era of ballrooms. Writer Josep Maria Carandell called it 'the most colourful island in Raval'.

The 'colourful island' opened in 1903. Three friends, señores Ustrell, Sorilla and Balliar, converted the Comas forgery on Carrer del Tigre into a ballroom called La Camelia Blanca. Business was rather poor. Pimps from surrounding *muebles* (apartment houses) used the hall for their knife fights, and soon the three friends were so deeply in debt with the soft drink producer Jaume Daura, that they had to hand over the premises to him. It became the greatest infatuation for his son, Ramón, who gave up his music studies at the age of 16 and decided to turn this converted warehouse into something Barcelona had never seen before.

He travelled to Paris, where he was fascinated by the Hall of Mirrors in Versailles. Ramón returned to his hometown, full of grand inspiration. He commissioned the well-known craftsman Manuel Mestre to design a late Baroque interior with carved boxes for the upper classes and an enormous candelabra. Salvador Alarmas, a stage designer from Barcelona's opera house, the Liceu, painted the walls and ceiling like Tiepolo, the Vatican church. The result was a magnificent combination of kitsch and art, sensuous colours and lush shapes, inaugurated in 1915. It has hardly changed on the outside to this day.

The former Camelia was renamed Venus Sport, and now not only attracted *putas* (prostitutes from the nearby port) but also maids, seamstresses and workers as well as *señoritos*, young gentlemen of the

LA PALOMA

bourgeoisie, looking for a fling. They danced the tango, the pasadoble, the waltz and the habanera, more or less under surveillance since the dictator Primo de Rivera came to power in 1923. During the Second Republic there was a brief honeymoon of liberal attitudes and proletarian morale. The establishment was only forced to close its doors for a short period in the Civil War during heavy and continuous bombing by Franco's planes and when the Catalan militia requisitioned the premises for target practice.

In 1940, one year after Franco seized power, Ramón Dauro was able to reopen his Venus Sport after replacing the Catalan word *sport* with the Spanish *deporte*. This is how the new rulers wanted it, and they also introduced a new element in true reactionary-Catholic fashion: now a supervisor wielding a stick watched over the dance floor. He was soon commonly known as 'La Moral' and would intervene when dancers, still following the old melodies, got too close or even tried a kiss. But when the first tourists from northern Europe arrived at the *costas* to bake in the sun, morals became a little looser. The population expressed its aversion to Franco's regime in the love of ballrooms and pride in Catalanism, and in the 1960s Barcelona's leftist intelligentsia, which included Joseph Maria Carandell and the Goytisolo brothers, joined the dancing proletariat in the Venus Deporte.

But public life in Spain only really began to bloom when, 'on Franco's death the bottles of champagne that had been waiting for years in fridges for this occasion could finally be opened', as described by the writer Manuel Vàzquez Montalbàn. By then Ramón Daura's great-nephew, Pau Sole, had taken over Venus Deporte, renamed it La Paloma, after a side street off Carrer del Tigre, and removed the man they called 'La Moral'. Otherwise, everything was the same.

Since then La Paloma has been opening to a full house four times a week for two shows nightly. Elderly people dance to the music of their youth in the early evening; forty to eighty-year-olds who have been regulars for decades meet friends, celebrate birthdays, pass around photos of their grandchildren and live a second or third spring. Some come back for the late show. When the orchestra Malibú strikes up the pasadoble, all the wild and crazy, sad and sweet characters a city like Barcelona can muster pile onto the dance floor.

As the ambience is intimate - many of those that come every night

LA PALOMA

know each other - La Paloma has its stars. Marga, for instance, a worker with gypsy blood from the Besòs suburb, turns up every weekend with the whole family, including her mother. No one dances flamenco and rumba quite like this well-rounded forty-year-old, who also enjoys introducing younger visitors to the art. El Tigre is another character, a short man who works as a bricklayer during the day and whose hallmark is his white scarf. He has a preference for dancing with black-haired beauties and sometimes even organises a clapping square-dance.

The black-suited waiters are as much a part of the interior as the heavy chandelier; they busily carry the ubiquitous ice buckets for the Catalan Cava. If you want, you can ask the orchestra to play your favourite tune and have your dedication read aloud. No one is bothered whether the dedication is from a husband to his wife, or from a gay guy to his friend. The ball rolls on into the early hours and enchants the faithful as well as those tourists who now and then venture off the Ramblas.

La Paloma. Tigre 27, tel. 301-6897. M: Universitat. Thurs.-Sat. 6 p.m.-9 p.m. and 11 p.m.-3 a.m., Sun. 6 p.m.-9:30 p.m.

THE ARTS

After forty years of cultural constraints and isolation under Franco's dictatorship, the arts in Spain not only flourished and leaped ahead, they almost went overboard. As a result, Barcelona's art scene can today compete with the most important international art centres such as New York and London.

Young artists eagerly absorb ideas from magazines and catalogues, but still try to preserve and demonstrate their national, and in Barcelona's case, their Catalan identity. A plethora of galleries, the result of a long tradition of trading in art, is now attempting to do this youthful scene justice as well as rescue many past Spanish artists from oblivion, at the same time as keeping pace with international trends. Museums, collections, exhibition halls and galleries are emerging everywhere, heavily subsidised by the state or funded by private patrons.

At the cost of $40 million (£22 million), the architect Richard Meyer is converting Barcelona's **Casa de la Caritat** from an 18th-century hospital into the Museo de Arte Contemporaneo, a museum of contemporary art, where a permanent collection of the Caixa de Pensions trust will be displayed over 1000 square metres. It is recognised as one of Spain's leading collections. The Ludwig collection will also be represented here once the museum opens its doors in 1993. But the question remains, will it be on a par with other great museums, and will there by regionalism without provincialism? This question equally applies to Barcelona's situation as a whole, where every artist and custodian must tread a path between ambition, dependency and self-interest.

20TH-CENTURY CATALAN ART

Catalan nationalism has had both a subtle and profound influence on the great Spanish artists of the 20th century. Pablo Picasso spent his youth in Barcelona from the age of 14 to 23. Here he received his academic training and absorbed many of what were to be the formative influences of his work. After his 'Blue Period' (1901-04) he left for Paris, and

while he spent the last half of his life in exile in France following the Spanish civil war, it is said that he always thought of himself as Catalan although he had been born in Andalusia.

When the artists Juan Gris, Luis Buñuel, Joan Miró and Salvador Dalí followed the young Picasso to Paris one by one in order to seek inspiration and fame in the world centre of art, they also found a common language which was closely linked to their Catalan homeland. They returned as Catalans with a new-found independence. A kind of drifting to and fro has since been the tradition. Antonio Saura and Antoni Tàpies both had ateliers in Paris, many others were even more nomadic.

The Catalan character, strikingly epitomised by Dalí's own legend, is often associated with political anarchism, which in its milder form manifests itself as Catalan nationalism. Time and again artists took up political causes. In the late 1950s, a group of surrealists came together under the name *Dau al set* (dice with seven) and published an art and poetry magazine of the same name. The publication had tendencies towards Automatism and Surrealism and served as an effective vehicle for political subversion and subliminal propaganda. However, Antoni Tàpies, the head of the group, dissociated himself from this style in order to develop his variant of Spanish Informalism. Together with Miró, who also had left Paris for Barcelona, he supported Catalan nationalism.

Another true Catalan, the artist and poet Joan Brossa, has not so far attracted much attention abroad, but is currently being honoured in many retrospectives. His origins as an artist go back to the civil war when he was allowed to recite his first poems to the troops on the republican front. In the 1970s he shocked Spanish TV viewers by including soft porn in his show, forbidden at the time. All the same, he is not only a great historic figure, but also one of the most vivacious contemporary personalities, and his *poema-objetos*, poetic pictorial objects, have had considerable influence, especially on younger generations of artists.

BARCELONA'S ARTISTS TODAY

Perejaume, one of the beneficiaries and self-proclaimed admirers of

THE ARTS

Brossa's art, works from a small fishing community. His principal theme is that of landscape, which he employs in everything from Romanticism to Surrealism. Like many of his contemporaries, he takes advantage of diverse media, such as photography, painting and sculpture, and yet he achieves a unique form of expression. In Barcelona, landscape is always mountain and sea, and through their proximity they both influence the aesthetic conscience.

Perhaps the most successful artist of his generation, Miquel Barceló, has won so many awards at the age of 33 that a forger has specialised in the style of this Catalan. The forged *Fish-Soup* changed hands for $90,000. The nomadic Barceló himself spends more time in New York, Paris and Mallorca than his hometown Barcelona and, typical of painters in the 1980s, makes a lot of money from galleries, although he's no longer the talk of the town.

The chasm between internationalism and regionalism is often the subject of the conceptual artists Antoni Muntadas. One of his works, entitled *Standard/Specific*, places credit cards side by side with photos of shop signs from the old Born quarter in order to draw attention to the imminent loss of a specific visual language.

These are only a few examples of artists who are characteristic of Barcelona, but like elsewhere in Spain, you must always be alert to new names.

THE ART TRADE AND CULTURAL ACTIVITY

Trading in art goes back a long way in Barcelona. The bourgeoisie have always been keen to improve their image by collecting and promoting art. As a result, a number of galleries trade in classic art without drawing much attention to themselves. The traditional competition with Madrid is therefore less of an economic question than one of cultural image. Catalans insist that theirs is the more artistically active town where, not just coincidentally, Surrealism has its roots, and they trade in their homegrown art and build their own museums.

In the old part of town, galleries cluster around the market in the **Born quarter**, and in the **Gothic quarter**, near the Picasso museum on Calle Montcada. When, a few years ago, the alternative exhibition centre, **Metronom**, opened in the Born in a beautiful Art Nouveau hall, it attracted many commercial galleries. It became the catalyst of a young scene already established in this quarter.

Most of the galleries are located in Carrer del Comerc. The most prominent of these is **Benet Costa**, whose influential programme includes the above-mentioned Antoni Muntadas. Other galleries include **Berini**, **Artual** and, just around the corner, **Lino Silverstein**, a branch of the **Fernando Alcolea** gallery. Incidentally, Alcolea is a family concern; Fernando's parents already traded in abstract art, and his brother Alfonso is an agent for a whole generation of Catalan conceptual artists. At Lino Silverstein you'll find internationally renowned names, such as Donald Baechler and George Condo, next to interesting new discoveries.

The well-established **Gallery Maeght** in Calle Montcada displays mainly abstract art, while the exhibition centre belonging to the **Caixa**, diagonally opposite, exhibits young experimental artists - site-specific works are the order of the day.

A second cluster of galleries can be found in the **Eixample** near Consell del Cent (Consejo del Ciento). One of Barcelona's most important galleries, **Joan Prats**, has its headquarters here. Names like Tàpies, Brossa, Perejaume, Longo and Bourgeois are listed in the programme. The director Elena Tatai runs a second exhibition centre, **Espai Poblenou**, where stars such as John Cage and Kounellis are celebrated in a museum-like atmosphere. This centre is located outside the concentration of galleries, but near the Olympic village in Poble Nou after which it is named.

The only remaining surrealist element of the gallery **Dau al Set** is its name. At **Ciento**, **Carles Tache** and **Alcolea** (the latter further north) the tried and tested blend of known and unknown, famous and young-and-hungry is evident.

Due to generous private and public funding, it is relatively easy to exhibit in Barcelona in venues other than the main commercial centres. Almost all the larger, uninhabited buildings, whether they are hospitals, monasteries or palatial residences, are converted into cultural facilities. Banks, above all Caixa de Pensions (Caja de Pensiones), are brushing up their cultural image. The **Caixa**, whose excellent collection was mentioned earlier, has had resounding success in their headquarters, an old palace on Passeig Sant Joan, staging high-quality temporary exhibitions, one of which ('Art and its Double') will go down in history. As the management of the trust has changed recently – the current director is Thomas Messer, a Spaniard previously associated with the Guggenheim Museum – you can expect innovation in its exhibition policy.

The **Palau de la Virreina** and **Convent de Santa Monica** have also been converted into art centres. The latter displays Catalan art in idyllic, though sometimes poorly constructed rooms, and, more recently, it has hosted thematic exhibitions from foreign collections.

The **Miró foundation**, located on a hill outside the city centre, invites you to admire the versatile works of this famous Catalan artist. The temporary exhibitions also attract attention, and the excellent restaurant will round off this trip into the hills. The **Tàpies Museum** also caught the public's eye with, for example, the Louise Bourgeois Retrospective, and an additional attraction is its public library.

ADDRESSES

Alfonso Alcolea Mallorca 327, tel. 215-1358. M: Diagonal.

Antic Hospital de la Santa Creu i Sant Pau. Hospital 56, tel. 424-7171. M: Liceu.

Artgrafic. Balmes 54, tel. 302-9975. M: Passeig de Gràcia.

Casa de la Caritat. Centre de Cultura Contemporania de Barcelona, Montalegre 5, tel. 301-0174. M: Universitat.

Carles Tache. Consell de Cent 290, tel. 318-1887. M: Passeig de Gràcia.

Centre d'Art Santa Monica. Ramblas 7, tel. 318-7591. M: Drassanes.

Ciento. Consell de Cent 347, tel. 215-6365. M: Passeig de Gràcia.

Dau Al Set. Consell de Cent 333, tel. 301-1236. M: Passeig de Gràcia.

Fundacio Caixa de Pensions. Centre Cultural, Passeig Sant Joan 108 (Palau Macaia), tel. 258-8907. M: Verdaguer.

Fundacio Joan Miró. Plaça Neptú (Montjuïc), tel. 329-1908. M: Espanya.

Fundacio Tàpies. Aragó 255, tel. 487-0315. M: Passeig de Gràcia. (See Museums.)

Joan Prats. Rambla de Catalunya 54, tel. 216-0284. M: Passeig de Gràcia.

Espai Poble Nou. Passage de Saladrigas 5. M: Poble Nou.

Lleonart. Palla 6, tel. 301-7626. M: Liceu.
Museum Picasso. Montcada 15, tel. 319-6310. M: Jaume I. (See Ribera.)

Palau de Virreina. Ramblas 99, tel. 301-7775. M: Liceu.

Theo. Enric Granados 27, tel. 323.0848. M: Universitat.

Thomas Carstens. Josep Anselm Clavé 4, tel. 302-5989. M: Drassanes.

GALLERIES

The following top art galleries can be found in and around the Ribera quarter:

Arcs & Cracs. Flassaders 42, tel. 310-3734.
Young gallery within the ancient walls of dark Flassaders. The floors are uneven and the steps down to the cellar are a medieval experience. The slide show about the Ribera quarter is a real eye opener! Pictures by Future 2000 and sculptures by Javier Garcés.

THE ARTS

Artual. Comerc 31, tel. 319-9975. M: Barceloneta.

Collective exhibitions with Vaccaro, Richard Díaz and Humberto Ribas.

Benet Costa. Comerc 29, tel. 310-1684. M: Jaume I. Tues.-Sat. 10:30 a.m.-1:30 p.m. and 5-8:30 p.m.

An enormous glass door leads into the exhibition room. Antoni Muntadas is also exhibited simply and plainly in the cellar. On opening days you can see the most ostentatious people in Barcelona.

Galeria Berini. Plaça Comercial 3, tel. 310-5443. M: Arc de Triomf. Tues.-Sun. 10:30 a.m.-1:30 p.m. and 5-8 p.m.

All over the building there are art works in hair and pictures by top designers Javier Mariscal, Paul Benney, Michael Byron and Juan Carlos Sabater.

Born Subastas. Plaça Comercial 2, tel. 319-5555. Mon.-Sat. 11 a.m.-8 p.m., Sun. 11 a.m.-2 p.m.

Exhibition room on two floors right next to Berini with monthly auctions on themes such as painting or 1920s furniture.

Galeria Ferran Cano-4 Gats. Fusina 6. Tues.-Sat. 10:30 a.m.-2 p.m. and 5-8:30 p.m.

Branch of the famous Quatre Gats in Palma de Mallorca. You have to ring the bell and go up to the first floor into office-like rooms to see pictures by Pepe Nebot, Serafin Rodrígues, Jose Aja and Xavier Puigmarti. Work by Idroj Sanicne and sculptures by Jordi Tolasa.

Gloria de Prada. Calders 2, tel. 310-2627. Tues.-Sat. 10 a.m.-1:30 p.m. and 5-8:30 p.m.

Up to now the newest gallery in the district. It opened with a homage to Jaume Torres i Estrade by Eric Maas.

Fundacio Caixa de Pensions. Montcada 14, tel. 310-0699. Tues.-Thurs. 11 a.m-2 p.m. and 4-8 p.m., Sat.-Sun. 11 a.m.-2 p.m.

Sala Montcada is the name of the room which was provided by this pension fund. The installations and interior design are beautiful.

THE ARTS

GU. Vidrieria 15, tel. 319-7931. Tues.-Sat. 10:30 a.m.-1:30 p.m. and 5-8:30 p.m.

Jewellery lovers will be impressed as the genial Ana Font reveals drawers full of designer jewellery and miniature objects from young artists all over Europe. Pieces in silver, platinum and gold sparkle in simple displays; some are very limited editions. Temporary exhibitions display silk paintings by Kima, sculptures by Manuel Rovira or exotica from India at moderate prices. Ana gives jewellery workshops for beginners and experts in her studio next door.

Lino Silverstein. Antic de Sant Joan 3, tel. 319-2439. M: Barceloneta. Tues.-Sat. 10:30 a.m.-2 p.m. and 4:30-8:30 p.m.

Small but beautiful. From the street you can view the works by Sergio Caballero, David Storey, Donald Baechler, and Ray Smith.

Galeria Maeght. Montcada 25, tel. 310-4245. M: Jaume I. Tues.-Sat. 10 a.m.-1:30 p.m. and 4:30-8 p.m.

A sister of the famous French Maeght gallery has found its way straight into the most beautiful Gothic palace on Carrer Montcada and displays top artists such as Tàpies, Broto, Barcelo, and Limos. In the courtyard you can buy prints and posters. Even art philistines should give it a try.

Metronom. Fusina 9, tel. 310-6162. Tues.-Sat. 4:30-8 p.m.

A must for aficionados of avant-garde and contemporary art. Green light falls through three magnificent modernist skylights into the exhibition hall. The Metronom now almost exclusively sponsors Spaniards such as Noguera, Franzesc Abad, Jordi Benito or Carles Pazos. The first floor houses a good library in this field, and next door is a bookshop.

THEATRE IN
BARCELONA

Perhaps even more than language, architecture and football, theatre is the very essence of Catalan culture. From the late fifteenth to the beginning of the nineteenth century there was virtually no literature written in Catalan. The language only remained truly alive in an oral form. When with the renewed Romantic interests in regional cultures, Catalan came to be used once more as a literary idiom, drama proved the most ostentatious form for the expression of a vibrant renaissance. Dramatists such as Frederic Soler (1839-95) and Angel Guimerà (1847-1924) thus became prominent figures.

Two important factors immediately established themselves in the characterisation of Catalan literature, and both help to distinguish it from its Castilian counterpart. Firstly, a highly receptive attitude enabled writers to keep abreast of European theatrical trends and quickly assimilate modern(ist) techniques. Maeterlinck's *L'Intruse* was produced in Catalonia soon after its French premiere, and Barcelona developed into an obligatory stopping point on the European tour, for performers such as Sarah Bernhardt and Fregoli. Erwin Piscator visited the city in 1936. Likewise, Santiago Rusinol (1861-1931) and Josep Maria de Sagarra (1894-1961) spent significant periods in Paris, observing and absorbing new artistic and literary currents. A parallel phenomenon can be seen in the art of Joan Miró and Salvador Dalí.

Secondly, to write in Catalan was to declare a political commitment, even if the subject matter treated was trivial or escapist. This commitment became more explicit during the Franco regime. And yet, in spite of the hostility of the Franco government towards Catalan, theatrical productions in the language recommenced in 1946 and small amateur groups provided outlets for avant-garde plays. By the 1960s Beckett, Ionesco and some works by Brecht had been translated into Catalan.

The post-Franco period (from 1975 onwards) has witnessed a considerable expansion of theatrical activity. After a fertile period at the Teatro Maria Guerrero in Madrid, the Catalan Lluis Pasqual is now

director of the Theatre de l'Europe in Paris and has already caused quite a stir with Shakespeare's *As You Like It* and Genet's *Le Balcon*. Pasqual comes from a vibrant background of Catalan theatre which has, in many cases, chosen to abandon any reliance on a written text.

Catalan groups such as Els Joglars, Els Comediants, El Tricicle and La Cubana have travelled widely in Europe and gained a reputation for exhilarating performance pieces. *Tier mon*, an extraodinarily violent representation of global conflict by La Fura dels Baus, involved striking images which were not merely designed to be contemplated: actors ran through the audience with chain saws and aggressively thumped spectators with giant inner tubes. This was playing for real; outside, ambulances waited on standby. These groups often perform in markets and other unorthodox locations. Even if they are, at times, pretentious, they are almost always thought-provoking and can be wickedly funny.

There is also plenty of original drama written in Catalan. The Theatre of the Absurd *avant la lettre* of Manuel de Pedrolo (1918-90) and Joan Brossa (b. 1919) is complemented by the poetic narratives of Salvador Espriu (1913-85) and the more overtly committed allegories of Joseph Maria Benet i Jornet (b. 1940). The Valencian Rodolf Sirera (b. 1948) has proved himself to be a master of an astounding variety of styles.

New works by Catalan writers are promoted above all through two theatres: the **Teatre Romea** (the Centre Dramàtic de la Generalitat) and the **Teatres de l'Institut** (sometimes called the **Teatre Adrià Gual**). Of the youngest generation, the works of Sergi Belbel (b. 1963) continue to be challenging for actors and audiences alike. Belbel now often works with José Sanchis Sinisterra, who has organised some fascinating sessions at the newly instituted **Sala Beckett**.

A comparable national identity (Catalonia is, after all, a *nacio*) has been evolved by the **Teatre Lluire**, run for a long time by one of the most talented set designers in Europe, the sadly missed Fabià Puigserver, and the Companyia Josep Maria Flotats, based at the **Teatre Poliorama**. Flotats worked for years in Paris and returned in triumph to form Catalonia's national company. The shows at the Poliorama are consistently professional. Flotats directs and performs in well-known foreign, especially French, plays. Some think he may be Spain's greatest living actor. He alone knows he is.

THEATRE IN BARCELONA

As far as musical theatre is concerned, an enterprising programme of international productions is followed at the **Liceu**, a historic opera house which is also a focal point for the Barcelona *beau monde*. Seats are reserved years in advance and passed on from generation to generation. The music-hall tradition is alive and (literally) kicking in places like **El Molino**, where a form of innocent pornography enjoys a continuing popularity. Audience participation is not so much provoked as expected, and selected members (the word is not used unwittingly) are touched (up) and searched for all their innate humour.

Finally, if you are especially interested in theatre, it is worth arranging your visit to Barcelona to coincide with one of its two major theatre festivals, the Grec (from June to early August) and the Festival de Tardor (from September to October).

THEATRES

Apolo. Avinguda Paral-lel 59, tel. 241-4006. M: Paral-lel.

Arnau. Avinguda Paral-lel 60, tel. 242-2804. M: Poble Sec.

Belle Epoque Teatre Musical. Muntaner 246, tel. 209-7385. FFCC: Muntaner.

El Molino. Vilà y Vilà 99, tel. 441-6383. M: Paral-lel.

Gran Teatre del Liceu. Sant Pau 1 bis, tel. 318-9122. M: Liceu.

Jove Teatre Regina. Séneca 22, tel. 218-1512. M: Diagonal.

Llantiol. Riereta 7, tel. 329-9009. M: Paral-lel.

Mercat de les Flors. Lleida 59, tel. 426-2192. M: Espanya.

Sala Beckett. Can Alegre de Dalt 55 bis, tel. 214-5312. M: Joanic.

Sat-Sant Andreu Teatre. Carrer de les Monges 2-6, tel. 311-9551. M: Fabra i Puig.

Teatre Condal. Avinguda Paral-lel 91-93, tel. 242-3132. M: Paral-lel.

Teatre Goya. Joaquim Costa 68, tel. 318-1984. M: Universitat.

Teatre Joventut. Joventut 4-10, tel. 448-1210. M: La Torrassa/Collblanc.

Teatre de la Penya Cultural Barcelonesa. Sant Pere Més Baix 55, tel. 310-2292. M: Jaume I/Urguinaona/Arc de Triomf.

Teatre Lliure. Montseny 47, tel. 218-9251. M: Fontana.

Teatre Malic. Fusina 3, tel. 310-7035. M: Jaume I.

Teatre Poliorama. Ramblas Estudis 115, tel. 317-7599. M: Catalunya.

Teatre Romea. Hospital 51, tel. 317-7189. M: Liceu.

Teatre Victoria. Avinguda Paral-lel 67, tel. 241-3985. M: Paral-lel.

Teatres de l'Institut (Sala Gran and La Cuina)/Teatre Adria Gual. Sant Pere Més Baix, tel. 317-2078. M: Urguinaona.

Teixidors Teatreneu. Terol 26-28, tel. 213-5599. M: Fontana.

Villarroel Teatre. Villarroel 87, tel. 451-1234. M: Urgell.

JAVIER MARISCAL
AN INTERVIEW WITH
SPAIN'S TOP DESIGNER

Javier Mariscal advanced from cartoon scribbling hippy to official designer of the Olympic mascots Cobi and Nosi. Cobi is a cheeky little dog with a pointed nose, who remotely resembles early Mickey Mouse figures from the 1920s. He can be found in more than 30 variations: from TV reporter carrying a camera under his arm, to sailor or athlete. Nosi, the female version and promoter of the cultural Olympiad, looks charming with her lopsided puckered lips, three locks of hair on her high fringe, and red jumper and green pleated skirt. This newest creation by the all-round designer is available on T-shirts, silk, key rings, towels, or as cuddly toys. As Mariscal points out slightly cryptically, 'everyone knows Cobi, and that's important for the Olympics'.

We sit in his office in Poble Nou, Barcelona's old industrial area, where he has converted a disused cement factory into a bright loft of glass and pure space. Surrounded by young graphic designers, design students and personal assistants, who coordinate meetings with clients from France, Japan and all over Spain, Mariscal sits at his white desk and doodles childish stickmen for soft drinks manufacturers, yapping dogs for liqueur companies and fading roses, bulls and Toreros for Tràfico, his brother's fashion company in Valencia.

'Just a little dash here on the mouth, and Cobi is a massive boxer who takes his job very seriously. And a friend of mine put the same friendly grinning mouth on my dog Julián, made of shiny aluminium, which is now being sold in an edition of 1,000 models in the design empire Vinçon. Of course, I check the quality of the brushstroke, which has to be just right.'

Talking to Mariscal, I get the impression he is poking fun at his job and a world that takes his scribblings so seriously. Still, he is proud, very proud, of his success in advertising, as restaurant designer for Barcelona, painter for the Olympics, and furniture designer. Mariscal is a brand name, and even his friends leave out the 'Javier'.

Mariscal has had a go at everything: from books and comics with Garris, his Mickey Mouse comic figures Lucas, Fermín and Piker, abstract plates and teapots, adorned with airplanes and New York's skyline, to wristwatches with the dog Juliàn on the face and white bed linen that wishes you 'Buenas Noches' in huge black writing.

'I don't compromise. My clients expect something special, they want surprises. I keep my eyes open, I see many things. Suddenly I feel a flutter in my stomach, it goes to my head, and the new design is ready. I like the obvious - things that a child can understand. A radio that looks like a girl chatting, a chair that looks like a torero's hat with silver slippered feet. But sometimes I improve on a design 25 to 40 times. It seems so quick and easy and it should, but a lot of work goes into it.'

Spain has understood Andy Warhol's lesson and no longer makes the distinction between art and crafts. In 1987 Mariscal was sent to the 'Documenta' in Kassel, Germany, and his unusual paintings and drawings sold very well.

'I need poetry in my life. I love artists like Paul Klee, Matisse, Picasso, of course, and my friend Miguel Barcelo, but also Germans such as Baselitz, Penck, and ecological art like that of Beuys. I live simply, and I have driven a Volkswagen bus for many years. Before I had an old red one, now a new white one. I love Spanish music, the Chunguitos, gypsy music, as well as the songs of Rosita Amores for whom I also made a video. Spain and Barcelona: for me it's like California. The feeling of sunny life in the Mediterranean, drinking with friends into the early hours, having fun. That's the life for me. It still is, even though I'm 43.'

And what does Mariscal like about Barcelona?

'I love riding on the cable car from the harbour in Barceloneta up to Montjuïc with my five-year-old daughter, Julia. And then we continue up to the Magic Mountain in Tibidabo to the roller coaster, slot machines and carousels, and drink Coca Cola.'

Mariscal draws the cable car in my diary and insists: 'You've got to go up there. The best views. You can only understand Barcelona from up there'. He pours himself a glass of mineral water and asks me whether I like his new yellow designer cardigan by Roser Marce. He claims that he's not normally too concerned with clothes. Jeans, baggy jackets, T-shirts are his daily work clothes.

'I'm a bit browned off at the moment. I offered city hall a proposal to open a bar on the cable car tower, designed and run by me. But I wasn't granted planning permission. The tower is probably too old and too small to take a lot of people. It's a pity. It could be the best bar in Barcelona. My restaurant, Gambrinus, down on Moll de la Fusta, looks great with its giant shrimp on the roof, but I only designed it and don't manage it. The paella is overpriced, with too few shrimps and too much rice. And the waiters are incompetent and unfriendly.'

However, Mariscal has since had his way. The city later granted permission for an alternative location, and he has designed the most outrageous nightclub of all in the Torre de Avila, the guard tower at the top of Montjuïc at the Poble Espanyol.

Mariscal's favourite restaurant is El Salmonete, a fish restaurant right on Barceloneta's beach, with lovely views of the sea. 'But the municipality wants to pull it down and relocate it further back, because suddenly there is a new beach law. You're not allowed to put up tables and chairs so near the sea. The beach belongs to everyone and not only the restaurant. And the Olympic village being built out there by the sea is probably another reason why the quaintly dilapidated district of Barceloneta is being sanitised. I'm all for the Olympics, but not generic and dull planning and architecture.'

Although he didn't do Gambrinus any favours, for the last 12 years he's been a frequent visitor to his other bar, Merbeye, designed with Fernando Amat, high up on Tibidabo by the terminus of the romantic Tramvia Blau. 'At night the view of the city is magnificent. You see, I love Barcelona from above.'

Eduardo Mendoza, the author of the paean to Barcelona 'The City of Miracles', stands here on the roof of Gaudí's La Pedrera in Eixample

EDUARDO MENDOZA,
THE MASTER OF MIRACLES

Eduardo Mendoza is Spain's most famous novelist. More famous even than Camilo José Cela, and that is quite something, considering Cela won the 1989 Nobel Prize for Literature.

The City of Miracles is Mendoza's fourth novel. A 600-page epic about Barcelona, it topped the bestseller charts for months. Critics compared the protagonist Onofre with James Joyce's Ulysses and raved: 'As Joyce did with Dublin, Mendoza has dedicated his city the novel it deserves.' This postmodern, picaresque story made the unknown cult writer a media personality and popular columnist, and led to numerous appearances on talk shows. But Mendoza is not only a great writer. Between 1972 and 1982 he worked as a simultaneous interpreter at the UN in New York, and even today Prime Minister Felipe Gonzalez invites him to translate important speeches or interpret for him at conferences.

We met at the Mauri, Barcelona's most sumptuous cafe in smart Eixample. Eduardo Mendoza is a handsome man of 46, slim with no trace of a double chin or plumpness. He is slightly tanned, and his neat brown moustache and well cut hair are streaked with grey. A Spanish girlfriend tells me he is a dandy and very charming. But he is not conceited. He jokes about Spanish clichés, laughs, orders three ham and cheese sandwiches with his espresso and loves to talk. 'Did you know that Franco's favourite actress was Anna Magnani? And that Gaudí is more famous and admired in the rest of the world than over here? My wife is an architect, and all architects detest Gaudí. He was too surreal, too organic. In Spain we prefer Domènech i Montaner. He built the Palau de la Música and the wonderful hospital Sant Pau. Make sure you put that down! This is what people should come and see, and not only flock to the horrible Sagrada Familia!'

EDUARDO MENDOZA

Do you like Gaudí?

'I wrote a book with my sister on Modernism, the Art Nouveau of Barcelona. Did you know that Gaudí was inspired by Morocco? By the Arab mosques and desert tents? What annoys me are these researchers. You don't always have to be something, either homosexual or heterosexual. According to the latest Gaudí experts, these chimneys on the roof respresent phallic symbols. And you could interpret some of these arches as female contours or genitals. But whether Gaudí saw it like this...'

I don't understand all the fuss about the Catalan language. As a Catalan, do you write in your mother tongue?

'It's tempting to write in Catalan, because there is hardly anyone who uses this language in literature. I grew up bilingual, speaking Catalan with my mother, as she is from Barcelona, but with my father I only spoke Spanish as he was born in Asturias. The children and my wife speak Catalan with each other. That is strange to me, as I always speak Spanish with my sister, because this is what we were taught at school and we are used to it. But from an historical point of view, Catalans have always been oppressed and exploited by the government in Madrid. It's understandable, then, that they are searching for an identity through their language. Catalan was strictly forbidden under Franco.'

Are the Catalans really so different from the Madrileños and Basques?

'Catalonia is a very poor country. Catalans were notorious mercenaries and pirates. For many centuries, Italian princes employed Catalan bodyguards. It has even been claimed that the Sicilian mafia was a reaction to the ruthless Catalan mercenaries. Because the country yielded so little agriculturally, we became merchants. The title of my book must really be understood considering the fact that the people of Barcelona are always waiting for a miracle, a radical change, a change for the better. Typical of merchants, who don't really love anything, but constantly exchange goods for money or other goods; they never own or enjoy anything. This was also the case at the turn of the century, when it was thought that electricity, new machines and scientific inventions would make our lives easier. Everything will get better! This was the dream up to the First World War, when we began to realise that science doesn't bring happiness, but, on the contrary, possibly the destruction and ruin of our society.'

Barcelona is said to be Spain's publishing capital, but I can hardly see anyone reading books.

'You hardly see anyone reading books, but the number of publishers is surprising for such a poor, small and uncultured country. My books have sold more than 100,000 copies here.'

Onofre was my favourite character in your novel, The City of Miracles. But Onofre is a gangster, an anti-hero.

'Originally, my hero was a good and upright man, but he had an antagonist, an enemy, and that was Onofre Bouvila. He was the black mirror. But then I couldn't develop the story any further. I had arrived at a dead end. Suddenly I tried to tell the story with Onofre alone and simply forgot about the hero. From then on everything was easier, it flowed. I was only thinking of the first world exhibition of 1888, and then it was a question of symmetry that the novel should end with the second world exhibition of 1929. The story was unstoppable. And strangely enough, it fitted better than I thought. Reality rescued me from my fantasy. Many young architects worked for the first world exhibition, and 41 years later, as very old and famous men, the same architects built a handful of exemplary buildings. The first exhibition was ultra-modern and forward-looking, the second was rather retrospective.'

Do you actually know many people like Onofre?

'I love crooks, shady characters, liars. All my friends are dishonest. Yeah, almost all. I like real thieves, and not industrialists. I don't believe Bertolt Brecht, who said that bankers are also thieves, not only bank robbers. People who steal money, from your handbag or my wallet. I like the fact that these people are also part of society. Society is a group of people with their own rules. There are written laws in statute books, and as a lawyer you can play around with them; but there are also secret laws that you can't find in any book, but which are equally important. Our society depends on the interaction of these rules, the legal and the secret. This is fascinating. Onofre has a foot in both worlds, he juggles with two different packs of cards, as he is very realistic. I like him very much, I find him very agreeable.'

But he is rather ugly. And also Delfina, his first wife, is not an attractive character.

'I find this essential. Ugly people have to fight harder in this world and use their brains a lot more. That's the story. Two ugly people fighting desperately to get a foot in the door and, once accepted by society, to become rich and successful. I also love Delfina, and the idea that her life began and came to an end in the night. Then she waits far too long to see her lover again, and it is too late. Tragic. She is too old and crazy to impress him. Perhaps she is a symbol for women in Barcelona. For a long time women were ignored.'

Because of Franco?

'I believe that Franco is just an excuse for many things. Franco was a stupid old man, a dictator I hated with all my heart. The army was behind him. The repression was far reaching. One million people emigrated. Hundreds of thousands were shot. It took generations to overcome this. But many Spaniards backed Franco. Franco did not invent Spanish society. He inherited all the bad traits of our society and made them still worse. But everything was there in the first place, in its crude form. He did not invent the oppression of women.'

How would you define Spain today?

'At the moment we are very modern. We are the most modern country in Europe. The bars, discos, new buildings. In our small town we have more postmodern bars than Los Angeles and New York put together.'

EDUARDO MENDOZA

How did you research the many historical details in your book?

I collected many tales about Barcelona, stories from the collective memory of the people, oral history. Sometimes cities forget what they are all about for long periods of time. This happens when new classes and new citizens arrive in the city and want to create a new image.'

Through your book I believe I know Barcelona better.

'I'm delighted. Sometimes it is more progressive to go backwards in order to understand the present. At the moment it is necessary for me to think intensely about the past. I don't know yet what the result will be, but I have a feeling that it will be important.'

Was the intention of your novel also to write a parable about the dangers of the Olympics? Do you regard yourself as a kind of male Cassandra?

'Not at all. Of course, it can be interpreted that way. But I started the novel when still no one was thinking about the Olympics. I only wanted to write the story of a man who is not only influenced by his personal history, but also by the fate of his city and country. Evolution, possibilities, opportunities, faults are not dependent on the individual but on his environment. This is what I had observed and experienced, but never read so clearly in a novel. This, then, was my aim.'

Mendoza smokes one cigarette after the other. He looks at his watch, as it is already half-past-six. He had promised his wife he would cook for the kids tonight. We walk up Rambla de Catalunya towards his flat near Avenida Diagonal.

What do you think about the Olympic games? Did you perhaps anticipate what would happen to Barcelona?

'You could feel it in the air, the idea of fever, of progress in leaps and bounds. I believe in intuition; it's always happening to me. People that now complain about all the construction works get on my nerves. It's a kind of renaissance for Barcelona and all Spain. It has a lot to do with

EDUARDO MENDOZA

1992 and the idea of Europe. The virus is here.'

Is Barcelona Europe?

'Yes. Africa does not begin at the Pyrenees! The ideal Europe is nordic Europe with its punctual people and hard workers. But Greece and Albania are also part of Europe. Here in Spain's northernmost city we, too, have always respected hard work and order.'

What do you think about when you walk through the city?

'Barcelona used to be a city of trees, greenery and parties in the backyard. They used to hang up paper lanterns and play music. It's not the Olympic games that have ruined the cities, but lies, intrigue, stupidity, bad planning. This destroys the quality of life in a city.'

How long have you been writing? Since you were a law student?

My first book was published in 1974, but I wrote it in 1969. The publishers didn't like it. The original title was *The Soldiers of Catalonia*. The censor didn't like the title, it was too militaristic. Subsequently it was called *The Savolta Case*. Sometimes I think that censorship is a good thing after all, because one has to make cuts.'

What is your favourite book?

'*The Secret of the Bewitched Crypt*. It was very successful in France, my most successful, a very strange book. I wrote it for fun in the space of one week in New York after a short visit to Barcelona. They were only impressions of my visit. I wrote as if I was dreaming and put the manuscript in an envelope without any kind of revision and sent it to my publisher in Spain. I wrote to him: "Have a look at the book. If you like it, publish it; otherwise throw it away." I don't know what it is. I didn't even have a copy. The critics didn't like the book, but it was an immediate success with the readers. It is still my favourite book. Of course, I love all my books, but I like the 'Crypt' most of all because it came to me so painlessly. Every minute was fun writing this book.

EDUARDO MENDOZA

The reader can sense the fun and energy of the book, and this is what makes it so attractive.'

After ten years in New York, why did you return to your home city, Barcelona, in 1982?

'For decades Spain was a snail. And suddenly everything accelerated. I felt I had to come back, if I didn't want to become a stranger in my own country and miss new developments. I also thought of my children. Manhattan life is no good for a kid. On the other hand, Barcelona is a city of miracles.'

Having said that, he throws his elegant beige linen jacket over his shoulder and strolls, smiling, home to the kitchen. It's time for dinner with the children. Definitely not a typical dandy. How first impressions can deceive.

LITERATURE

BOOKS

THE SPANIARDS, A Portrait of the New Spain. John Hooper, Penguin.

The best book on modern Spain. Well researched and amusingly written by *The Guardian*'s Spain correspondent.

BARCELONA AND BEYOND. Annie Rankin and Karen Taylor, Lascelles City Guides, 1991.

This newest guide is not bad, perhaps a bit chaotically put together.

SPAIN. Robert Elms, Heinemann, 1992.

Funny book, with interesting facts and stories about young Spaniards.

SPAIN. Jan Morris, Penguin.

Elegiac adventures in Spain by Jan Morris, one of the world's best travel writers.

THE SHELL GUIDE TO SPAIN. Angus Mitchell, Simon and Schuster.

Well-written and informative book by a young English author.

NUEVA GUIA SECRETA DE BARCELONA. Josep Maria Carandell, Martinez Roca, Barcelona.

Why on earth has this collection of short stories and historical facts on downtown Barcelona not yet been translated into English?

GUIA DE ARQUITECTURA DE BARCELONA. Col.legi d'Arquitectes de Catalunya.

A must for lovers of architecture. Photos and descriptions of all the important buildings in Barcelona.

LITERATURE

MAGAZINES

Most visitors to Barcelona will hardly speak Spanish well enough to read a daily newspaper. But if you want to keep informed about daily events, cinemas showing non-dubbed films, theatre and pop concerts, opera or classical music, then buy the **Guia del Ocio** guide which comes out every Friday. This low-cost publication lists hours, addresses and sometimes even telephone numbers of almost every interesting bar, gallery, restaurant and museum.

VIVIR EN BARCELONA is a colourful publication with limited information. Only selected restaurants that probably pay for the privilege are listed in the information section. Sometimes there are interesting interviews, for example, with the mayor of Barcelona.

BARCELONA CONCEPT is only published twice a year, spring/summer and autumn/winter. But this glossy magazine offers the most up-to-date insider tips for shopping, eating and drinking, and fashion. Innovative photography and lavish layout.

DIAGONAL and **NEON** are only published sporadically and offer information on alternative events; they sometimes include critical or witty articles on the Olympiad and other local issues. You'll rarely find these magazines in kiosks, but you'll come across them in trendy bars and clubs such as Universal, or in the designer shop, Vinçon.

CATALUNYA VIVA will be of interest to those who want to explore Catalonia beyond Barcelona. Well-illustrated features (also translated into English and French) on the various wine and Cava cellars of Penèdes, or about seaside resorts such as Sitges. Published quarterly.

REVISTA is published quarterly by the city authorities and the cultural department. Long and almost scientific articles on, for instance, the Olympic village in Poble Nou, the clean beaches or new architecture in planning policy. Almost everything is translated into English. Probably indispensable for serious Barcelona aficionados.

LOOK OUT is the only English language magazine on Spain.

NEWSPAPERS

EL PAIS is without doubt Spain's most important daily. It is published in Madrid and Barcelona, though the head office is in Madrid. Although the paper is liberal and independent, it tends to side with the socialist Felipe González. Interesting on Fridays for its comprehensive, classified entertainment listings, on Saturdays for the art guide, and on Sundays for the glossy magazines which include restaurant reviews and interviews with stars and starlets.

LA VANGUARDIA was founded in 1881 in Barcelona, and during Franco's regime was a prominent voice of opposition – too important to have been closed down or censured for its critical opinions. It is the paper with the highest circulation in Spain, as Catalans generally read more books and newspapers than the rest of Spain. Of course, *La Vanguardia*, which also publishes articles in Catalan, does not only specialise in Catalan issues, but is a proper national newspaper, rather like *The Times*, and somewhat conservative. A bit like the hard-working Catalans themselves! On Sundays it also comes with a glossy magazine and scientific supplement.

Also look out for **EL MUNDO,** an independent, Madrid-based paper launched in 1989. *El Mundo* appeals particularly to younger readers and has already established itself as a rival to *El Pais*.

AVUI and **DIARI DE BARCELONA** are the city's Catalan newspapers, with empahisis on local issues and full of national pride.

MERCAPRESS is an advertising publication only marginally relevant to tourists. You can advertise in this paper free of charge no matter what you're after, from a cat to a flat, an old olive press, a job as a waiter or translator, an iron bed, or a guitar. *Mercapress* comes out weekly and is a bargain at 150 pesetas.

MEDIA IN
BARCELONA

Spanish television dozed when Franco ruled the airwaves. So did the
people who watched its dull mix of propaganda, Spanish B-movies and
cheap, American TV shows. All imports were dubbed and censored so
that they became acceptable to the church. Viewers yawned.

Then, in 1990, viewers woke up to the possibilities of private
television. Now Madrid and Sevilla were at last able to get a taste of
modern television. But they were already behind Barcelona, where in
1983, TV3 had started to dent the state monopoly.

The government of Catalunya was behind TV3. The autonomous
regional government wanted to control its own media. With typical
Catalan dynamism they studied the way the rest of the world made
television programmes. Then they invested the money in technology
and found the talent to make the most of it.

TV3 only broadcast in Catalan, but it showed Spain what television
could be like. Young professionals were offering the audience
programmes they would never have seen on the state-owned channels.
One of TV3's biggest successes was to bring the Catalan language, in
the form of good and popular television, into all homes, not only
Catalan-speaking ones. J.R. Ewing, of *Dallas* fame, dubbed into
Catalan, was particularly helpful in this respect.

Now viewers in Barcelona have six different choices. Two
channels are state-run, TVE-1 and TVE-2; and two, TV3 and Canal
33, are run by the local government, the Generalitat. Three are private:
Antenna 3 (controlled by Conde Javier de Godo, who also runs
Antenna 3 Radio and the *La Vanguardia* newspaper); Tele 5 (run by the
blind organisation, ONCE, and the Italian magnate Silvio Berlusconi);
and, finally, Canal + (controlled by Prisa S.A., the same company that
owns the *El Pais* newspaper and Radio Ser).

Canal 33 aims at the cultural fringes of television, a bit in the style
of England's Channel Four. Private television was free to begin
broadcasting at Christmas 1990. Since the birth of private channels,
viewers have seen major changes in television output every September,

when new programmes are launched with a fresh collection of stars and presenters. The strong competition between programmes means there are very few long-running ones. Antenna 3 aims at a mass-market audience; Tele 5 offers mainly light entertainment, including game shows and soap operas, but with little emphasis on current affairs; and Canal + (the subscription channel) aims to be more exclusive, with film premiers and exclusive sports coverage.

Since the advent of competition, TVE has turned increasingly to commercial, mass-market television. Compared to British television, Spanish output, as a whole, has a greater focus on light entertainment. It also offers many cheaply and quickly-made programmes, with little continuity.

For news, TVE and TV3 have the usual lunchtime and evening programmes, and Tele 5 and Canal + have only evening programmes. In general, they are more racey and fast-moving than British news, but they have less distinctive profiles. There are also weekly current affairs programmes, such as *30 minuts* (TV3 on Sunday, *En portada* (TVE-1 on Tuesday) and *Linea 900* (TVE-2 on Wednesday). The latter relies on audience participation, in the form of telephone tip-offs and home videos. The sports programme, *Forca Barca* (TVE-2 on Wednesday), is not precisely an information programme but a humorous look at the Barca football team's performance on the previous Sunday.

In the musical and cultural field, there are video clips in *Los 40 principales* (Canal +, daily), *Rockpop* (TVE-1 on Saturday) and *Rapido* (TVE-2 on Monday). They present the latest on the mainstream music and arts scene, while the late-night *Metropolis* (TVE-2 on Thursday) concentrates on fringe offerings.

Game shows are increasingly popular, though most of them are foreign import formulas. *Amor a primera vista* (TVE-3 on Tuesday) is very successful, and so is the long-running *El precio justo* (TVE-1 on Monday). *El tiempo es oro* (TVE-1 on Saturday), which is like the British *Mastermind*, is presented by Constantino Romero. The only major game show conceived in Spain is *Un, dos, tres* (TVE-1 on Friday) which has been running for many years. In Great Britain the game is called *3, 2, 1*.

Other favourite game shows - which video companies are happy to sponsor - are based on competitions for the funniest home video. The shows are called *Videos de primera* (TVE-1 on Tuesday), *Betes i films* (TV3 on Monday), *Clip, clap, video* (TVE-2 from Monday to Friday) and *Que gente tan divertida* (Tele 5 on Thursday).

A new phenomenon on Spanish television is the success of South American soap operas, very cheaply made, and in which the stories are very simple and make many Spanish housewives cry. The main topics of conversation in food markets are the plots of the love stories.

But not only love and passion are shown on Spanish television. Many channels have special 'erotic nights' during which they broadcast soft porn. TVE-2 has the *Noche erotica* on Sundays, where they have cartoons of animals making love. On Fridays it's *Sesion especial X* on Canal + and *Erotisimo* on Tele 5.

Among many magazine programmes, there is Jesus Hermida's magazine (Antenna 3, weekends). This veteran and polemic star of the Spanish media conducts interviews, presents reports and comments on news in a very personal style. There is also the fashionable Emilio Aragon and his magazine *Vip noche* (Tele 5 on Sunday). He first appeared on television singing and dancing in a clown's programme.

La vida en un xip (TV3 on Friday) is not a magazine programme, but with its debates on everyday topics and audience participation, it gives a good picture of Catalunyan society. A unique offering from TV3 and Canal 33 is a dual television system which allows viewers to switch to the English-language version of many films and serials if they have stereo television or video. TV3 also has *International Headlines* in the summer, a news programme made by different European professionals and in different languages.

TUNING IN

In radio, the real audience battle is raged by the morning magazines. Their formula is a series of soundbites of information, politics, human interest stores and humour.

The veteran presenter, whose voice everybody knows, is Luis de Ormo on *Protagonists* (Onda Cero). Other presenters include Inaki Gabilondo on *Hoy por hoy* (Cadena ser); and Antonio Herrero on *El primero do la mana a* (Antenna 3 Radio). Xavier Sarda's *La bisagra* (RNE-1) is quite unique. He presents the programme with 'Senior

Casamajor', a charismatic old man with a very strong Catalan accent, who comments on what people say. But what many listeners do not know is that crusty old Casamajor - who refuses to have his picture taken - is, in fact, Sarda.

We mustn't forget Encarna Sanchez (Cope) who for years has been talking to lower-middle-class women, and Julia Otero, an aggressive journalist who presents a late evening magazine on Onda Cero with outside broadcast interviews.

But the man leading the audience battle is José Maria Garcia, with his aggressive sports programme *SuperGarcia* (Antenna 3 Radio). After 25 years on the air, he is no stranger to speaking out about scandal and dishes the dirt on personality feuds both inside and outside the sporting arena.

OLYMPIC GAMES 1992

The Olympic games will begin on Saturday, 25 July and end on Sunday, 9 August 1992. It is not advisable to visit Barcelona during this time, nor one week before or after this gargantuan event. In all probability, pensiones, hostales and hotels will be fully booked, and there will hardly be a berth available on the 15 ocean liners from all over the world, chartered by the city to serve as floating hotels over the 16 days of the Olympiad. For two weeks Barcelona will not be itself, the city's own character and relaxed atmosphere will give way to pandemonium and traffic chaos. This is to be expected. However, sport aficionados won't be deterred. Therefore, here are the most important addresses and Olympiad survival tips.

The Olympic games will take place in all four corners of the city. Spectators will have to travel between venues. One area, above Diagonal, comprises Camp Nou, F.C. Barcelona's stadium, and the Royal Polo Club near the university. Then, on Montjuïc, there is the athletic stadium, the Bernat Picornell swimming pool, the Catalan Institute of Sport (INEFC) and the Palau Sant Jordi. Third is the cycle track and volleyball venue in Vall d'Hebron and finally the Olympic village in Parc de Mar.

Barcelona's city planners and the organisational committee COOB '92 are attempting to improve transport links between these far-flung centres. Frantic efforts are still underway to complete a ring road, but it is not likely to be operational in time. The same is true for the Montjuïc Metro station, intended to serve the main venue. Therefore, gigantic escalators are being built to transport visitors from the old Metro station at Plaça d'Espanya all the way up Montjuïc.

INFORMATION

COOB '92. Comite Organitzador Olimpic Barcelona '92, Edificio Helios, Mejia Leguerica sin, tel. 411-1992, fax: 411-2092.

The Olympic committee organises everything.

OLYMPIC GAMES 1992

EDIFICIO OLIMPICO. Travessera de les Corts 131-159; 08028 Barcelona, tel. 010-34-3-490-1992, fax: 010-34-3-490-9200.

You can obtain information about the Olympic games directly from here.

OCSA. Olimpiada Cultural, S.A., Torre Llussana, Cami de Sant Genis a Horta 6, tel. 429-0009, fax: 429-0607.

Information concerning plans of the company which since 1990 has been organising a cultural Olympiad including music, art, theatre, literary and architectural events in Barcelona. Very active in summer.

SPORT IN THE OLYMPIC CITY

The people of Barcelona love sport. It's no surprise, then, that you can find 1,200 sports clubs and 1,300 sportsgrounds around the city. Approximately 250 signposted running and walking tracks wind through the city's many parks and green spaces. Barcelona is ideally situated for many types of sports. The coastline is crowded with sailing boats, surfers, water skiers, swimmers, fishermen and windsurfers. In the mountains around the city you can ski or climb steep rock faces, and in the spacious valleys of Barcelona's smarter suburbs you can play golf, tennis, squash and football. The tourist bureau distributes free pamphlets on golf in Catalonia and sports in Barcelona.

INFORMATION

Biblioteca de l'Esport. València 3. M: Tarragona. Mon.-Fri. 11 a.m.-2 p.m. and 4-7 p.m.

This new bookshop stocks thousands of sports books as well as magazines, posters and videos. Mostly in Spanish and Catalan, and some in English.

Museu i Centre d'Estudis de l'Esport, Dr. Melchior Colet. Buenos Aires 56-58, tel. 439-8907. M: Hospital Clínic. Mon.-Fri. 10 a.m.-2 p.m. and 4-8 p.m., Sat.-Sun. 10 a.m.-2 p.m.

Sports museum.

Billiards. Federacions Catalanes de Billar, Casanova 57, tel. 253-5310.

Bowling and Boccia. Federacions Catalanes de Bitlles i Botxes, Jonqueres 16, tel. 301-0142.

Football. Federacions Catalanes de Futbol, Sicilia 93, tel. 232-0013.

Golf. Federacions Catalanes de Golf, Aribu 282, tel. 200-2478.

SPORT IN THE OLYMPIC CITY

Gymnastics. Federacions Catalanes de Gimnàstica, Avinguda Josep Tarradellas 40, tel. 230-1256.

Riding. Federacions Catalanes de Hípica, Infanta Carlota 40, tel. 239-9053.

Sailing. Federacions Catalanes de Vela, Passeig Manuel Girona 2, tel. 203-3800.

Ski and Wintersports. Federacions Catalanes de Esports d'Hivern, Casp 38, tel. 318-6028.

Squash. Federacions Catalanes de Squash, Napols 218, tel. 258-7317.

Swimming. Federacions Catalanes de Natació, Diputació 237, tel. 301-8270.

Tennis. Federactions Catalanes de Tennis, Infanta Carlota 40, tel. 239-2491.

Waterskiing. Federacions Catalanes de Motonàutica, Avinguda Madrid 118, tel. 330-4757.

FITNESS

Most top clubs require expensive membership, but some fitness centres accept bookings by the hour.

Club Esportiu Gran de Gràcia. Gran de Gràcia 37, tel. 218-2264. M: Diagonal.
   Super centre with squash courts, roof terrace, jazz dance, aerobics, weights, massage and restaurant.

Holidays Centre. Entenca 102, tel. 325-9286. M: Tarragona.
   Sports centre on three floors with gymnastics classes, sauna, roller skating, squash and karate.

Sport Corsega. Còrsega 371, tel. 257-5002. M: Diagonal.

Swimming pool, sauna, gymnastics and body building classes. Good value.

GOLF

El Prat Royal Golf Club. Apartado de Correos 10, 08820 El Prat de Llobregat, tel. 379-0278. 15 kilometres from Barcelona.

International tournaments are played on three courses. After telephone booking, non-members can also hire equipment and play.

Sant Cugat Golf Club. 08190 Sant Cugat del Valles, tel. 674-3958. 20 kilometres from Barcelona, you can get there by train.

Eighteen holes and three driving ranges as well as equipment hire.

RIDING

Club Hipic de Barcelona. Ciutat de Balaguer 68, tel. 417-3039. FFCC: Tibidabo and then a long walk.

Riding classes also for non-members after telephone booking. The club organises horseback excursions into the mountains.

SPORT IN THE OLYMPIC CITY

SQUASH

Squash Barcelona. Avinguda Dr. Marañon 17, tel. 334-0258. M: Zona Universitaria. Daily 8 a.m.–12 mid. Reservations essential.

Tibidabo Squash Club. Lluis Muntades 8, tel. 212-4683. FFCC: Avinguda Tibidabo and Tramvia Blau. Reservations. Mon.-Fri. 9 a.m.–11 p.m., Sat. 10 a.m.–10 p.m., Sun. 10 a.m.–5 p.m.

SWIMMING

Bernat Picornell Piscina. Avinguda del Estadi 34, Parc de Montjuïc, tel. 325-9281. M: Espanya or Paral-lel, then the funicular. Daily 10 a.m.–3:30 p.m. Open air.

Club Natacio Montjuïc. Reina Amàlia, tel. 241-0122. Mon.-Fri. 11:30 a.m.–1:30 p.m. M: Paral-lel. Indoor.

Parc de la Creueta del Coll. Castelltercol, tel. 213-2514. Bus: 25, 28. Mon.-Fri. 10 a.m.–4 p.m., Sat.-Sun. 10 a.m.–7 p.m. Open air swimming mid-June – mid-Sept. At other times only boating.

Piscina Club Natacio Barceloneta. Passeig Marítim, tel. 309-3412. M: Barceloneta. Mon.-Fri. 7 a.m.–9 p.m. Indoor.

Piscina Ronda. Ronda de Sant Pau 46, tel. 329-9806. M: Paral-lel. Mon.-Fri. 7 a.m.–9 p.m. Indoor.

Sant Andreu Piscina. Riera d'Horta, tel. 346-5603. M: Montbau. Summer, daily 10 a.m.–4 p.m. Open air.

TENNIS

Private tennis courts are a status symbol in the Zona Alta - the smart quarters of Pedralbes, Sarrià and San Gervasi. The visitor will hardly gain access to them as they are mostly hidden in gardens, on rooftops of high-rise buildings and atriums of residential 'urbanizations'.

Can Caralleu Complejo Deportivo. Esports, tel. 203-7874. FFCC: Reina Elisenda, and a long walk. Daily 8 a.m.-11 p.m.

Courts cost almost twice as much in the evening.

Vall Parc Club. Carretara a Sant Cugat 79, tel. 212-6789. M: Penitents, and a long walk. Daily 8 a.m.-12 mid.

Court fees are twice as expensive in this exclusive club as in Carralleu.

The weird mountain-shapes above the cloister of Montserrat, just 90 minutes outside Barcelona.

EXCURSIONS IN CATALONIA

Barcelona can be a demanding, time-consuming mistress. It can wear you out. If you have been seduced by this city you will have noticed that Barcelona can turn into an absorbing monster that requires uninterrupted attention. The solution? A trip into the enchanting, no less overwhelming surroundings in order to recover from your adventures.

INFORMATION AND LITERATURE

You can obtain the following useful publications free of charge from the tourist office: 'Tours of Modernism in Catalonia', 'Tours of Gothic Art in Catalonia' and 'Tours of Romanesque Art' as well as (in Spanish) pamphlets on the different Catalan regions (*comarques*), 'Catalunya Camping' and 'Catalunya Museums'. The 'Catalunya Hotels' guide, which also lists pensiones and restaurants, is available in bookshops for 325 pesetas.

In order to plan the best possible bus and train connections, you should go to the tourist office. The staff speak English and are willing to coordinate your trip as they have access to bus and train timetables. On arrival at your destination the local tourist bureau will give you more detailed information on places to visit and accommodation.

Officina de Turismo. Gran Via de les Corts Catalans 658, tel. 301-7443. M: Passeig de Gràcia. Mon.-Fri. 9 a.m.-7 p.m. Sat. 9 a.m.-2 p.m.

COSTA MARESME

A comfortable train serves the flat and sandy coastline northeast of Barcelona towards Blanes, the Costa Maresme. You can get off wherever you want: in **Argentona**, for instance, to visit the summer house of the modernist architect Puig i Cadafalch, or to look for the

EXCURSIONS IN CATALONIA

many curious Art Nouveau buildings in the holiday resort **Canet de Mar**. In **Blanes** visit the botanical gardens, Jardí Botanic Mar i Murtra, laid out by the German Carles Faust. This oasis is home to 3,000 different plant types, mainly cacti, from all over the world.

Tourist Office: Plaça de Catalunya, tel. (972) 330318.

Train: from Estació de Sants. **Journey time**: approximately one hour to Blanes.

COSTA BRAVA

The 'wild coast' extends north from Blanes via Lloret de Mar, Tossa de Mar, Palamós and Cadaqués, all the way to the border at Port-Bou. The tourist masses bake on the beaches of **Tossa de Mar** and **Lloret de Mar**, where there are more hotels than in the whole of Madrid. The coastline in the regions of **Baix Emporda** and **Alt Emporda** is less developed and you can escape the crowds by exploring the little fishing villages.

BAIX EMPORDA

Begur. This holiday resort of the Catalan bourgeoisie slumbers beautifully in the shadow of a medieval castle, the starting point for a series of small hidden inlets (*calas*) with crystal clear water. Not all calas are accessible by car. In the summer months there is a half-hourly bus service to two of at least six calas, Sa Riera and Aiguiblava. The modern parador Costa Brava, a state-run four-star hotel, is built on the peninsula Punta dels Munts and offers beautiful views of the pine forests leading down to the calas. Juanita does some excellent cooking at El Bodegón, in a small alley of Begur: meat and fish grilled on a wood fire. And then it's off to the pubs such as L'Orangerie or the Arc Blau. For romantics there are concerts in the village church San Pere.

Tourist Office: Edifici Casa Gran, Avinguda Onze de Septembre, tel. (972) 623479.

Bus: Sarfa, Plaça Duc de Medinaceli 4, tel. 318-9434. M: Drassanes. **Journey time**: approximately 2 $^1/_2$ hours.

Pals. This picturesque medieval village with its Torre de les Hores (the tower of hours), which you must climb, is situated six kilometres from Begur. You will find many shops selling handicrafts and the Museum of Marine Relics. Pals prides itself on one of the few nudist beaches of the Costa Brava, and there is even a handful of dunes. Nearby is the restaurant Sa Punta, where Josep Font makes heavenly anchovy salads.

Tourist Office: Plaça de Espanya 7, tel. 636161.

Bus: Sarfa, from Barcelona to Begur (see above); change at Begur, Pi i Ratllo 7, tel. (972) 622135. **Journey time**: Barcelona approximately two hours, from Begur half an hour.

Peretallada. This pleasant little place with stone houses built into the cliffs, lies 12 kilometres inland from Begur. The gigantic graveyards, Dolmen dels Tres Peus, are in Fitor, about 10 kilometres from Peretallada. There is good food in the rustic ambience of La Riera: what about stuffed duck's neck or marinated pears? The local cooperative's wine tastes great: *vinos tintos i rosados del Empurdán*.

Information: tourist offices in Barcelona and Begur.

Train: from Estació de Sants on the Barcelona-Port Bou line. **Journey time**: approximately $2^1/_2$ hours.

Foixa. On the way to Foixa, 27 kilometres from Begur, you'll even come across Begurenses. In all likelihood you'll run into the famous Catalan singer-songwriter Lluís Llach, whose reason for being in this little place is the Can Quel restaurant: exquisite cuisine for a few pesetas.

Information: tourist offices in Barcelona and Begur.

Train: from Estació de Sants on the Barcelona-Port Bou line. **Journey time**: approximately $2^1/_2$ hours.

La Bisbal d'Emporda. If you visit La Bisbal d'Emporda (15 kilometres from Begur), don't forget to go into the old town to look for ceramics in Carrer Aigüeta. The traditional cakes are delicious: *Hojaldres de Piñones*!

Tourist Office: Plaça Francesc Macià 10, tel. (972)642593.

Bus: Sarfa, from Barcelona or Begur. Local Sarfa-office: Les Voltes 10, tel. (972) 640964. **Journey time**: approximately $2^1/_2$ hours from Barcelona.

EXCURSIONS IN CATALONIA

L'Estartit: The Illes Medes protrude from the sea at l'Estartit. Information regarding the hire of diving equipment and boats can be obtained from the tourist office. A walk to the ruins of Castell de Montgri ($1^{1}/_{2}$hours) will reward you with super views. The solitary coves can only be reached on foot; head towards Roca Foradada.

    Tourist Office: Passeig Marítim 47, tel. (972) 758910.

    Train: from Estació de Sants to Girona. Right next to the station there is the Estació d'Autocares, where you catch the bus to l'Estartit. **Journey time**: approximately $3^{1}/_{2}$ hours.

ALT EMPORDA

L'Escala. Freshly caught anchovies are canned immediately. You're sure to enjoy Els Pescadors. You must also visit the ruins of Empuries – fantastic panoramic sunsets and sunrises from among the mosaic remains.

    Tourist Office: Plaça de les Escoles 1, tel. (972) 770603.

    Train: from Estació de Sants to Girona. Change at the bus station for l'Escala. **Journey time**: approximately $3^{1}/_{2}$ hours.

Cadaques. The pleasant fishing village atmosphere is popular with artists and cranky French women loaded with jewellery. In nearby Portlligat you can admire Dalí's house from the outside. The Museu Perrot-Moore houses a comprehensive collection of European painters. In July and August a music and art festival takes place in Cadaqués. Many an artist has found inspiration from the trip to the old lighthouse at Cap de Creus (six kilometres away) and a good walk among the bizarre rock formations. In the restaurant Casa Anita, you're more or less in the kitchen itself and you can watch Anita at work. You'll sit around long, wooden tables together with other guests. Cool Sammy is the owner of El Barroca, where he serves cuisine francaise in the flower-filled patio. Later on, you can mingle in the Bar Casino or l'Hostal on the Paseo for a traditional *cermat*, coffee with rum.

    The Benedictine monastery San Pedro de Roda is a must for early risers. Fantastic views at sunrise. You can get there via Port de la Selva, which is ideal for watersports (information from the town hall, Ajuntament). The place starts to bustle when they bring in the fish for auction in the early afternoon.

Tourist Office: Cotxe 2a, tel. (972) 258315.

Bus: Sarfa, Plaça Duc de Medinaceli 4, tel. 318-9434. M: Drassanes. **Journey time**: approximately three hours.

Port de la Selva. Ajuntament, Carrer Mar 1, tel. (972) 387025. You can get there by foot from Cadaqués ($1^1/_2$ hours) or direct by train from Barcelona's Estació Sants to Llançà and onwards by bus ($3^1/_2$ hours). The walk to the monastery will take about an hour.

Figueres and Peralada. In Figueres you can visit Dalí's scurrilously eccentric theatre-cum-museum, where you will also find different works by his wife Gala. You can stroll around the gardens of a fascinating castle in Peralada. There is also the wine cellar, Cavas del Empurdán, a casino and a library containing 60,000 volumes and many rarities. A first-rate international music festival is held during the summer, where the diva Montserrat Caballé and the tenor José Carreras are among the regular performers. The Spanish jet-set have an annual rendezvous here.

Tourist Office: Plaça de l'Estació, Figueres, tel. (972) 503155. Information of guided tours and visits to the Castell de Peralada: tel. (972) 538125.

Train: from Estació de Sants to Figueres, the next station is Peralada. **Journey time**: approximately three hours.

THE INTERIOR

Montserrat. The monastery of Montserrat clings onto a massif in the Baix Llobregat region, 50 kilometres northwest of Barcelona. Its rugged beauty attracts not only pilgrims but also mountain climbers, hang gliders, herb pickers and roaming adventurers. Potholers have recently taken an interest in the gigantic subterranean lakes. Gaudí fans will find evidence of their idol in the chapel: a museum for modern Catalan art. The complex has turned into an international faicground and there is no shortage of supermarkets, hot dogs and fast-food restaurants. It's best to take the cable car still further up and visit the scatterd hermitages. Take the bus if you like winding roads and want to really feel the landscape, and go early in the morning to avoid the hordes of pilgrims.

Bus: Julia, Placa Universitat 12, tel. 318-3895. M: Universitat. First bus around 9 a.m. **Train**: Ferrocarrils Catalans, entrance Plaça de Espanya, to the Aeri de Montserrat, then the cable car. Information on timetables, tel. 205-1515. First Ferrocarne around 9 a.m. **Journey time**: a good hour.

Covas Salnitre de Collbato. Visits to the caves and subterranean lakes Tuesday to Sunday; it's best to call in advance, tel. 777-0309.

Bus: Hispano Ignaladina, Europa II, tel. 230-4344.

Sant Sadurni d'Anoia and Vilafranca. The wine region Alt Penedès lies to the west of Baix Llobregat. The architect Puig i Cadafalch built a modernist temple for the Cava producer Codorniú in Sant Sadurni d'Anoia. It is quite exciting to walk around the 26-kilometre-long vaults which store millions of bottles of Cava. After lunch you should make tracks for Vilafranca, Europe's oldest wine centre. The Palacio Real houses the wind museum. The Cellar Miguel Torres, famous for its Sangre de Toro, will surprise you with its Waltraud Riesling, recommendable with oysters. Vilafranca is full of modernist town houses and the Farmacia Güell is especially impressive. Try the *Caquas de matafaluga* (aniseed cookies) in patisseries. The food is good at Casa Juan on Plaça de la Estació: produce comes fresh from the market.

Cavas Codorniu. Caseria, tel. 891-0125. Visits Mon.-Fri. 8 a.m.-1:30 p.m. and 3-5:30 p.m. Telephone booking recommended. Closed August.

Tourist Office: Vilafranca, Cort 14, tel. 892-0358. Sant Sadurni, Plaça Ajuntament 1, tel. 891-1212.

Train: from Estació de Sants. **Journey time**: approximately half an hour.

Banyoles. This romantic village in the Girones region, with its stone houses and marketplace surrounded by beautiful arcades, nestles

between soft hills and pine forests near the only natural lakes in
Catalonia (120 kilometres northeast of Barcelona). It is also the venue
for the 1992 Olympic rowing events. You can hire rowing boats,
canoes, waterski equipment and sailboards from the Club Natació
Banyoles. You can eat well and spend the night comfortably in Fonda
Flores. If you can pluck up the courage, ask for the Museo de las
Bestias.

Tourist Office: Passeig de la Industrial 25, tel. (972) 575573.

Bus: Teisa, tel. 318-1086; departure, Pau Claris on the corner
with Consell de Cent. **Journey time**: approximately three hours.

Castellar de N'Hug and Pobla de Lillet. Castellar de N'Hug lies
2,000 metres up in the Pyrenees in the Bergada region, 150 kilometres
north of Barcelona. It has been declared the most beautiful village of
Catalonia, but it comes over as rather stiff. The real attraction is the
springs of the river Llobregat that shoot out of the rocks south of the
village – a natural wonder. Further downstream you'll find La Pobla de
Lillet, where you can discover forgotten ruins in the style of Gaudí, and
a crazy natural stone garden.

Bus: A.T.S.A., departure from Barcelona at Balmes 117; from
Berga change to a A.T.S.A. bus for either village. A.T.S.A. Berga,
Passeig de la Pau 2, tel. 821-2000. (No office in Barcelona.) **Journey
time**: approximately four hours.

COSTA DORADA

Sitges. If the Costa Dorada to the south of Barcelona is less crowded
and touristy than the resorts of the Costa Brava, it's probably because it's
largely drab and unexciting. One big exception, however, is Sitges.
This attractive, former fishing village has become one of Spain's
trendiest (and pricey) resorts, frequented by young Barcelonese and
stylish Europeans who generate a vibrant nightlife. It's also a popular
gay resort, known for its outrageous Carnaval, with several nudist and
exclusively gay beaches.

While such popularity makes accommodation tight (arrive early if
you plan to stay), Sitges also makes a great daytrip from Barcelona.

EXCURSIONS IN CATALONIA

Trains leave Sants station approximately every half hour and drop you at the station about 10 minutes walk from the seafront and town centre. Apart from the beaches, there's a long promenade beside the seafront. When you tire of people-watching, explore the town with its Baroque parish church, white-washed mansions, and three museums.

Tourist Office: Oasis shopping mall (turn right out of the train station and right again on Passeig Vilafranca), tel. (93) 894-4700.

Trains: from Barcelona Sants station, about every half hour. **Journey time**: 35 minutes.

Sitges is permeated by an atmosphere of tolerance and deference towards gay tourists, on whom much of the economy of the resort depends. It is a bustling, safe haven, which is especially busy during the May to October season. Here are some of the more popular places to visit, or perhaps stay, in Sitges.

BARS AND CAFES

Bourbons. San Buenaventura 13, tel. 894-3347. Open 10 p.m.-3 a.m.
Air conditioned bar/disco used by men of all ages. Very popular.

Spray. San Buenaventura 37. Open 10 p.m.-3 a.m.
Mainly young men at this bar.

Planta Baja. Santa Tecla 4. Open midnight onwards. Air-conditioned bar/disco, popular with younger men.

El Meson. Uno de Mayo 4, tel. 894-2807. Open 1 p.m.- 6 a.m.
Terrace cafe/bar. Pleasant atmosphere.

El Horno. Juan Tarrida Ferratyes 6, tel. 894-0909. Open 12 noon-4 a.m. Mixed age groups, with leather/denim bias. Very popular.

Mediteraneo. San Buenaventura 6. Open 10 p.m.-3:30 a.m.
Very large, popular bar which has recently been refurnished. All age groups.

Lord's Club. Marques de Montroig 14, tel. 894-1522. Open 10 p.m.-4 a.m.
This bar is more popular with older men. Air-conditioned.

Parrot's Club. Plaza Industrial. Open 4 p.m.-4 a.m.
A terrace/cafe popular with gay men and women of all ages.

Capricorn. San Bartolome 60, tel. 894-6299. Open 6 p.m.-1 a.m.
A friendly bar, used by mainly younger men.

El Candil. Calle de la Carreta 9, Sitges. Open 10 p.m.-4 a.m. One of the most popular bars in Sitges. A must for all gay visitors to the town.

Le Leman. Bonaire 35, tel. 894-4667. Open 5 p.m.-3 a.m. Early opening, with leather/denim leanings.

DISCOS

Trailer. Angel Vidal 36. Open 12 mid.-5 a.m. Closed Oct.-April.
Busy disco with good atmosphere. Popular with young crowd.

RESTAURANTS

El Trull. Mossen Felix Clara 3, tel. 894-4705. Open 8:30 p.m.-1 a.m.
The best gay restaurant in Sitges. A must for visitors.

El Xalet. Isla de Cuba 35, tel. 894-5579. Open 9 p.m.-1 a.m. Expensive but chic restaurant. Good food.

HOTELS

Hotel Romantic de Sitges. Sant Isidre 33, tel. 894-0643. Ancient mansion. Not exclusively gay, but very charming and comfortable. Located in the centre of town.

EXCURSIONS IN CATALONIA

Hostal Incognito. Honos Maristas 3, tel. 894-2698.
Popular with older gays.
Comfortable rooms, all with private bathrooms.

Liberty. Isla de Cuba 45, tel. 894-4650.
Friendly hotel catering for all ages.

Hostal Madison. Sant Bartomeu 9, tel. 894-6147.
Comfortable hotel at the lower end of the market.

GAY SAUNAS

Sauna Sitges. Espalter 11.
Open 4 p.m.-10 p.m.
Weekends only Oct.-Apr.
Exclusively gay sauna with massage and videos.